W9-BPJ-313

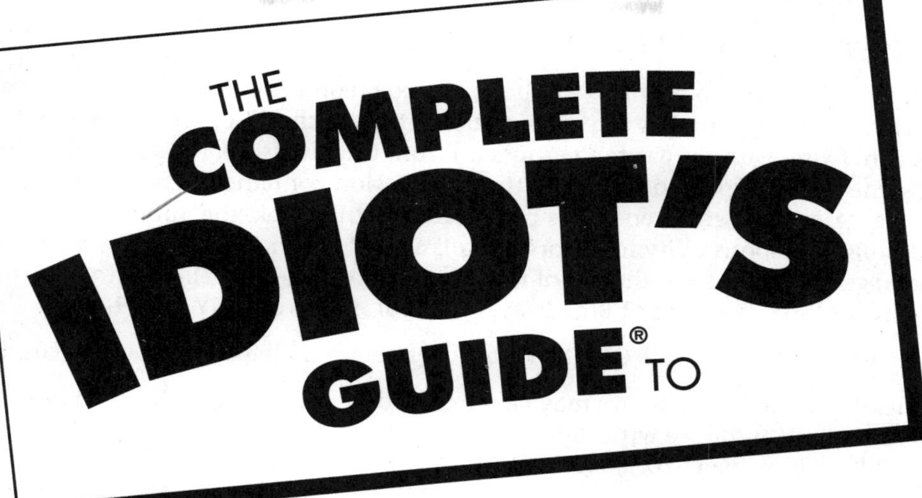

Jazz

by Alan Axelrod

alpha
books

A Division of Macmillan General Reference
A Pearson Education Macmillan Company
1633 Broadway, New York, NY 10019-6785

ABINGTON FREE LIBRARY
1030 OLD YORK ROAD
ABINGTON, PA 19001

For Anita.

Copyright © 1999 by Alan Axelrod

All rights reserved. No part of this book shall be reproduced, stored in a retrieval system, or transmitted by any means, electronic, mechanical, photocopying, recording, or otherwise, without written permission from the publisher. No patent liability is assumed with respect to the use of the information contained herein. Although every precaution has been taken in the preparation of this book, the publisher and author assume no responsibility for errors or omissions. Neither is any liability assumed for damages resulting from the use of information contained herein. For information, address Alpha Books, 1633 Broadway, 7th Floor, New York, NY 10019-6785.

THE COMPLETE IDIOT'S GUIDE TO and design are trademarks of Macmillan, Inc.

Macmillan Publishing books may be purchased for business or sales promotional use. For information please write: Special Markets Department, Macmillan Publishing USA, 1633 Broadway, New York, NY 10019.

International Standard Book Number: 0-02-862731-8
Library of Congress Catalog Card Number: 98-87600

01 00 99 8 7 6 5 4 3 2 1

Interpretation of the printing code: the rightmost number of the first series of numbers is the year of the book's printing; the rightmost number of the second series of numbers is the number of the book's printing. For example, a printing code of 99-1 shows that the first printing occurred in 1999.

Printed in the United States of America

Note: This publication contains the opinions and ideas of its author. It is intended to provide helpful and informative material on the subject matter covered. It is sold with the understanding that the author and publisher are not engaged in rendering professional services in the book. If the reader requires personal assistance or advice, a competent professional should be consulted.

The author and publisher specifically disclaim any responsibility for any liability, loss or risk, personal or otherwise, which is incurred as a consequence, directly or indirectly, of the use and application of any of the contents of this book.

MAY 2 2 2008

Alpha Development Team

Publisher
Kathy Nebenhaus

Editorial Director
Gary M. Krebs

Managing Editor
Bob Shuman

Marketing Brand Manager
Felice Primeau

Acquisitions Editor
Jessica Faust

Development Editors
Phil Kitchel
Amy Zavatto

Assistant Editor
Georgette Blau

Production Team

Production Editor
Mark Enochs

Cover Designer
Mike Freeland

Illustrator
Brian Mac Moyer

Designer
Nathan Clement

Indexer
Nadia Ibrahim

Layout/Proofreading
John Bitter
Angela Calvert
Mary Hunt
Jeannie McKay

Contents at a Glance

Contents

Appendices

Foreword

Jazz has been called "America's classical music." And, as any jazz fan can tell you, your enjoyment of the music is greatly enhanced when you know something about it.

It's been a hundred years since Scott Joplin's "Maple Leaf Rag" first appeared—and sold a million copies in sheet music—changing American music forever. The "Maple Leaf Rag" is in the form of a four-part march, one of the most popular musical styles of the day. But there's a difference between John Philip Sousa and Scott Joplin's works—syncopation. The oom-pah emphasis of the march is still there, but the melody dances around it, like a slightly drunken soldier. They called the result "ragtime," which in turn gave birth to something called "jazz."

Dr. Alan Axelrod takes you through this history step-by-step, beginning with the roots of jazz in African and African-American traditional music. Then, you'll swing through New Orleans, where Buddy Bolden and Joseph "King" Oliver created the first real jazz bands. You'll meet the young guns who spread the message, including trombonist Kid Ory, the Dodds brothers (clarinetist Johnny and his younger brother, nicknamed Baby, who played the drums), and, of course, a young orphan named Louis Armstrong.

Then hop a freight and follow the thousands of immigrants to Chicago, where you'll encounter the first great bands, black and white—ensembles led by Oliver and Armstrong, and the first band to make a recording, the all-white Original Dixieland Jass Band. You'll also meet the first great jazz fans, who adopted the music themselves—a group of college and high-school age Midwesterners led by a cornet player with a sound that was clearer than a bell: Leon "Bix" Beiderbecke.

In the "Big-Band Era," from the mid-'30s through the mid-'40s, jazz became America's most popular music. Zoot suits, cool cats, crazy gals, jitterbugging to the beat—it's all here, along with a discussion of the legendary bands of Duke Ellington, Benny Goodman, and Count Basie.

And just when you think you've got the beat—it changes! After World War II, a group of young outlaws decided that jazz had become too popular, and lost its original direction as an improvised, creative music. Playing after hours in small Harlem clubs like Minton's, musicians like Thelonious Monk, Dizzy Gillespie, and Charlie Parker created a high-paced, angular, intense music that perfectly suited the times. As Gillespie said, the question was, "To be or not to bop"—and, although the old guard resisted, bebop soon went downtown to become the sound of the day.

The generation that wanted to "do their own thing" added another dimension to jazz in the 1960s—total freedom. Ornette Coleman ushered in "free jazz," where each musician could improvise without the constraints of melody, rhythm, or harmony—and jazz stretched to its ultimate limits. While players like John Coltrane and Sun Ra explored the outer limits of the musical universe, many listeners were left scratching their heads, wondering if jazz would ever return to earth.

Enter Miles Davis—an influential voice on the jazz scene since the late '40s. He had pioneered "cool jazz" in the '50s—a laid-back response to bebop that emphasized muted tones and introspective works—and then nurtured some of the most important young players of the '60s. Determined to reclaim jazz's place as America's popular music, Davis wed his improvisational style with the rhythms of funk and the instruments of rock—and created fusion, the most popular jazz style of the '70s. Again, the old guard was upset, but the fans didn't care.

The '80s and '90s have been eclectic times. Some, most notably trumpeter Wynton Marsalis, have revived past styles, reaching all the way back to early Ellington and Armstrong as well as bop. Others continue to push the boundaries without regard to profit or popularity. And so jazz continues—innovative and traditional, avant-garde and conservative, popular and edgy.

Dr. Axelrod explains everything you need to know to begin enjoying jazz music. He describes the instruments and the styles, the great players, arrangers, and behind-the-scenes movers and shakers; and introduces the clubs, key recordings, and festivals. For anyone new to the music—and even for the experienced listener—this book will enhance your knowledge and enjoyment of America's classical music.

—**Richard Carlin** has been writing on music for over 20 years. He is the author of *The Big Book of Country Music, The World of Music* (five volumes), and *Classical Music: An Informal Guide*. He has also written liner notes and articles for numerous publications. He is currently executive editor at Schirmer Books, a publisher of books on music and the arts.

Introduction

If you think jazz is about a bunch of musicians getting together and "jamming," making it all up as they go along—you're not entirely wrong. A big part of the appeal of jazz is its freedom and spontaneity. Listening to a great soloist take a tune into outer space and back again creates the kind of thrill associated more commonly with a sporting event than with a musical performance: a hard-fought basketball game, maybe a great prizefight, tennis pairing—any contest involving a combination of imagination, invention, skill, courage, and endurance.

Sporting events aren't spontaneous anarchy, of course. They have rules. Not only is it impossible to play if you don't know these rules, it's also pretty difficult to enjoy the game as a spectator if you lack knowledge. Jazz is like that. While it's about freedom, it's also about rules, traditions, and styles, and the more you, as a listener, know about these things, the more pleasure jazz will give you.

Knowledge of the "rules," the history, and the lore of jazz is important to understanding and enjoying the music. In a musical marketplace where a CD can cost anywhere from about $12 to $16—with boxed sets priced higher, of course—such knowledge is also essential consumer advice.

The Complete Idiot's Guide to Jazz will not make you a jazz expert, but it will give you all the knowledge you need to choose your music wisely and to listen to it intelligently and with pleasure.

Part 1, "Downbeat" begins by defining jazz, this wonderful blend of African and African-American folk tradition with the strains of Euro-American classical and popular music. We go on to a survey of where to find jazz these days—in clubs, concert halls, on the air, and on disk. Finally, this introductory section ends with a primer on what to listen for when you listen to jazz.

Part 2, "The Sounds of Jazz" brings together the basic elements of jazz, sorting through the African, African-American, and Euro-American threads of this musical cloth, the instruments on which jazz is played, and the way in which jazz uses the human voice.

Part 3, "Backbeat" begins the narrative history of jazz, from the music's precursors (including work songs, field hollers, the blues, and ragtime), to the "birth" of jazz in New Orleans, to its early "classic" period in Chicago and New York, and to the emergence of the first great jazz soloists. From here, we explore the joyous phenomenon of swing and the two later styles swing spawned: bebop and the "cool school."

Part 4, "The Elements of Style" continues the narrative history with a look at mainstream jazz and third stream jazz, as well as Latin jazz, from Cubana Bop to the bossa nova. The section ends with a survey of the exciting style known as hard bop.

Part 5, "Wild Side or Mild Side?" shows how the makers of jazz pushed the envelope of their music, introducing highly challenging and controversial avant-garde and "free jazz" styles and then incorporating rock 'n' roll into jazz to produce fusion styles. The section continues with a tour of the borderlands between jazz and pop and surveys those performers who freely crossover from one to the other. We conclude with a snapshot of the fascinatingly fragmented world of jazz today, a music pulled in many directions and a field rich with exciting new performers. Finally, you get some guidance on building your own jazz archive and connecting with other jazz sources and resources.

At the very back of the book, you'll find a jazz who's who, a brief chronology of jazz, some ideas for expanding your collection of jazz CDs beyond the essentials, a basic jazz bibliography, and a glossary of jazz terminology.

Extras

In addition to the main narrative of *The Complete Idiot's Guide to Jazz*, you'll find other types of useful information, including classic jazz anecdotes and quotations, discussions of must-have albums, mini-essays on special jazz topics, warnings about mistakes to avoid, and definitions of key terms. Look for these features:

Take Five

Here you will find mini-essays on special jazz topics, ranging from capsule histories of the key record labels to highlight discussions of one-of-a-kind musicians.

Talk the Talk

These boxes define the terms and jargon every jazz insider needs to know.

Real Square

Here is a box that points out the pitfalls awaiting those new to jazz—and how to avoid them.

Dig This

This feature points out must-have jazz recordings and highlights key jazz facts.

Riffs

Jazz is full of classic anecdotes and pithy quotations. These boxes present some of the best.

Part 1

Downbeat

Jazz—what is it, exactly? That's the ground zero of this discussion, and it's where Chapter 1 takes us. Once we know what jazz is, we can go out looking for it, and that's the subject of Chapter 2, which takes us to the great live jazz venues of the past and present, then talks about where to find jazz on the air and on disk.

Anyone can listen to jazz, but it takes a little work really to hear *it. The last chapter in this section is a primer on just what to listen for when you tune your ears to a piece of jazz.*

Chapter 1

If You Have to Ask, You'll Never Know

In This Chapter

- Do I need lessons to like jazz?
- Rock vs. jazz
- The building blocks of jazz
- Improvisation: the soul of jazz
- Instrumental and vocal categories

They tell the story like this: Louis "Satchmo" Armstrong had just finished a set in a Harlem club patronized, as these places were in the 1920s and '30s, by well-heeled white nightclubbers. A society matron approached Satch and asked him to "define jazz."

"Lady," he replied, mopping his brow with his trademark handkerchief, "if I have to tell you, you'll never know."

The remark isn't as rude as it sounds. Volumes have been written in an attempt to nail jazz, to define it once and for all. But after all the ink that's been spilled, the heart of jazz remains feeling, not intellectual definition.

But I won't leave you hanging the way Satchmo left that poor lady. This chapter will talk about some of the things jazz is (and isn't), and how knowledge of some of the history and styles of jazz can enhance the pleasure you derive from the music.

One last thing, though. Sooner or later, *everyone* who writes about jazz brings up that old Satchmo story. Trouble is, it probably never happened. It's a myth. When you get into jazz, you enter a territory filled with myths and legends. Some are true. Some not. But the very existence of so many does convey a key truth about jazz: It's powerful music and a compelling force.

I Already Dig Jazz. So Who Needs a Book?

Maybe you already feel the power and the force. Jazz already moves you. Why do you need a book?

History, If You Want It

The fact is, you *don't* need a book. Go ahead, enjoy!

But it's also a fact that knowing more about what you already like only increases your enjoyment. This may seem obvious, but some people are afraid they're in danger of having the things they love explained to death.

Maybe being forced as a kid to memorize 112 facts about the War of 1812 killed any interest you had in American history. But jazz is filled with so many passionate, daring, even desperate characters that it's pretty hard to make it boring. The more you know about the men and women who've made and continue to make jazz, the more you'll love the music.

And there's even more.

When I was a boy of eight or nine, just starting piano lessons, I looked at the score of a Beethoven sonata my teacher happened to have on the piano. Looking at the score, thick with chords, I turned to her.

"I can play one note at a time," I told her, "but how will I ever learn to play all these notes at once?"

She explained that, in music, you don't read one note at a time, any more than you read one letter at a time when you read a book. You learn to recognize groups of notes, just as you learned to recognize groups of letters. You learn how one note relates to another.

This is true of learning to appreciate jazz or any musical tradition worth spending time with. You learn not to listen to a particular musician or piece of music in isolation, but in the context of what came before, what came after, and what's going on now. As you become familiar with the history of jazz, you start to hear and appreciate how one composer or performer relates to another. You start to understand how and why something is (or was) new and exciting, because you hear where it came from and dig where it's going.

Jazz is a conversation. Any piece of music worth calling jazz is a conversation among the players, a partly planned and partly spontaneous dialogue in tone and rhythm and color. But jazz is also a conversation with the past. Even the most avant-garde jazz players engage in a musical dialogue with the musicians who came before them.

Let's say you're a fan of Bud Powell (Chapter 13), a truly great bebop pianist. Learn about Art Tatum (Chapter 10), who came before Powell, and you'll hear how Powell talks with (and back to!) his musical predecessor. Then listen to such "stride" piano masters as Willie "The Lion" Smith, James P. Johnson, and Fats Waller (Chapter 10), and you'll hear more of Tatum's side of the dialogue. You'll hear where he comes from. You can go back even further, if you want, to the kings of ragtime, such as Scott Joplin and Tom Turpin (Chapter 7). They *started* the conversation in the first place.

I'm not suggesting this as an intellectual or academic exercise—what would be the point?—but instead, a way of deepening the pleasure you already take in jazz. Jazz is exciting because it is spontaneous, of the moment, a conversation in the here and now, anchored firmly and lovingly in the past.

Consumer Advice, If You Prefer

The 17th-century English poet Andrew Marvell addressed these lines "To His Coy Mistress": "Had we but world enough and time/This coyness, lady, were no crime."

As we approach the 21st century, most of us have even less world and time than the poet. Career, family, car payments, mortgage, all of these and more press down on us with demands for time and cash. We don't want to squander what little of each we have left. And while there are thousands of worthwhile jazz CDs waiting for you, who can afford the money or the time to plow through them all?

This book doesn't offer history alone, but also straightforward consumer advice: tips on where you might want to invest your jazz-dedicated budget of cash and time—now and later.

Someone to Bounce Off of

This book offers the jazz lover at least one more benefit. If you've been listening to jazz for awhile, you've doubtless developed some opinions about the music: who's great and who ain't, what's better and what's best. Opinions are like tennis balls. It's always more fun if you can bounce them off someone else's racket.

My racket is ready.

> **Dig This**
>
> You'll find advice on building your own jazz archive in Chapter 23. But start thinking now about building a collection. Don't junk your old turntable. Since CDs have made relics of vinyl LPs, you can pick up plenty of great jazz bargains in used record stores.

Jazz Is Boring. So Who Needs a Book?

Chances are, if you don't like jazz, you aren't reading this book. So to whom am I speaking? The only people who do *not* buy *Complete Idiot's Guides* are complete idiots. You're smart enough to know that jazz is an important subject you know too little about. And this makes you, a *Complete Idiot* reader, smarter than most.

Real Square

Beware of so-called "expert" opinions on individual jazz musicians. They are a lot like "expert" opinions on the right way to make a martini: rigid. Afficionados of the music enjoy making absolute pronouncements. You'll have more fun if you keep an open mind.

Or maybe people you admire and respect enjoy jazz. You've heard a lot about how great it is. But...well, you just can't get into it. Your mind drifts. There's no driving beat. The melody seems to get lost in a flurry of notes.

Typically, jazz is complex. It has a lot going on at once in terms of melodic line, harmony, and rhythm (all terms we will explore later). It makes demands on the listener—demands that most popular music, especially rock, does not make.

This is not intended to knock rock. In fact, jazz and rock are not necessarily mutually exclusive, as the "fusion" phenomenon has demonstrated (Chapter 20). But rock is fundamentally simpler than jazz and requires less from the listener. If you come to jazz expecting the same experience you get from listening to rock, you'll be disappointed.

"Bored with Life"

But if jazz *demands* more from listeners, I believe that it *gives* more in return. "The man who is bored with London," the great 18th-century writer Samuel Johnson declared, "is bored with life." Much the same can be said about jazz. Like Dr. Johnson's London, it is bustling, raucous, and, in some ways, demanding. Yet it is so rich in variety that you just can't be bored by it.

If you feel that you are "bored by jazz," well, just try a different kind of jazz. If swing doesn't turn you on, maybe bebop will. If the cool school leaves you cold, try fusion. Jazz is *many* musics, but you don't *have* to take them all. Certainly not all at once.

Bored or Just Bewildered?

Only exceptional people are interested in what they don't understand. I think that's the chief difference between great scientists and the rest of us. Most of us become disengaged once we fail to connect with something, whether it's a Physics 101 lecture or an avant-garde piano performance by Cecil Taylor (Chapter 19).

Fortunately, jazz is not rocket science, and a book like this one is enough to get you started on the road to understanding what you hear. With understanding, interest and enjoyment will follow. Trust me on this.

Elementary, My Dear Reader

There are many ways to approach jazz: historically, sociologically, musicologically.

Ugh!

Let's just start with the elements from which the music is built.

We Got Rhythm

Ask just about any musician to identify *the* most basic element of music, and melody will be number *two* (or even number three, after harmony).

In the first place? *Rhythm.*

Rhythm is a beat pattern or set of patterns formed by a series of notes of varying duration and stress. Rhythm is what makes you tap your foot or nod your head in response to the music—even complex rhythms are often *felt* as simple, infectious movement. The way jazz uses this basic musical element is what most distinguishes it from any other type of music. You'll read more in Chapter 4, but the point is that the subtle and varied use of distinctive rhythmic devices is what makes jazz jazz. Competent musicians in any musical style can learn to imitate the tone, melodic gestures, and harmonies we associate with jazz, but you can't fake true jazz rhythm. A jazz musician internalizes it so thoroughly that it becomes as natural as breathing.

Talk the Talk

Rhythm is a beat pattern or patterns formed by a series of notes of varying duration and accent or stress.

Melodies Merry and Melancholy

Important as rhythm is, melody is what appeals to most non-musicians. It's what sticks in your head. A good predictor of a Broadway musical's success was whether the audience left the theater humming the tunes. You can define *melody* as a series of notes arranged rhythmically to form a musical phrase. But that's pretty lame. What makes a melody more than just a series of notes? A true melody invites repetition. We want to hear it again, and we even want to reproduce it ourselves.

Why? Because it's cool, or beautiful, or funny, or sad, or it makes you want to jump or dance or sip a martini. Who knows?

Entire philosophies have been constructed in answer to this question. Suffice it to say that a beautiful melody moves us. The emotions evoked may be cheerful or melancholy or haunting or exciting.

Now, jazz is full of some very wonderful melodies. But a characteristic of most jazz is that melody takes a back seat to rhythm, improvisation, and harmony (which we'll discuss in a moment). In much popular music, the melodic line—the regular arrangement of notes we call melody—is the main thing and you get it right up front, obvious and with relatively little adornment. The simple pleasure of a melody is the whole point of popular music.

Talk the Talk

Melody is a series of notes arranged rhythmically to form a recognizable musical phrase.

In jazz, however, melody is not a final product, but a raw material. The melodic line is subjected to all kinds of manipulation and variation, so that even familiar tunes, given the jazz treatment, may not be recognizable.

The jazz attitude toward melody opens up dazzling musical worlds, but it also gives some listeners problems. They miss the tunes and, therefore, feel frustrated, even cheated.

The "Changes"

If you didn't sleep through all of Physics 101, you may remember the law of conservation of matter and energy. You know: Matter and energy are neither created nor lost, they're just transformed.

The same is true of melody in jazz. It's not lost, just transformed, both rhythmically and harmonically. *Harmony* combines two or more notes simultaneously to produce chords, which are, in turn, combined successively to produce chord progressions. A *chord progression* is a succession of chords that have a certain harmonic coherence, a recognizable harmonic pattern.

Casual listeners (non-musicians) naturally tend to focus on the melodic line, just as an ordinary person might look at a beautiful face and see skin, cheeks, mouth, nose, and eyes. A jazz musician, in contrast, focuses on the series of harmonies, the chord progressions, that underlie the melody, much as a sculptor, looking at a beautiful face, will visualize not the external features, but the underlying musculature and the structure of the bones.

Talk the Talk

Harmony is the combination of two or more notes *simultaneously* to produce chords, which are, in turn, combined *successively* to produce chord progressions. A **chord progression** is a succession of chords that have a certain harmonic coherence, a recognizable harmonic pattern.

Jazz musicians call this series of harmonies the *changes,* and these, more than any external melody, give jazz much of its structure and coherence.

Combined with rhythm, manipulation of the changes is much of what makes jazz sound like jazz. It is a source of great musical richness, but, again, the emphasis on the changes may present a problem for some listeners in some jazz music.

Let me explain why. Maybe you're familiar with those record albums, usually advertised on TV by some guy with a British accent and a smoking jacket, offering "101 Best-Loved Classical Melodies." Who buys these albums? Well, they're people who like the opening theme of Schubert's *Unfinished Symphony*, but don't want to wait around to hear what Schubert does with the theme. Yet the heart of classical music is this process of development. This is even truer of most jazz, which may consist of about 1 percent theme and 99 percent development.

Does this mean you have to become a musicologist to enjoy jazz?

Of course not. The wonderful thing about development, whether in classical music or in jazz, is that its beauty and logic have a way of sneaking up on you. They emerge, sooner or later, for just about anyone willing to listen—repeatedly, if necessary. Don't give up. Play the CD until it opens up for you. You may not be able to deliver a musicological lecture on the harmonic variations Charlie Parker plays in "'Round Midnight," but you'll quickly learn to love them.

Talk the Talk

Changes are what jazz musicians call the chord progressions on which a jazz piece is based.

Colors for the Ear

In addition to characteristic approaches to rhythm, melody, and harmony, jazz is rich with instrumental and vocal color. *Color* may be defined simply as tonal quality. Color is both the sound produced by a particular instrument and by the way that instrument is played. For example, the same melody played on a flute, a piano, and a saxophone will sound different because each of the instruments creates a different color. Additionally, the same melody played on tenor saxophone by a swing-era Coleman Hawkins (Chapter 11) would sound quite different played on the same instrument by a post-bop John Coltrane (Chapter 19).

Color is the fine seasoning of jazz music. Orchestral color is very important in classical music. Tchaikovsky knew when to use a clarinet and when to use an English horn. But there are generally fewer differences between one classical clarinetist and another than there are among one jazz trumpet player and another. Color is part of a jazz musician's signature.

Talk the Talk

Color, in music, refers to tonal quality and is a product of the instrument as well as the player.

Bent but Not Broken

One of Wolfgang Amadeus Mozart's many works is something called *A Musical Joke*. In this piece, Mozart pokes fun at clumsy composers and rustic musicians (the piece is sometimes called *The Village Musicians*). In this piece, Mozart writes "wrong" notes and has the musicians slide from them up to something like the "right" notes. In the context of 18th-century classical music, this passed for comedy, even painfully so. Jazz musicians, however, routinely and intentionally slide from note to note or, even more frequently, produce *bent notes*, attacking the note at its true pitch ("on key"), then bending it up or down just a bit, before coming back again. This "impure" sound is part and parcel of jazz and adds considerable flavor.

Talk the Talk

A **bent note** is produced by attacking it on pitch, then sliding up or down before returning to the "correct" pitch.

While any note may be bent, jazz players typically bend "blue notes." The blue note was a hallmark in jazz from the earliest days of the music, and we will define and discuss it in some detail when we get to Chapter 4. For now, just know that blue notes are certain notes that are bent or intentionally played "off key"—how far off depends on the instinct of the player. Mozart might chuckle at their impropriety, but to jazz musicians, it's serious business: one more way of expressing something.

Close Enough for Jazz

The prejudice classical musicians once felt against jazz musicians has pretty well died, though it died hard. For much of the 20th century, many classicists looked down on jazz musicians as sloppy and undisciplined. Of course, you can find mediocre musicians anywhere—in classical, jazz, rock, whatever. But while the greatest jazz musicians have always been as skilled as their classical counterparts, it is true that the "rules" of jazz tend to be much looser than those governing classical composition and performance.

Writing It

To begin with, much of jazz isn't written down. Musicologists may devote themselves to a Bach or a Brahms, attempting to ensure that the *B-minor Mass* or the *Second Piano Concerto* is performed precisely as the composer intended it. A jazz "composition" may consist of conventional musical notes fully written out on paper, or it may be nothing more than a sketchy indication of chords and a beat. In the latter case, the musicians are expected to use the chords as a framework on which to build an improvisation. Basically, they fill in all the notes.

Many jazz *charts* (as musical scores are called) written for big bands fully notate the main ensemble parts—where the whole group plays—but leave room for soloists to improvise.

Faking It

The extensively or even fully written-out jazz chart became common with the growth of the big bands in the late 1920s and '30s (Chapters 11 and 12). Before this, much of jazz was improvised. This is not to say that the musicians just made it up as they went along. Typically, the players were working with tunes they all knew and had rehearsed together, planning out who would do what. But when the moment of truth came, a lot of the sound was spontaneous, improvised on the spot.

Talk the Talk

A **chart** is what jazz musicians call sheet music or a musical score.

Even in the mature big bands, the soul of jazz was still spontaneity. Solos were too complex, too subtly inflected to be written out, so a big band might play the same tune in the same arrangement over and over again, and each time the soloists would do something a little different.

As smaller-ensemble jazz developed in intimate nightclub settings, improvisation became more important than ever. Quintets, quartets, trios, duets, and solo performers would routinely perform entirely without charts. Sometimes they would *jam* (playing in a group *jam session*), improvising with great boldness and intensity.

Dig This

The personality of individual soloists shapes and defines their playing. This is a signature of jazz and one of its greatest strengths. Becoming familiar with individual players and learning to recognize the differences between them is one of the main pleasures of jazz.

A jam session might be viewed as a collaborative venture, a jazz dialogue in the truest sense, the musicians leading and following one another. But jazz improvisation always had a macho, competitive edge to it, and jam sessions might become *cutting contests*, gladiatorial competitions between soloists to see who had superior skill, inventiveness, or just plain stamina.

Categorically Speaking

Jazz, I've pointed out, is not a single music, but encompasses a wide variety of styles. Some of these evolved chronologically. Some have gone out of style and are now considered old-fashioned—if they're played at all, it's strictly for historical interest. Others came into being more or less simultaneously. At any given time, more than one style of jazz has been regularly played.

Talk the Talk

To **jam** is to improvise, usually with other musicians. A **jam session** is an occasion of such improvisation.

Talk the Talk

A cutting contest is a type of jam session in which musicians compete to determine who has superior skill, inventiveness, and stamina. When entire bands compete in this way, the cutting session is often called a "battle of the bands."

Many of the chapters in this book are devoted to discussion of major jazz styles. For now, it's enough to recognize two major categories of jazz: instrumental and vocal.

Instrumentals

Instrumental jazz includes everything from music played by symphonic orchestras to dance orchestras of varying sizes, to big bands (which usually don't have strings), to smaller ensembles, down to chamber-size groups (quintets, quartets, trios, or duets) and solo performers. As you'll see in Chapter 5, the range of jazz instruments is wide.

Vocals

Jazz singers have been associated with dance orchestras and big bands since the 1920s and may also sing to the accompaniment of small ensembles or a pianist. In the 1930s and 1940s, jazz vocal groups, not just individual singers, were also popular. Yet, as you will learn in Chapter 6, singers haven't played the central role in jazz that they do in the blues, a musical style closely associated with jazz. This is not to say that jazz lacks important singers. There are many. But the vocalists, unlike the great instrumentalists, were not usually the pioneers and groundbreakers. This is ironic, because most of the important instrumentalists played their instruments in conscious imitation of the human voice. In fact, this may be considered a hallmark of jazz instrumental style: Play your horn as if you are singing.

Why Jazz?

Jazz rewards whatever effort you devote to it. Some of its pleasures are immediate. Others come with increased understanding. Still more benefits reach you more slowly and subtly, as you find yourself engaged in your own private dialogue with a variety of artists. Moreover, as you begin to discover the history behind the music, you find yourself connected, as never before, to American heritage, its glory and its pain, its nobility and its injustice. Jazz is an intensely American music, drawing on folk, African American, and European traditions, and on the feelings associated with living in this nation over the past century or so. To appreciate and savor jazz is to know something more about ourselves.

And if all this isn't reason enough to dive into what jazz musician and scholar Billy Taylor calls "America's classical music," dig this: Jazz is just plain cool.

The Least You Need to Know

- ➤ Jazz is a conversation. The players carry on musical dialogues with each other in the present, and also with the musicians and traditions of the past.
- ➤ The more you know about the history of jazz and the evolution of its different styles, the more pleasure you'll get from hearing any particular piece of jazz music.
- ➤ Jazz is built on rhythm, melody, harmony, and color. All are important, but rhythm and harmony are the most important of all.
- ➤ Even when jazz musicians play from a written score, spontaneous improvisation is at the heart of the music.

Chapter 2

Changing Venues: Where to Find Jazz Today

In This Chapter

- Finding jazz: sometimes you have to search
- A compact guide to jazz clubs
- Jazz in the concert hall
- Tapping into the collegiate jazz scene
- Finding out about festivals
- Jazz at home: radio, TV, and CD

The great American humorist of the 1920s and '30s Will Rogers used to say, "All I know is what I read in the papers." Let me paraphrase for myself: "All *I* know is what I see on *The Simpsons*."

Maybe you remember an episode in which saxophone-playing Lisa Simpson attempts to stage a memorial radio broadcast for her jazz idol, "Bleeding Gums" Murphy. Springfield's local jazz station is willing to cooperate—but the deejay points out that, being a *jazz* station, broadcast range is limited to about 30 yards ("which makes us the most powerful jazz station in the country").

Let's face it: You won't find as much jazz on the radio as you will country, rock, or easy listening. Nor will you stumble across a jazz club on every corner, and, in most cities, jazz festivals don't exactly elbow each other out of the way.

But the jazz scene is hardly as bleak as *The Simpsons* suggests. Actually, there is a *wealth* of jazz to be found—on the air, in clubs, in concerts, in festivals—if you are willing to poke around a little. And since you're obviously interested in jazz (or you've bought the wrong book), you probably won't mind stepping out from the crowd and strolling a side street or two. This chapter will help you find your way.

Endangered Species?

Question: *Where do you look when you're on 52nd Street between Fifth and Sixth avenues in Manhattan?*

Answer: *Up.*

This stretch of New York City real estate is all sleek office towers nowadays. Apart from a couple of signs the city has affixed to lampposts—"W.C. Handy Way" and "Swing Street"—there is nothing left of this block's former glory as the nation's jazz mecca.

During the decade before World War II, from about 1930 to 1940, 52nd Street was lined with such celebrated nightclubs as the Onyx, the Famous Door, Hickory House, Downbeat, the Three Deuces, Jimmy Ryan's, the Spotlite, and Kelly's Stable. Every jazz style could be found here, from ultra-traditional New Orleans to what was then the cutting edge: bebop. Art Tatum, Coleman Hawkins, Erroll Garner, Charlie Parker, Billie Holiday, Hot Lips Page, Count Basie, Woody Herman, Buddy Rich, Charlie Barnet, Fats Waller, and other jazz legends you'll meet in these pages all played 52nd Street.

To see this now reduced to a couple of street signs makes one think of the fate of the dinosaurs.

It's true that 52nd Street is no longer a jazz hotbed, and it's also true that you won't find anyplace like the 52nd Street of old in this or any other country today. However, jazz is hardly extinct, and the jazz club—the intimate, loose setting in which so much jazz has traditionally flourished—hasn't vanished from the face of the earth.

Dig This

New York may have been a jazz mecca in the '30s and '40s, but don't make the mistake of thinking it was the only place to ever find jazz. Many cities contributed to the development of jazz, with New Orleans, Chicago, Kansas City, Los Angeles—and New York—being the most important.

In fact, there are jazz clubs in most of the world's major cities. In the United States, you can find important clubs in Atlanta, Austin, Boston, Chicago, Cincinnati, Cleveland, Columbus (Ohio), Dallas, Detroit, Honolulu, Houston, Indianapolis, Kansas City, Los Angeles, Madison (Wisconsin), Memphis, Miami, Minneapolis-St. Paul, New Orleans, New York, Oakland (California), Orange County (California), Philadelphia, Pittsburgh, Portland (Oregon), San Antonio, San Francisco, San Jose, Santa Cruz, Seattle, St. Louis, Washington, D.C., and elsewhere. It's 52nd Street, spread all over the map.

"Can You Direct Me to the Nearest Speakeasy?"

"Reports of my death have been greatly exaggerated," Mark Twain wrote in response to erroneous news stories. And the same must be said in reply to anyone who bemoans the fate of jazz.

Not only is it not dead, it's unique among musical genres, popular or classical, for enjoying performance in just about every setting imaginable: the concert hall, the college auditorium, and the dedicated music festival, as well as on radio, TV, and CD.

But for the majority of jazz aficionados, the music is enjoyed most in nightclubs.

The reason for this goes to the very heart of jazz. In Part 3 of this book, we'll explore the heritage and history of this incredibly rich music, but let's skip ahead a little right now. As we will see, jazz fuses European and African-American musical traditions. On the African-American side, the music reaches back, ultimately, to West Africa and, later, to the music black slaves made to pass time, to ease pain, to accompany work, and to make the most of whatever joy they could find.

The point is this: At its deepest, jazz is rooted in life and everyday activity. By the late 19th century, in New Orleans, one of the "nursery" cities of the music, jazz developed not from show music or concert music, but from music that accompanied funeral processions (still a big part of the city's musical life) and from music that accompanied the commerce of "sporting houses"—brothels—in the red-light district. That is, beginning with its prehistory and early history, jazz was the sound of life at its most basic and unvarnished.

Little wonder, then, that jazz early on developed a deliciously unsavory reputation and found a home in deliciously unsavory settings, the *speakeasies* of the Roaring '20s, where folks could whet their whistles in a country decreed "dry" in 1919 by the 18th Amendment to the Constitution.

Talk the Talk

A **speakeasy** was a place where illegal alcoholic drinks could be obtained during Prohibition. Many speakeasies featured jazz entertainment and were important in the early history of the music.

The novelist F. Scott Fitzgerald called the '20s the "Jazz Age." As he saw it, the music set the era's social tempo: devil-may care hedonism flying in the face of official sobriety. The band played on while speakeasy patrons sipped illegal gin served in perfectly legal-looking tea cups. And, from that decade forward, jazz has been associated with woozy late hours and the rather wonderful, naughty pleasures of the nightclub scene.

The Club Scene

Prohibition was repealed in 1933, and, today, there is nothing illegal about jazz clubs. They aren't particularly "naughty," either. In fact, as the club scene goes, the establishments catering to a jazz clientele tend to be more sophisticated, civilized, and downright pleasant than most—albeit still informal and intimate.

If you like nightlife and good music, but you don't want to be hustled, hassled, jostled, or deafened, today's jazz clubs are great places to be.

The Classic Clubs

While it's true that many of the legendary clubs, such as those that once lined 52nd Street, are no more, a good many classic venues, clubs with an established reputation for hosting the most important musicians in an atmosphere conducive to great listening, survive and prosper. Let's talk about a few.

Boston proper once had many classic clubs, of which Wally's Paradise (617-562-8804), long a venue for local musicians, survives. In adjacent Cambridge, two clubs from the 1980s are already considered classics:

- **Regattabar** (617-876-7777) is a nightclub in the Charles Hotel on Harvard Square and features a stellar line-up.
- **Ryles** (617-491-3418) has built a reputation as a venue for the more popular avant-garde performers.

Chicago, with New York, has been a top jazz city since the 1920s. If you're in the Windy City, check out these:

- **Andy's** (312-642-6805) has been presenting jazz since 1977.
- **Green Mill Ballroom** (713-878-5552) was hosting jazz musicians as early as the 1920s. It closed in the 1940s, but reopened in the 1980s—retaining its Roaring '20s decor.
- **Jazz Showcase** (312-670-2473) was opened as Joe Segal's Jazz Showcase back in the late 1940s and is often considered the single most important jazz club in the city. It was the focus of much bebop activity during its early days.

New Orleans, usually deemed the cradle of jazz, today has disappointingly few jazz venues; however, two are especially important:

- **Preservation Hall** (504-523-8939) opened in the city's celebrated French Quarter in 1961 specifically to keep alive the traditions of early New Orleans jazz.
- **Snug Harbor** (505-949-0696) also occupies the Quarter, but is the city's most important venue for modern jazz, featuring local musicians as well as those with national reputations.

New York has more high-profile classic clubs than anywhere else on the face of the planet. Any jazz fan should visit at least one of the best-known clubs:

- **Birdland** (212-581-3080) is currently on 44th Street between 8th and 9th avenues. It is named in honor of its spiritual predecessor, which had been housed on Broadway near 52nd from 1949 to the 1960s and was itself named after the great alto saxophonist Charlie "Bird" Parker, who regularly performed there.
- **Blue Note** (212-475-8592) opened in Greenwich Village in 1981 and quickly became a leading venue for the most important jazz and bop-style musicians, including Dizzy Gillespie, Gerry Mulligan, and the Modern Jazz Quartet, among many others.
- **Bottom Line** (212-228-7880) is another Greenwich Village club, but was opened primarily as a folk venue. Jazz, however, has always played a significant part in its offerings—especially jazz at the cutting edge.
- **Bradley's** (212-473-9700) is in the vicinity of New York University and is a particularly intimate setting that specializes in duos.
- **Fat Tuesday** (212-533-7902) opened in 1979 and, since then, has been a major bop, blues, and mainstream jazz venue.
- **J's** (212-666-3600) offers traditional and mainstream jazz.
- **Knickerbocker's Saloon** (212-228-4890) is another New York University–area club. This one features jazz in intimate duo and trio settings.
- **Sweet Basil** (212-242-1785) has offered a very wide range of jazz styles since its opening in 1975 in Greenwich Village. Some of the world's most respected jazz musicians regularly appear at this venue.
- **Village Vanguard** (212-255-4037) has its origins in Max Gordon's Village Fair, opened in 1932 as a Greenwich Village haven for poets and artists. It moved to its present location on lower Seventh Avenue in 1935 and began to offer jazz, becoming a full-time jazz venue in the 1950s. *Everyone* has played the Vanguard, which is one of the very great places to hear—and experience—jazz. Although it occupies a basement, the Village Vanguard is a New York monument at least as significant as the Empire State Building.
- **Zinno's** (212-924-5182) opened in 1982 in a former speakeasy. The club specializes in piano and bass duos.

Philadelphia once sported a good many jazz clubs, and while several still flourish, the best known is the Painted Bride (215-925-9914), which opened in the late 1970s, closed in the 1980s, and is now reopened. It is more of a performance space than a club, but it presents good music.

The combo at Eddie Condon's, late 1940s: seated left to right are Cutty Cutshall, trombone; Wild Bill Davison, cornet; Edmund Hall, clarinet; Gene Schroeder, piano; standing: George Wettling on drums and Walter Page on bass.
Image from Lawrence Cohn.

Guitarist Eddie Condon, himself a regular performer at his club, appears in the other photograph.
Image from Lawrence Cohn.

Of San Francisco's numerous jazz clubs, at least one has enduring national standing. Kimball's (415-861-5555) has hosted jazz greats since the 1980s. For more genteel, cocktail-style jazz, the city's older hotels are a good choice, most notably the Top of the Mark (415-392-3434) at the venerable Mark Hopkins Hotel.

Finally, our nation's capital boasts one undeniable classic, Blues Alley (202-337-4141), which opened in Georgetown in 1965 and has continuously featured one jazz giant after another.

Where to Find More

The preceding roster is hardly exhaustive. It's just a rundown of a very few of the nation's jazz clubs that aficionados consider the classic venues. How can you find more?

- Try the Yellow Pages first. Look under "Nightclubs" and read the ads.
- Look in the entertainment section of your local newspaper. In larger cities, the "alternative" papers are often your best sources of information—in New York, for example, *The Village Voice;* in Chicago or Los Angeles, *The Reader;* in Atlanta, *Creative Loafing*. You get the idea.
- Log onto the Internet. Try pointing your Web browser to www.angelfire.com/fl/jazzchannel/, which lists many clubs in many U.S., Canadian, and European cities, and also offers links to other jazz-related Web sites.

"How Do I Get to Carnegie Hall?"

While many believe that live jazz is best heard in the informal and convivial club setting, jazz is no stranger to the classical concert hall. Indeed, for listening to large ensembles—big jazz orchestras, rather than duos, trios, quartets, and the like—the acoustics of a large symphony hall are hard to beat.

Making "a Lady Out of Jazz"

There was a time when concertgoers (especially American concertgoers) drew a sharp line separating the music of the concert hall (which was *classical* music—period) from the music of the speakeasy (jazz). Yet as early as 1912–14, the important African-American band leader and songwriter James Reese Europe (1881–1919) conducted what might be called proto-jazz orchestral concerts in New York's Carnegie Hall, and jazz programs became regular items on that hall's calendar by the 1930s.

The popular bandleader Paul "Pops" Whiteman (1890–1967) first made a consistent effort to bridge the gulf between jazz and classical music—"to make," he said, "a lady out of jazz." Toward this end, he commissioned the premier American composer, George Gershwin, to write Rhapsody in Blue (see Chapter 16), which was premiered in another New York City classical venue, Aeolian Hall, in 1924. But not until the late 1930s was jazz heard regularly in New York's Carnegie Hall and Town Hall, in Chicago's Orchestra Hall, and in other major symphonic concert halls throughout the nation.

Dig This

Of course you know the story of the bewildered New York City tourist who asks a native passerby, "How do I get to Carnegie Hall?" and is told in reply: "Years of practice, my boy. Years of practice."

Take Five

The most notable Carnegie Hall jazz concerts were initiated in the late 1930s by producer John Hammond under the series title "Spirituals to Swing." Featured performers included Sidney Bechet, James P. Johnson, Count Basie, Benny Goodman, Duke Ellington, and others. Goodman came back numerous times to Carnegie Hall, as did Ellington.

In 1946, Woody Herman and his Herd premiered *Ebony Concerto*, a jazz concerto for clarinet and orchestra, which Herman had commissioned from no less a figure in classical music than Igor Stravinsky. Charlie Parker, Miles Davis, Charles Mingus, and others have also played Carnegie Hall, and it became a major venue of the JVC (formerly Newport) Jazz Festival, after that annual event moved from Rhode Island to New York in 1972.

The Concert Experience

Just as classical music and jazz were once strictly segregated, so was there a time when concertgoers dressed to the nines—women in formal gowns, men in dinner jackets. Those days are long gone, but when you attend a jazz concert in a symphony hall, you'll probably be most comfortable in *neat* casual wear. If in doubt, don casual business attire.

"Concert manners" have nothing to do with maintaining stuffy formality, but do remember that you are among people who want to hear and enjoy the music. Accordingly,

- Don't converse while the music is playing.
- Don't snack.
- Don't fidget or fish in purse or pocket.
- If you have a cold or cough, come equipped with cough drops. (Then try to unwrap them quietly!)
- Avoid wearing a watch with an audible alarm or carrying a turned-on pager or cellular telephone.
- Don't wander in late.

Higher Education: Tapping into Your Local College

The college and university circuit has been good to jazz since at least the 1930s, and most touring musicians are eager to take as many college gigs as they can get. Traditionally, these audiences have been both enthusiastic and appreciative. In most college communities, institution-sponsored events are open to the public.

Tap into any jazz programming your local college or university may offer. A phone call to the main switchboard should point you in the direction of the appropriate box office. If they offer to put you on a mailing list, accept!

These days, most colleges and universities maintain home pages on the World Wide Web. Log onto www.clas.ufl.edu/CLAS/american-universities.html to locate the Web page of your local institution, then point your browser to it, and see if you can locate concert and ticket information.

Finally, student bars and clubs often feature jazz—and, often, with low cover prices or nominal drink minimums. Check out these places where you live.

Real Square

Latecomers be warned! Show up after the music begins, and you'll be seated only between numbers, not in the middle of a selection. You'll just have to wait.

Festive Occasions

In 1926, an outfit called the International Jazz Association held a six-day International Jazz Congress in Chicago. You might call that the first jazz *festival*—a series of performances by a large number of performers over a limited period of time. But the first true jazz festival was probably the Australian Jazz Convention, first held in 1946. Two years later came the first festival of international significance, the Nice Jazz Festival, in Nice, France.

In the United States, jazz festivals began to catch on big in the 1950s, with the inauguration of the Newport (now JVC) Jazz Festival (Newport, Rhode Island, 1954) and the Monterey Jazz Festival (Monterey, California, 1958). Since then, festivals have proliferated.

Talk the Talk

A jazz **festival** is a series of performances by a large number of performers over a limited period of time.

Make a Day of It

Jazz festivals can be a great way for you, your friends, and your family to enjoy a day or two or more of jazz. Here are some of the principal U.S. festivals and the year they first began:

- **Atlanta:** Atlanta Free Jazz Festival (1978)
- **Berkeley, CA:** Berkeley Jazz Festival (1967)
- **Boston:** *Boston Globe* and Jazz Heritage Festival (1966)
- **Chicago:** Chicago Jazz Festival (1979)
- **Davenport, IA:** Bix Beiderbecke Memorial Jazz Festival (1972)
- **Detroit:** Montreux-Detroit Kool Jazz Festival (1980)
- **Monterey, CA:** Monterey Jazz Festival (1958)
- **New Orleans:** New Orleans Jazz and Heritage Festival (1968)
- **New York City:** JVC (formerly Newport) Jazz Festival (1954)
- **Pittsburgh:** Pittsburgh Jazz Festival (1984)
- **St. Louis:** Mid-America Jazz Festival (1982)
- **Saratoga Springs, NY:** Newport Jazz Saratoga (1978)

That list hits only the biggest festivals. There are many more smaller events throughout the year as well. If there's no festival close to you, consider planning a travel vacation around a multi-day festival. Many festivals are all-outdoor events, usually located in a park or even out in the country. For more information, point your Web browser to yahoo.com and type in the search words "jazz festivals." You'll get a rich listing.

Jazz on the Couch

Club setting not intimate enough for you? Well, there's no place like home. There's a lot of jazz to be heard on the airwaves, and your local record store is not only a treasure trove of current jazz, but, if it stocks a good selection of reissue albums, can serve as your personal time machine back into jazz history.

TV Time

Broadcast network television offers distressingly little jazz, but public television (PBS) has a fair amount of jazz programming, and many of the arts channels on cable television offer even more. Tune in and turn on.

The Radio Dial

Lisa Simpson's experience with a 1-watt jazz radio station notwithstanding, most metropolitan areas support at least one FM station that plays jazz during at least part of its broadcast day. Sometimes such stations are associated with local colleges or universities. Sometimes they are part of the National Public Radio (NPR) network. But larger cities typically also offer commercial, jazz-oriented stations. Surf the stations. And, while you're at it, why don't you pledge a few bucks to the local NPR station? Not only will you be supporting a good thing, you'll receive a programming guide that will clue you into jazz broadcasts you might otherwise miss.

Waxing On

You'll find recommendations for CD purchases throughout this book, and Chapter 23 and Appendix C offer specific advice on building your own library of jazz recordings. In Chapter 3, you'll even find a few words of advice about choosing a sound system. Sure, the typical jazz record doesn't sell anywhere near the numbers of the latest rock or country release; still, record companies know that jazz listeners tend to be collectors (at least to some degree), and there's no danger of a serious shortage of new jazz recordings. Just as exciting is the fact that many of the great older recordings are readily available as well, often as "remastered" CDs—that is, recordings that not only have been reissued in CD format, but have also been electronically cleaned up to remove hiss and crackle. Some remastered jazz classics actually sound better than the original releases!

Jazz is a very personal music—personal to the performer as well as to the listener. For this reason, it particularly invites the collector who wants to build his or her personal musical library. In acquiring a collection of jazz recordings, you have the opportunity not only to partake of great American music, but, in doing so, to express your personal taste.

The Least You Need to Know

- Jazz is not as popular as rock or country, but it is readily available. You just have to know where to look.
- Most jazz fans believe the nightclub is the natural environment of jazz.
- In contrast to most other types of music, jazz is available in a range of venues, including clubs, concert halls, festivals, radio, TV, and recordings.

Chapter 3

Sharp Ears, Cool Head, Big Heart

In This Chapter

- How to listen to jazz
- Thinking of jazz as a conversation
- What to listen for: the basic elements of the jazz sound
- Musical structure
- Tips on choosing audio equipment for jazz listening

You don't need a Ph.D. in musicology to learn how to listen to jazz—not that you couldn't *use* one. At its best, jazz is rich and complex enough to satisfy any college professor, but it can also be fully enjoyed by anyone willing to lend their ears, head, and heart. Listening to most jazz is more like listening to classical music than pop or simple rock 'n' roll. It requires a concentration and a certain commitment. This chapter outlines what you need to help you really *hear* the jazz you listen to.

In the Mood

At no time in history have people had access to more information than we do. The Internet, e-mail, television, radio, books, newspapers, magazines, billboards—it all comes streaming in at us. Voices, tunes, songs pour in, too. You hear them over the supermarket Muzak system. You hear them on your car radio. You hear them over the phone when you're put on hold.

The fact is, unless you lock yourself in your room, it's difficult to experience true silence these days.

Ready access to information and music is mostly a wonderful thing, of course, but it can bring on a numbing sensory overload after awhile. The noise of the day, day after day, can make it difficult to get in the mood to listen—really listen—to good music.

Deep Background

If you know you have trouble concentrating on music, don't try. At least, not too hard. Instead, tune your radio to a jazz FM station and let it play in the background. If you get tired of listening, shut it off. Don't just tune to another station. Shut off the radio.

Do this over the course of several weeks. Soon, you'll find yourself pausing to listen more closely to a particular piece of music. Let it happen.

After using your radio as selective background music for awhile, you may get some idea of the kinds of jazz or the particular artists who appeal to you. If not, read through this book and take note of the recommendations given throughout. When you're ready, purchase a CD or two. Take it home. Pop it in. Start listening to it as background music. Listen to the same CD for the next few days.

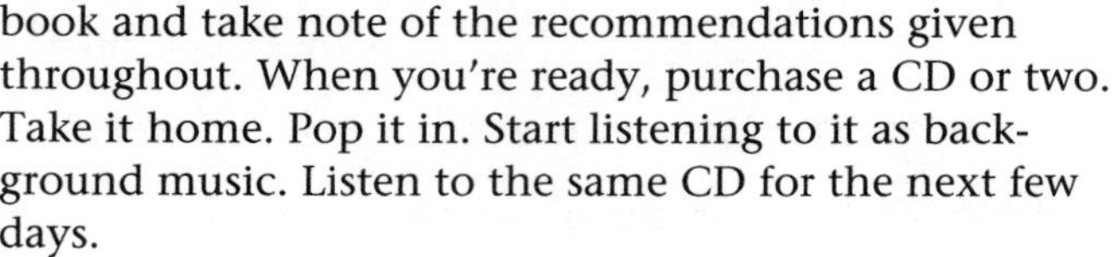

Real Square

Beware of becoming *too* focused on the radio when you are driving. Mind and eyes should be on the road. If something you hear really turns you on, pull over (if it is safe to do so) and listen. Also remember that headphones of any kind are dangerous to use when driving and are illegal in most states.

Now, one of two things will happen. Either you'll grow tired of the music, or it will grow on you. That is, one day, the music will "suddenly" seem familiar and comfortable, and stimulating.

Listening to unfamiliar music is a lot like looking for very faint stars in the sky. Astronomers know that you can see the faintest celestial objects by not looking too hard. You try to look out of the corner of your eye, where vision is less acute but more sensitive to low-light levels. When you approach unfamiliar music, try listening out of the corner of your ear. Don't try too hard. At least, not at first.

Dig This

Got a library card? Get one. Many public libraries lend CDs. For free.

It Ain't Muzak

Now here is a word of warning. While you can play jazz as background music, good jazz is *not* elevator music. It just can't stay tucked away in the background. It makes too many demands. Nor does it deserve to be ignored.

Approaching jazz through the background can ease you into the music—if, harried by the daily information flood, you *need* to be eased into it. But don't start thinking of it like the hum of an electric fan. Once you get comfortable with a piece of music, bring it out front. Really listen. Devote some time and attention to it. The payback is pleasure.

A Party

You can listen to any Louis Armstrong recording from 1925–27, say, or Miles Davis from the early 1950s, the way you'd listen to an old Jascha Heifitz recording of the Beethoven *Violin Concerto* or Glenn Gould playing Bach on the piano, giving it your utmost concentration. But remember from Chapter 2 that jazz is rooted in music that was meant to accompany life's basic (and baser) activities.

By all means, give jazz its due, but don't think of it as sacred, to only be enjoyed in private. Much jazz makes great party music—and not just music for the background, but music that *creates* the party. Listening need not be a solitary pleasure. Call your friends! Have them bring their favorite recordings.

A Party of One

There's a lot to say about jazz, but it's also hard to talk about. Why? Because the music offers so much variety that you begin to feel foolish when you try to explain or describe it. Really, we should invent a plural form of the word—call it *jazzes*—because, whatever "jazz" is, it's more than one kind of music.

At the very least, jazz runs a gamut of moods from intense introspection (take *Sunday at the Village Vanguard*, a 1961 album by pianist Bill Evans rereleased on Original Jazz Classics) to full-out extroversion (put on just about anything from the swing era—Benny Goodman, Count Basie, you name it).

While enjoying an evening alone, you may naturally gravitate toward reflection and introspection. But why not try something loud and fast? Make it a party of one. And let's face it: "Alone" may be the only way your housemate(s) will let you listen to that fabulously frenetic Coltrane *At the Village Vanguard* album.

Time and Place

When you're ready for something more than casual listening, find the right time and place.

- ➤ You need a time and place where you won't be disturbed—and when your listening won't disturb others.
- ➤ You need to be free from distraction. You don't want to feel like you should be catching up on that work you brought home or organizing that shoebox full of tax receipts. On the other hand, something mindless like doing dishes or folding laundry lets you listen *and* be productive.

Zeroing In

Much of this book is about "what to listen for" when you listen to jazz. Part 2 explores this subject in some depth. Before plunging in, however, let's get an overview of some basic elements to listen for in jazz.

The Jazz Conversation

Think a moment about any nonvocal piece of music that holds your attention—jazz, classical, or otherwise. What grabs you? It could be the beat, the melody, the orchestration. But something else is also happening to catch and hold your attention.

Dig This

Headphones can help, especially in distracting environments or wherever you could disturb others. You can choose the heavy studio-type phones, which block out most external noise, or the feather-weight designs, which bring the music close to you without totally excluding the outside world.

Say you're riding the morning commuter special to work. Same old train. Same old scenery. Same old stops. Then you catch a fragment of conversation from the seats behind you.

"… he's the one, then?"

"Oh, yeah. I think I'm in love. There's just one problem."

"What's that?"

"Well, he's married …"

And now you're no longer reading the paper, you're listening to this suddenly very interesting conversation.

You eavesdropper!

At its best, jazz, too, is a conversation, and if we can't fully participate, we can at least eavesdrop. This idea of conversation is basic to most good—and by "good," I mean consistently interesting—music. It's very typical of classical music. Listen to an orchestral piece, or especially a chamber work like a string quartet, and you become aware of the different instruments trading musical comments with one another.

In truly classical music—the music of the era of Mozart and Haydn—this "conversation" may be highly structured, like a series of questions and answers. For example, if the theme of a Haydn symphony begins with three notes running up the scale (a kind of musical question mark), it will soon be answered by three notes running down the scale.

In jazz, the conversation is usually spontaneous. Whether recorded or on a stage in front of you, it's live at that moment, not read from a script. It's sometimes more subtle and sometimes more intense, frenetic, and charged than in classical works. Sometimes it's an argument—a brawl, even. Sometimes it's emotionally charged: the dialogue of lovers. Often it's carried on at breakneck speed—rapid-fire syllables traded back and forth.

But behind what may at first seem like a lot of babble and chatter, there is almost always a question-and-answer structure. Listen to the thoroughly delightful bossa nova classic *Jazz Samba* (Verve), a 1962 recording featuring tenor saxophonist Stan Getz and guitarist Charlie Byrd (see Chapter 17). Don't just get caught up in the tunes and rhythms; listen to the exchange of ideas between these two masters.

Keep this in mind when you listen to great orchestral and big band recordings, too—like Benny Goodman, Artie Shaw, Woody Herman, Count Basie, or Duke Ellington. It's not just a lot of sound or even a lot of tunes, harmonies, and rhythms. It's a conversation: lively, absorbing, and provocative.

Picking Out Colors

In Chapter 1, I mentioned the great importance of rhythm in jazz, and we'll return to that subject repeatedly. I also mentioned the subject of color, which, in music, is the word used to describe the unique sound of each instrument. A tenor saxophone has a very different color from a trumpet, and Stan Getz on tenor sax creates a very different color from Sonny Rollins on the same instrument.

Listening for the different colors of the different instruments in an orchestral piece helps you concentrate more clearly on the conversation. It's like listening to the different voices of a conversation when you can hear but cannot see the participants. If everybody sounded the same, it would be hard to figure out who was talking and make sense of the whole thing. Fortunately, we all have different voices—and the same is true of jazz instruments and jazz players.

Theme Song

Thinking of conversation—a give-and-take—and instrumental color can really help you get into a piece of music. But the elements of jazz—rhythm, melody, harmony, conversation, color—actually take things one step further, beyond ideas, into the realm of feelings. Jazz is a paramount example of the way philosopher and educator Susanne Langer (1895–1985) described music: "Feeling as form."

Jazz gives musical form to feelings. Whatever else it is (and it is many things), it is the musical expression of emotion.

Feeling Feelings

That's what makes jazz so exciting, and, ultimately, enables anyone who's willing to listen to enjoy jazz fully. We all have emotions. We're all human. And no music is more emotional, more human, than jazz.

But as anyone who's ever been in a serious relationship knows, feelings aren't always easy to share, or understand. It takes commitment.

Allow yourself to feel what the musicians are inviting you to feel. Commit yourself to getting involved in the emotional world of the music. If you're determined to remain aloof and detached, jazz will always be alien and not a little boring.

Feeling Structure

The idea of musical "structure" scares just about anyone who is not a performer, composer, or musicologist. After all, you don't have to be an architect to live in your house or to work in your office building. These are structures you enjoy and use without knowing a thing about them.

Or so you think.

Actually, the way your house or workplace looks affects you very much, each and every day. The structure of these places produces certain emotions in you. Who doesn't want to live in a pretty house? Who wants to work in an ugly environment?

Like any complex music, jazz moves and affects us, not with sound or beat alone, but with structure. And just as you don't have to be an architect to enjoy your house, neither do you have to be a musicologist to get pleasure from the way a jazz piece is put together.

If you allow yourself to enter the world of feeling created by a good piece of jazz, you will start to *feel* how that piece hangs together. You'll perceive a kind of emotional logic. If you had a Ph.D., you might be able to put those feelings into academic verbiage—and, as you get into jazz, you'll find *plenty* of that on album covers and in CD booklets (more on that in a minute). That probably doesn't matter to you, but don't let it put you off. The point is this: Give yourself over to the music, and it will take on a new reality, the sounds coming together as a kind of architecture.

A Line or Two on Liner Notes

But why stop with feeling? Remember, jazz is "feeling as form," not just raw emotion. While you don't have to be a musical scholar to get a kick out of jazz, the more you know, the more you'll enjoy. In this regard, you're in luck. Most jazz records and CDs come packaged with *liner notes*, a brief essay usually by a jazz expert who illuminates some aspect of what's on the recording. Liner notes typically tell you…

- Something about the composer(s).
- Something about the performer(s).
- Something about the compositions.
- Perhaps something about the historical background of the music.

Most liner notes make for very interesting, very helpful reading.

Dig This

The great American architect Louis Sullivan called architecture "frozen music." Why not think of jazz as fluid architecture?

From the Audio File

You don't *have* to have your own audio system to enjoy jazz, but it sure helps. Sure, there are clubs and radio stations (in most metropolitan areas and college towns) that offer a wealth of jazz, but so much of our jazz heritage is recorded—from almost the turn of the 20th century right up to the present—that, without a good turntable or CD player, you're cut off from a lot of the music.

You don't have to go into deep debt to buy a decent audio system, though you can spend a fortune on a very elaborate system, if you so choose. Here are some guidelines.

Talk the Talk

Packaged with a CD (or found on the back of an LP), **liner notes** are a brief essay by an expert or the performers explaining some aspect of what's on the recording.

Choosing a Sound System

At minimum, you'll need a receiver and a CD player, as well as speakers. If you already own or plan to collect LP records (you remember, those 12-inch disks made out of black vinyl), you'll need a turntable as well. If you want a more elaborate system, you could get separate tuner, preamplifier, and power amplifier units. But I'll assume you're just going for a good, basic system.

You might want to purchase an integrated system, which consists of components sold together. These tend to be on the lower end of the price as well as the quality range. If you decide to invest in individual components, choose carefully to match the CD player, receiver, and speakers. Don't splurge on one item only to cheap out on the others. As the cliché goes, a chain is only as strong as its weakest link. In particular, don't be tempted into thinking that great speakers will make up for a cheesy receiver or a distortion-prone CD player. Speakers are only as good as the signal going into them.

You can pick up a very good receiver for $400 to $600. Go for at least 100 watts per channel and look for a unit with low distortion. You'll find this information on the unit's spec sheet.

CD players range widely in price. You are best off with a CD changer (a machine with multi-disc capacity), for which you shouldn't have to spend more than $300, unless you are reaching for the highest end.

Dig This

Invest a few dollars in a couple of the leading audio magazines, such as *Audio, Stereo Review,* or *Stereophile,* to get an idea of the latest products available. Andrew R. Yoder's *Home Audio: Choosing, Maintaining, and Repairing Your Audio System* (McGraw-Hill, 1997) is a very useful introduction to the subject.

Varying even more in price are speakers, which can get into thousands of dollars. For a moderately priced system, expect to spend $200 to $400 for a pair. These days, you don't have to buy monster-sized speakers, either. Many very small and elegant speaker systems on the market nowadays deliver powerful, high-quality sound.

Fine Tuning

Audiophiles (folks who are fanatics about stereo equipment) will tell you that a sound system ideal for rock 'n' roll is not necessarily the best for classical music or jazz. The whole area of taste in music systems is highly subjective; however, there is more than a grain of "absolute" truth in what the audiophiles say.

Talk the Talk

An **audiophile** is someone who is both fanatical and knowledgeable about hi-fidelity sound.

If your main listening interest is jazz, invest in high-quality (that is, low-distortion) equipment rather than in raw wattage and big speakers. You want a system geared to reproducing acoustic instruments, not the amplified guitars and keyboards of rock. While some jazz—especially fusion (see Chapter 20)—uses amplified instruments, it's still primarily an acoustic medium, and clarity of reproduction is your primary goal. You might also give some thought to what kind of jazz you're most likely to listen to: big bands and orchestras, or intimate duos, trios, and the like?

Also give thought to the room you'll be listening in. If it's small, you won't need a monster amplifier or speakers to fill it with sound. Anyway, *most* jazz doesn't call for the kind of volume rock fans want.

The Listening Room

This brings us to the listening room. It pays to purchase your equipment at a store that specializes in audio and offers a listening room where you can audition the equipment. Take along a favorite CD, something you know well, and make your tests with that.

When auditioning equipment, don't be impressed by raw volume. Listen for the following:

- **Distortion** Does the sound break up or get fuzzy?
- **Noise** One of the great advantages CDs offer over old vinyl LPs is a virtual absence of background noises, including hiss and the various snaps, crackles, and pops that often made phonograph records sound like a breakfast cereal. The music you hear should be free from background noise, especially hisses or hums of any kind.

- **Dynamic range** Test the equipment with a recording that has a lot of dynamic range—from very soft passages to very loud. The equipment should be able to handle the entire range comfortably without break-up of sound.
- **Transient response** This means how the equipment reproduces subtle, brief, high-frequency musical sounds, such as brushes on a snare drum or cymbal or the sound of the double-bass player's fingers sliding across the strings on the fingerboard.
- **Bass handling** You should hear clean, full bass notes. Poor equipment makes the low notes sound like they're coming from the bottom of a tub.
- **General clarity** Poor-quality equipment produces a "boxy" sound; that is, a sound that continually makes you aware that you are listening to music reproduced through speakers. The music should sound as if it is coming from instruments positioned right in front of you.

Real Square

A hum in a brand-new audio system is a signal of poor electrical grounding, which is, in turn, a sign of faulty workmanship. Listen for any hum, no matter how faint. Do not purchase equipment that hums.

The Headphone Experience

If you are serious about your music, you don't want to be disturbed when you're listening. And if you care about your family, roommates, or nearest neighbors, you don't want to disturb them. Consider investing in a good pair of headphones.

While headphones come in a variety of styles and prices, you have one major choice to make. Do you want to wear rather large and heavy phones, which will totally cut out noise from the outside? Or do you want small, feather-light phones that reproduce sound beautifully, but do not isolate you?

In recording studios, the heavy, isolating phones are used, and they provide probably the best-quality sound; however, wearing them for long periods can be fatiguing. Moreover, you're always aware that you have headphones on. For some people, this interferes with fully enjoying the music.

The Digital Revolution

There is no denying that the compact disc (CD) has many advantages over vinyl records. CDs have less unwanted background noise, they're more durable, they don't wear out with repeated playing, and they're far less likely to suffer from manufacturing defects. They're also easier to store and take up less room.

Nevertheless, many diehard audiophiles insist that digital sound reproduction is inferior to the analog reproduction techniques used to create LP records. This is a question of personal taste. Probably a more important consideration is whether or not you will want to listen to vinyl recordings as well as CDs. While many, many historical jazz recordings have been reissued on CD, many others are available only on vinyl, still to be found in used record stores. If you have access to a substantial collection of LP recordings or you wish to begin collecting them, invest in a good turntable in addition to a CD player. Put your money in a high-quality basic table—no changer—with a high-end phono cartridge.

Dig This

Got a problem CD? A note that "gets stuck" and repeats like a machine gun? Chances are the CD just needs cleaning. Eject it and *gently* wipe the non-label surface with a spotlessly clean cloth. Be careful not to scratch the CD. Most CD problems can be easily wiped away.

One Man's Meat...

...is another man's poison. In other words, let's not argue about taste. Aside from certain basic issues of quality—the handful of points I've just listed—choosing a sound system involves highly subjective choices, just like choosing the music you listen to. Learn all you care to learn about audio equipment and about jazz, then listen for yourself. Give the sound system as well as the music a fair shake. Then make your own choices.

But *hearing* jazz isn't *all* subjective. The music follows certain traditions and even certain rules. Now that you have read some ideas about how to listen to jazz, dig into the next part of the book, which will guide you in just what to listen *for*.

The Least You Need to Know

- Full enjoyment of jazz requires more than passive listening. It requires a commitment of focus at a time when you are free from distraction.
- A great way to get into a piece of jazz is to think of it as a conversation. Listen not just to the sounds, but to the exchanges among the instruments and among the musical phrases.
- Becoming accustomed to the tonal color of each instrument enhances your enjoyment of jazz.
- You don't have to spend a fortune on audio equipment, but listen to the equipment at a reputable audio store before you buy it. Take along a favorite CD for the test hearing.

Part 2

The Sounds of Jazz

Jazz comes from a rich tradition, with a complex heritage that blends African folk music with African-American folk and popular music, the blues, a dash of Spanish ethnic music, and various strains of Euro-American folk, popular, and classical traditions. We begin this section by sorting out the various strains of this background, then combine them with the improvisational spirit that is (as many see it) the single most important defining characteristic of jazz.

But jazz is not just a collection of musical ideas. It is, after all, about sound, and sound requires instruments. Here you'll find a discussion of the major—and some important minor—instruments of jazz, ending, in the last chapter of this section, with the human voice.

Chapter 4

Black and Blue

In This Chapter

- The African, African-American, and European roots of jazz
- Relation of blues and ragtime to jazz
- The meaning of "swing"
- About harmony and melody in jazz

The distinguished musicologist and jazz musician Billy Taylor calls jazz "America's classical music." This is an interesting way to think about it, but most students and enthusiasts see jazz as more immediately rooted in African-American folk music and a combination of American and European popular music traditions. The point is this: Jazz is not classical music, or folk music, or black music, but, rather, *American* music. It draws on the culture and genius of many people of many backgrounds. Jazz is a democratic music, a plural music, inclusive rather than exclusive. Whatever our musical, cultural, or ethnic background, we are all invited to listen and enjoy.

America, it has often been said, is a great melting pot. Maybe. Musically, it's more of a stew pot, and jazz is one of its spicier creations. This chapter will define some of the key ingredients.

Deep Rooted: Africa, Europe, Slavery, Freedom

We'll delve into the history—and even the prehistory—of jazz beginning in Chapter 7. But if we want a snapshot definition of jazz, we have to take a glance back now. Jazz is a highly improvisational form of music primarily developed by African Americans who combined European harmonic structures with African rhythmic complexities, which are, in turn, additionally overlaid with European and white American dance and march rhythms. Let's add a bit more to this nutshell: Part of the "feel" of jazz also comes from another African American musical tradition, the blues, a form of music that makes eloquent use of the intonations and rhythms of speech—in instrumental as well as vocal music.

The peoples of West Africa, hundreds of thousands of whom fell victim to the slave trade between the 16th and 19th centuries, had vocal and percussive music that was quite different from anything that had developed in Europe or white America. Scales and harmony, subject to rigid rules in the European tradition, were more intuitive in the African tradition. Indeed, African music is closer to speech in the way it conveys subtle shades of meaning and emotion. Variation in the pitch of a note or the inflection of the voice could carry worlds of meaning and emotion.

Talk the Talk

Jazz is a highly improvisational form of music, primarily developed by African Americans, combining European harmonic structures with African rhythmic complexities. These are, in turn, overlaid with European-American dance and march rhythms and with elements borrowed from the blues tradition.

The **blues** derives from a southern African-American folk tradition, usually characterized by slow tempo and the use of flatted thirds and sevenths ("blue notes"). Emotionally, the blues is typically intense and plaintive.

For those brought in slavery to the New World, music was poignant and precious. A link with what had been lost, it also grew and developed in the plantation fields. While it is doubtless true that some slave owners discouraged song, most saw it as a harmless aid to production. Slave songs made good work songs, and the echo of this tradition can be heard in such early jazz as King Oliver's "Lift 'Em Up, Joe."

As we'll see in Chapter 7, African musical traditions met Euro-American traditions in music for worship (the spiritual) as well as entertainment. Many scholars believe that plantation brass bands, popular in the 1830s, were the first direct precursors of jazz. These African-American bands led to minstrel shows, popular entertainment in which *white* performers blackened their faces with burnt cork and performed for white audiences what they called "darky" songs and dances.

While the conclusion of the Civil War brought an end to slavery, it did not end the oppression of African Americans. Nevertheless, freedom—such as it was—promoted the development of new forms of black popular music, the most important of which was ragtime.

A West African musician, about 1919. Image from arttoday.com

Where's the Beat?

Ragtime is so crucial to the early history of jazz that we'll devote part of Chapter 7 to it. What's important to know now is that it was wildly popular not only among black audiences, but among whites as well.

The first ragtime musicians wandered from dive to dive in the Mississippi country and on the eastern seaboard in the late 1880s. They played piano in honky-tonk joints, cheap restaurants, bordellos, and saloons. But the music really took off in the final decade of the 19th century and the first decade of the 20th.

Talk the Talk

Ragtime is a jazz precursor characterized by elaborate **syncopation** in the melody played against a steadily accented accompaniment. It was most popular at the end of the 19th century and in the early 20th, before the 1920s.

Syncopation: "Ragged Time"

The source of this music's appeal can be guessed by looking more closely at its name. Ragtime is short for "ragged time," which is how people described the syncopation that was this music's driving force. The most popular ragtime instrument was the piano, and "ragged time" was ideally suited to that instrument. Typically, the left hand played a steady bass in a duple (one-two) rhythm—a standard dance-orchestra beat—while the right hand played the melody with a syncopated triple (one-two-three) rhythm.

Syncopation, putting the emphasis unexpectedly on weak beats rather than the main beats, was nothing new in Euro-American musical tradition—classical composers and others had been doing it for years. But ragtime played syncopation to the hilt, raucously, joyously, sometimes eloquently exploring and exploiting the full range of this novel beat.

Talk the Talk

Syncopation is a rhythmic device whereby weak beats rather than the main beats are accented. The beat becomes at once freer and yet more compelling to listeners.

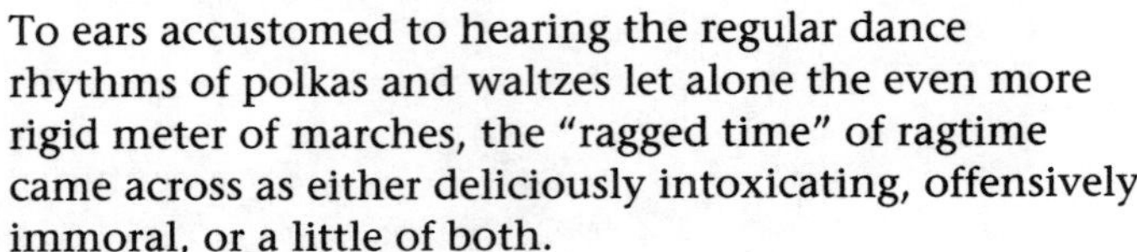

To ears accustomed to hearing the regular dance rhythms of polkas and waltzes let alone the even more rigid meter of marches, the "ragged time" of ragtime came across as either deliciously intoxicating, offensively immoral, or a little of both.

The best ragtime music, works by Scott Joplin (1868–1917), for example, still sounds fresh today. But there is also an innocence about such music that seems a far cry from the more sophisticated forms of jazz. Nevertheless, the "ragged time" of ragtime is the direct predecessor of the kind of beat that is typical of all jazz: playful, inventive, variable, sometimes elusive, never rigid or regular.

Dig This

Get a taste of ragtime as it was played in 1910. *The Elite Syncopation: Classic Ragtime from Rare Piano Rolls* (Biograph) features digital transcriptions of player piano rolls recorded by Joplin and other ragtime immortals.

Rubato: A Musical Slinky

Syncopation plays with rhythm by repeatedly delivering the unexpected, purposely putting the emphasis where it doesn't belong—not on the strong beats, but on the weak ones. This stretches our ears and our imagination. Another element typical of jazz literally stretches the music itself.

In the preceding chapter, I mentioned that jazz is a lot like conversation. Try a little experiment. Tune your TV or radio to a talk show in a language that is foreign to you. If you don't speak Spanish, for example, find a Spanish show.

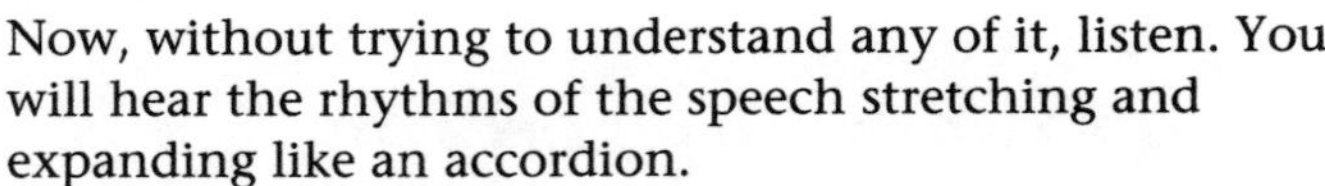

Now, without trying to understand any of it, listen. You will hear the rhythms of the speech stretching and expanding like an accordion.

Talk the Talk

Rubato is a relaxation of strict musical time; a rhythmic flexibility within a musical phrase or measure. It is very widely used in jazz.

Just as speech is characterized by accordion- or Slinky-like rhythmical patterns, so is jazz. The musical term for this is *rubato,* and it means a relaxation of strict time, a rhythmic flexibility within a musical phrase or measure. Jazz musicians often "violate" strict rhythm, stretching and compressing the beat as the spirit moves them. The real trick is for ensemble players to learn to do this together, so that no one gets lost or left behind.

Rubato gives great flavor to jazz and also lends it the intimacy of conversation. It is a way of treating rhythm that is instinctive and highly personal. Much of a jazz musician's "signature sound" is the result of how he or she uses rubato.

Swing It

Syncopation—or ragged time—and rubato are important to jazz, but they're not unique to the music. Listen to piano pieces by the 19th-century German romantic composer Robert Schumann (1810-56), for example, and you will hear plenty of syncopation. Attend any grand-opera performance, and you'll get an earful of rubato in every aria.

But another rhythmical element is absolutely unique to jazz and truly separates it from any other music.

Musicians call it *swing*. Now, that's a word applied to a specific style of jazz most popular in the 1930s and '40s and especially associated with big bands (see Chapters 11 and 12); but *swing* also applies to a quality attributed to all jazz music and performance.

Talk the Talk

Swing has two meanings in jazz. It is a style of music, chiefly associated with big bands, popular in the 1930s and 1940s. It is also a difficult-to-define rhythmic quality that characterizes most jazz, an interplay or conflict between the accents and duration applied to musical notes versus the overall fixed pulse of the music.

Why John Philip Sousa Wasn't a Jazz Musician

Unfortunately, in this sense, *swing* can't be defined precisely. It's one of those things you "know" when you hear. It's something you *feel* more than hear, and often unconsciously sway or tap your foot or respond physically in some way. But essentially, swing is the way a jazz player creates a kind of interplay or even conflict between the accents and duration he applies to the notes versus the fixed pulse of the music.

If you want a quick lesson in swing, hum to yourself the familiar song "April in Paris." Now listen to what Count Basie does with the tune on the 1956 Verve album *April in Paris* (a classic available on CD). You'll understand the concept in a flash.

On paper, most jazz is not written in exotic meters, but in the familiar time signatures of dances and, yes, even of marches. Yet no honest-to-goodness jazz musician ever plays a tune "straight." She *swings* it.

The *Stars and Stripes Forever* by John Philip Sousa (1854–1932) is a stirring march, but it's not jazz. The rhythm is regular. It never swings.

Dig This

John Philip Sousa was no jazz musician to be sure, but America's celebrated "March King" did win a prize at the 1900 Paris Exposition not for a rousing march, but for a rendition of "My Ragtime Baby" (1898).

Why Elvis Presley Wasn't a Jazz Musician Either

Often, swing involves high energy. Often, it imparts a moving soulfulness to the music. Well, these same qualities can be found in really good rock 'n' roll as well. No one put more energy and soul into a song than the King himself, Elvis Presley.

But he was not a jazz musician. He delivered a driving, highly charged beat, to be sure, but he did not swing. That is, he did not consistently play his signature sense of rhythm *against* the pulse of the music. And therein lies the heart of the jazz performer's approach to music: a playing of one rhythmic pattern against another.

What's the Key?

Just as you'll be disappointed if you search for a four-square beat in jazz, so you may find yourself bewildered by what might be described as a murky or hazy quality about the music. Just as jazz stretches our rhythmic sensibilities, so it compels us to exercise our tonal sense.

Key is one of the most basic and yet most difficult of musical concepts. All we need to know is that the music most Euro-Americans have been raised on is based on a scale of seven tones in fixed relationship to a *tonic*—the "keynote," or first note of a particular scale. We are so accustomed to this system that we automatically define music according to it. Anything that "violates" it seems, to a greater or lesser degree, not just different, but *wrong*.

Some modern "classical" music (the works of Arnold Schoenberg are prime examples) refuses to get pinned down to a key and scale. We call this music *atonal*, and most people find it downright hard to listen to—a collection of random noises. While a handful of avant-garde jazz pieces are atonal, probably 98 percent of jazz music is written in a specific scale. Nevertheless, just as jazz musicians bend rhythm while still being highly rhythmic, they bend tonality, while still being tonal.

Harmony: A Backward Glance

The loose approach to key probably derives from the music's roots outside of the familiar Western concepts of tonality. West African music isn't based on a seven-tone scale; indeed, much of it is hardly based on any scale at all. To varying degrees, jazz performers look back to the roots of the music, and, therefore, the harmonies are inherently looser. A jazz player often purposely plays off-pitch or attacks a note off-pitch, then slides up to and even slightly above the "correct" pitch, before settling down to it.

Color It Blue

Typically, the harmonic looseness of jazz is not random. In Chapter 1, I mentioned *blue notes*, notes that are slightly lowered ("flatted") below their "correct" pitch. Most of the time, these blue notes are the third and seventh steps in the scale. Occasionally, the fifth is also treated as a blue note.

If you've taken any music lessons at all, you're familiar with the C-major scale: C, D, E, F, G, A, B, C. This scale has no sharps or flats (the black keys on the piano). A jazz musician, however, would likely flat the E (third step in the scale) and the B (seventh step). If she was playing the piano, she might hit the black key instead of the white, fully flatting the note. But if she were playing an instrument capable of hitting tones *between* E-natural and E-flat, she'd probably hit a note somewhere between the two. As her musical instincts moved her, she might slide around that note, too.

Blue notes, especially when they are combined with chords, give jazz a very characteristic sound. Combined with swing rhythm, blue notes are among the most important elements that make jazz sound like jazz.

Where's the Melody?

In Chapter 1, you were warned that melody can be a tantalizingly elusive thing in jazz. Jazz composers have, in fact, written some of the world's most beautiful melodies. Think of Duke Ellington's "Mood Indigo" or "Sophisticated Lady" or Thelonious Monk's "'Round Midnight." Yet jazz musicians rarely play melodies straight. To jazz people, tunes are for bending, stretching, twisting, disassembling, juggling, and generally playing around with.

Variation

As with many other musical devices, variation is hardly unique to jazz. Composers have been writing various variations for centuries. As usual, though, jazz players take a less formal approach. They may play an original melody or a familiar tune from a pop song. They may play all of it or just enough of it to give you a taste of the familiar. After this, the tune becomes fair game for improvised variation.

If you like your tunes straight and simple, you probably will never get seriously into jazz. If, on the other hand, you are willing to let the musicians take you on a ride that wanders far from the familiar, the jazz adventure is for you.

Invention

In the days before cue cards and teleprompters, politicians and other professional speakers were expected to take any subject and, on a moment's notice, speak on that subject extemporaneously. Few speakers today would measure up. But for the jazz musician, something very much like this is his stock in trade.

Some jazz is completely written out, just like classical music; some is completely spontaneous; most is a combination of the two. Chord patterns may be specified. Maybe a tune will be written out. But it's up to the performer to take these hints and make jazz out of them. The jazz musician is an inventor who produces his inventions on the spot, putting them together out of a few musical hints, phrases from familiar tunes, and chord patterns (called—remember from Chapter 1—changes).

The result is music that, at its best, is intensely spontaneous and improvisational, but not random. The rules of music familiar to us are still there. They are often bent, stretched, and even broken, but we're still aware of them.

That's the real kick of jazz. It's no fun to break the rules unless you know what those rules are. Then, provided they are violated imaginatively, daringly, inventively, soulfully, or playfully, breaking the rules is a supremely creative act that is something very like a miracle to hear.

The Least You Need to Know

- Jazz is rooted in African-American as well as Euro-American musical traditions; open to many traditions, it is a highly democratic form of music.
- Ragtime is an important precursor to jazz, while blues is a prominent relative of the music, from which jazz has borrowed a number of key elements.
- "Swing," a characteristic approach to rhythm, is a difficult-to-define quality that is unique to jazz and, indeed, is the rhythmic essence of the music.
- Melody (a pretty tune) is important to jazz more as a musical element or building block than as an "end product."
- While jazz encompasses impromptu as well as written-out music, spontaneity and improvisation are almost always crucial elements.

Chapter 5

It's Instrumental

In This Chapter

- Make-up of the early jazz ensembles
- The rhythm section
- The important solo instruments
- Saxophone and double bass: jazz icons
- The piano as jazz instrument
- Unconventional instruments

Chapter 4 pointed out some of the musical and stylistic features to listen for and enjoy when you put your ears to jazz. But you're not just hearing music and style when you listen to jazz. You're hearing instruments.

Most of the instruments of jazz are familiar. Many find homes in both a symphony orchestra and a jazz band. A trumpet can play Haydn or Miles Davis, and a musical genius like Wynton Marsalis can do—and has done—both. The classicism or the "jazzism" isn't in the instrument, it's in how the instrument is played and, to some extent, in how instruments are combined. We'll talk about it all in this chapter.

Talk the Talk

To **cover** is to borrow (in some cases, steal) a song or a style composed or originated by another performer.

Dig This

Although none of five ODJB members were standout musicians, their recordings have an innocent and infectious energy and are well worth checking out. *75th Anniversary* (Bluebird) offers the best of their 1917–21 recorded output. *The Complete Original Dixieland Jazz Band* (RCA) is a two-CD set for those who also want to hear the band in its second incarnation, during the 1930s.

The Original Dixieland Jass Band

They were five journeymen white musicians who *covered* (copied) and simplified the black music they heard. "Original" they weren't, but that didn't stop them from calling themselves the *Original* Dixieland Jass Band (ODJB). And while they were hardly the first to play jazz, they were the first to record it, releasing *Livery Stable Blues* in 1917 and *Tiger Rag* the following year. They enjoyed great success, especially in New York, through the mid 1920s.

In another sense, too, the Original Dixieland Jass Band was neither original nor even unusual. They had drums, trombone, cornet, clarinet, and piano: the standard instrumentation of a small dance band of the period.

And that's how jazz bands began, developing from nothing more or less than dance bands or "social orchestras." Many black jazz musicians in New Orleans got their start in the brass bands that officiated at funeral processions, playing solemn dirges on the way to the burying grounds and full-out hot jazz on the way back. Such groups may still be heard during any of New Orleans' Mardi Gras parades. No one can deny that their sound is unique, yet their instrumentation is ordinary: standard late 19th- and early 20th-century brass marching bands, from eight to 14 pieces, with cornets or trumpets, trombones, alto or baritone horns, sousaphone or tuba, snare drums, and at least one bass drum, with a cymbal attached.

From "Jass" to "Jazz"

Gradually, as *jass*—an early name for the music—evolved into jazz by the mid- to late 1920s, the instrumentation of jazz diverged, taking on greater variety. Some of the instruments introduced during the '20s continue to figure as prime jazz instruments today. A few have fallen out of favor.

Take Five

The origin of the term "jass"—or "jazz"—is obscure. Musicologists as well as etymologists (students of the origins of words) speculate that *jazz* may be derived from an Afro-Caribbean word meaning "to speed up." It may also be derived from the name of an early performer, Jazbo—or "Chas"—Brown. Many others have suggested that the clue to the word's origin lies in its early "jass" spelling, which suggests "ass" in the sense of sexual intercourse. Additional interpretations abound. Whatever its precise origin, the word first appeared in print in 1913 in the *San Francisco Bulletin,* but, in many places, the older term *ragtime* persisted to describe jazz well into the '20s.

Rhythm Section

To describe the "rhythm section" as the accompanying instruments or the rhythm keepers is accurate, as far as it goes. But when you consider that rhythm is the root sound of jazz, this description clearly doesn't go far enough.

The rhythm section is the heartbeat of any group. It gives the band life, kicks it along, makes it go.

In small, early groups like the Original Dixieland Jass Band, the rhythm section consisted of drums and piano. In later ensembles, rhythm sections might include drums, piano, guitar or banjo, and double bass or tuba.

Percussion Pieces

If the rhythm section is the heart of a jazz ensemble, the drums are the heart of the rhythm section. In the traditional New Orleans marching bands, percussion consists of snare drums (a small, double-headed drum with "snares"—wires—stretched across the lower skin to increase reverberation), a bass drum (a big, upright drum that produces a low-pitched boom), and a simple set of cymbals.

Dance-type bands, such as the ODJB, added tom-toms (bigger than a snare drum, smaller than a bass drum, with a sound that was full-bodied and tunable) and, sometimes, a cowbell.

How a snare drum works: wires ("snares") stretched across the bottom of the drum vibrate, giving the drum its characteristic highly reverberative sound. Image from arttoday.com.

By the 1930s, large, sophisticated orchestras sported an array of percussion instruments. In addition to the basics just mentioned, there were…

- **Floor tom-toms** A bigger tom-tom for a bigger, "jungle-like" sound.
- **More and more cymbals** These supplemented the traditional 14-inch-diameter Turkish cymbal. Chinese cymbals are larger in diameter and sound lower and more brittle than the standard Turkish cymbal. Splash cymbals are about half the diameter of a standard Turkish cymbal and provide a high, bright sound. Crash cymbals are larger than Turkish cymbals but smaller than Chinese and are used to provide accents rather than keep time. Hi-hat cymbals are two cymbals mounted on a stand and worked by a foot pedal; they are used to keep time. The sizzle cymbal has rivets loosely placed in holes drilled around the edge of the cymbal to create a sizzle sound. The top or ride cymbal is large—up to about two feet in diameter—and was very popular in big band ensembles.
- **Tam-tams** Gongs of various diameters and tones.
- **Woodblocks and temple blocks** These are hollow "slit drums" or blocks that produce a percussive tone. Woodblocks sound like horses' hooves; temple blocks are subtler, because they are actually tuned to musical notes.
- **Timpani** Also called kettle drums, this instrument is found in symphony orchestras and in large jazz orchestras. It is a completely tunable drum, capable of playing a range of notes.
- **Tubular bells** Another tuned percussion instrument, this is a set of metal tubes hung on a rack and played with a mallet or mallets.
- **Vibraphones** Also called vibes, this is essentially a xylophone with an electric resonator that produces a much fuller, louder sound. The instrument became a member of the rhythm section of some of the bigger big bands in the 1930s. We'll discuss it a bit later in the chapter.

Take Five

The "drum kit" found in most jazz bands since the 1930s was developed and standardized by jazz drummers, and the agility and independence of limbs necessary to play different rhythmic accents between both feet and both hands was carried over from complex African polyrhythms. The 1920s drummer Vic Berton is said to have invented the hi-hat cymbal and possibly the bass drum foot pedal as well, and while percussionists like Duke Ellington's drummer Sonny Greer used an extensive setup of drums and cymbals as much for showmanship as functional music-making, others like Count Basies's drummer Papa Jo Jones proved that an entire big band could swing based upon the beat provided by a single snare drum and hi-hat cymbal. Some jazz students suggest that the introduction of the hi-hat and snare drum was a central influence on jazz rhythms and is at the root of the development of increasingly swinging and sophisticated jazz styles through the 1930s, '40s, and beyond.

Pickin' and Strummin': Banjo and Guitar

In early jazz ensembles, a banjo (an instrument with African-American folk roots) was often used as a part of the rhythm section. It was not regarded as a melody instrument. By the 1930s, as big bands became increasingly popular, the banjo was replaced by the acoustic guitar—again primarily as a rhythm instrument until a few giants of the instrument, most notably Eddie Lang (in the 1920s), Django Reinhardt (from the late '20s into the early '50s), and Charlie Christian (during the '30s), put the instrument front and center by turning it into a single-line *solo* instrument.

Christian pioneered the use of electric guitar, which became increasingly important in jazz during the 1940s and into the present. These days, if a jazz ensemble includes guitar, it is probably an electric instrument.

ABINGTON FREE LIBRARY, 1030 OLD YORK ROAD, ABINGTON, PA 19001

It's 1926, and behold the very well-equipped jazz musician of the era. Bandleader Roger Wolfe Kahn displays his musical arsenal, which prominently features both guitars and banjos. Image from arttoday.com.

That's Some Brass

The earliest jazz bands included all the brass instruments of the typical marching band. The tuba is found in relatively few jazz ensembles nowadays, but in early jazz it figured very importantly as the bottom-line instrument—a role assumed by the double (string) bass by the 1920s. From the 1940s through the '70s, the tuba was used in highly imaginative arrangements by Claude Thornhill and Gil Evans. (Evans made the most extensive and innovative use of the tuba in modern jazz arrangements, including those for Miles Davis's celebrated nonet. See Chapter 14.)

The baritone horn, also called a euphonium, is a tenor tuba, widely used in marching bands and early jazz, but only sporadically used in jazz after World War II.

The most enduring brass in jazz are the trombone and trumpet, with cornet and flugelhorn also figuring importantly. We'll discuss these instruments in a moment. But first, lend an ear to the reeds.

A Walk Among the Woodwinds

Not all of the woodwind family is made of wood. Of course, there are the bassoon, oboe, and English horn—major and genuinely wooden woodwinds familiar in symphonic classical music and occasionally even heard in symphonic jazz music. The clarinet, first of the woodwinds to become supremely important in jazz, may be made of wood or plastic (ebonite).

Take Five

There are six members of the modern clarinet family. The soprano, or B-flat clarinet is most familiar and most widely used in jazz. A high-pitched, piercing, E-flat instrument, called the sopranino, is rarely heard in jazz—though it was the favored instrument of Odell Rand, in his recordings with the Harlem Hamfats (1936–39). The deeply resonant B-flat bass clarinet has found favor in jazz and may be heard in large ensembles (as played by Harry Carney in the Duke Ellington Orchestra); Eric Dolphy introduced the instrument to modern jazz in the late '50s and early '60s. Avant-garde musician Anthony Braxton often plays the highly impressive contrabass clarinet, a brass instrument comfortable in the very lowest musical registers. Lower than the soprano but higher than the bass clarinet are the alto clarinet (another E-flat instrument) and the basset ("little bass") clarinet (tuned in F).

The other woodwinds aren't wooden at all. We'll meet the saxophone family in a moment. Made of brass, they are classed with the woodwinds because their sound is produced by a vibrating reed. The oboe, bassoon, and English horn use a double reed (two reeds bound tightly together), while the other woodwinds employ a single carefully shaped reed.

That leaves the flute, an instrument originally fashioned of wood, but for many years now made exclusively of metal. It has no reed, but produces its sound by the air blown across—not into—its mouthpiece. Unlike any of the other wind instruments, the flute is held transversely—that is, parallel to the lips.

The ancestors of the flute predate recorded history; however, the instrument was little used in jazz before the late 1950s, when a number of saxophone players began to take it up. If you want to sample jazz flute, listen to Herbie Mann (*Flute Souffle*, a masterpiece 1957 recording on Original Jazz Classics), Hubert Laws (*Afro Classic* on CTI, 1970), Bud Shank (*The Lighthouse All Stars: Oboe/Flute* on Original Jazz Classics, 1954–56), and Lew Tabackin (*I'll Be Seeing You*, Concord Jazz, 1992).

Dig This

In addition to the familiar concert flute in C, there is the higher-pitched piccolo (little used in jazz) and the lower-pitched alto in G (played masterfully by jazz musician Herbie Mann) and the bass in C.

A *bass* flute!?

Yes—and extremely difficult to play: Listen to Henry Threadgill on "Air Song" from the *X-75* album (Novus, 1979).

The Soloists Stand Up and Step Out

It was with brass and clarinet that the first important soloists in jazz made themselves heard. They were the most expressive instruments associated with traditional brass bands.

Trumpet, Cornet, Trombone

When the cornet was invented in France, in the 1830s, its sound was quite distinct from its older relative, the trumpet. By the 20th century, however, the differences between the design of these instruments virtually disappeared, and, listening to early jazz recordings, it is often impossible to tell whether a performer is playing cornet or trumpet. In any case, by the 1930s, most cornetists had switched to trumpet, which has endured as a leading jazz solo instrument.

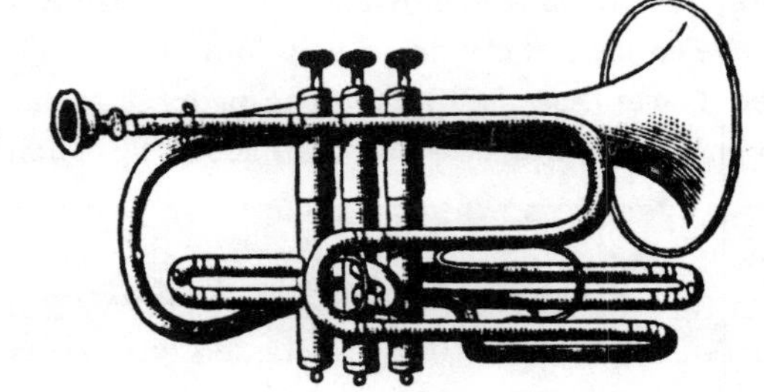

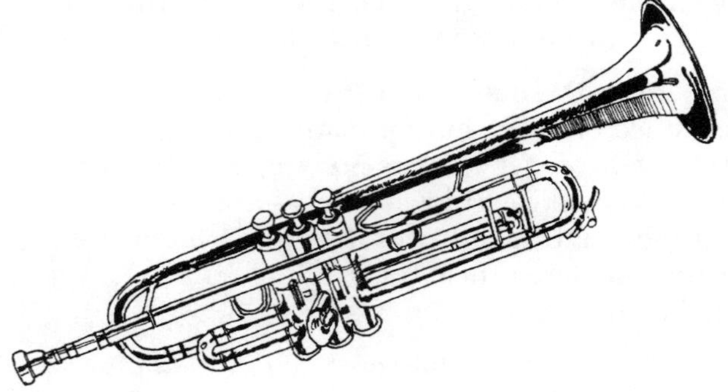

The cornet is stubbier or more squat than the trumpet, although later cornet designs were more elongated. The cornet, which developed from the hunting horn, produces a mellower tone than the trumpet.
Image from arttoday.com.

Louis Armstrong (*much* more on him later) is not only recognized as one of the greatest masters of jazz cornet and trumpet, but also as one of the first important jazz soloists. Armstrong's 1928 solo work with pianist Earl "Fatha" Hines is a breakthrough for the cornet/trumpet and a milestone in jazz history. "West End Blues" (on *The Louis Armstrong Collection,* Vol. 4, Columbia, 1928) is the first truly great jazz solo and endures to this day as one of the most remarkable jazz utterances.

The trombone produces a deep, rich sound that makes it ideal in many jazz settings. More importantly, its slide allows for great freedom of movement *between* pitches, either sliding between notes or creating a pronounced *vibrato* effect. Although the trombone's ancestry dates to the 17th century (and even back into the Middle Ages, if you look hard enough), it seems to have been invented for the very purpose of gliding in and out of blue notes. Yet, as a solo instrument, the trombone is not without limitation. It's much less supple than the trumpet, so it's far more difficult to *articulate* rapid musical passages.

Talk the Talk

Vibrato is a tremulous or pulsating musical tone. Trombonists create vibrato by rapidly moving the instrument's slide back and forth. To **articulate** in music is to separate musical notes precisely rather than to blur them or run them together.

While there have been a few trombonists capable of playing at the breakneck speeds demanded by the bebop idiom (Bill Harris and J.J. Johnson are prime examples; see Chapter 13), the trombone's heyday was the swing era (Chapters 11 and 12) of the '30s and '40s, when a thick, rich, vibrato-filled sound was called for. However, the first important trombone soloist was Miff Mole (1898–1961). If you're interested in hearing great early jazz trombone, check out Mole's work with the Red Nichols band during 1927–28 (*Red Nichols*, vol. 2, Classic Jazz).

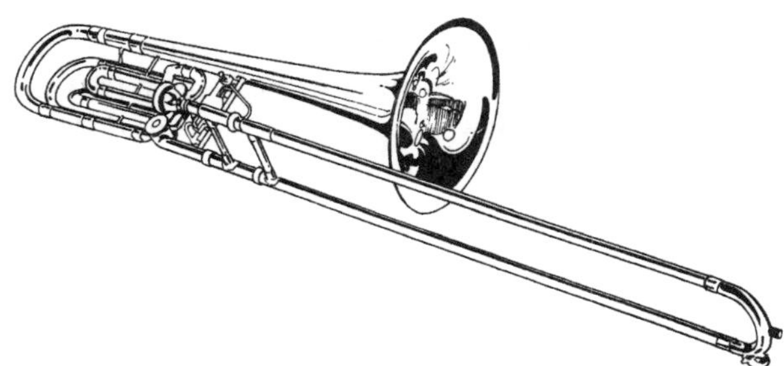

A slide trombone. The instrument is also available with valves, like a trumpet, rather than the slide.
Image from arttoday.com.

Clarinet

The clarinet was the instrument of choice for important early soloists. Mention the clarinet, and the name Benny Goodman (1909–86) comes instantly to mind. To be sure, Goodman was one of the greatest exponents of the instrument, with a career spanning the 1920s until his death in 1986. He was a jazz clarinetist without peer (and you'll hear much more from him in Chapter 12), but he wasn't the first great clarinet soloist. That honor goes to the New Orleans clarinetist (and soprano saxophonist) Sidney Bechet (1897–1959), whose groundbreaking early work can be appreciated on *The Chronological Sidney Bechet, 1923–1936* (Classics).

A b-flat "concert" clarinet and its bass cousin. Image from arttoday.com.

Real Square

Although it is commonly done, true jazz aficionados frown on abbreviating *saxophone* to *sax*. Avoid doing so. However, in a jazz context, you may refer to the saxophone simply as a *horn*.

Talk the Talk

Timbre (sometimes spelled *timber* and pronounced either "tamber" or "timber") is the distinctive tone of an instrument or instruments or singing voice. A flute, a clarinet, and a piano may play *exactly* the same note, but each instrument imparts a different and distinctive sonic character to that note. This is timbre.

Enter Saxophones

The early swing era—through the 1930s—was the heyday of the clarinet as the jazz instrument supreme. Artists such as Goodman and Artie Shaw revealed its potential both as a vehicle for astounding virtuosity and for emotional expression (although most connoisseurs believe that Shaw was more interested in dazzling technique than emotion).

By the late 1930s, *emotional expression* had become increasingly important to musicians, and it drew increasing numbers of them to the instrument that, more than any other, would come to symbolize jazz: the saxophone.

The saxophone is the chameleon of jazz, capable of shooting out sharp shards of sound at warp speed, capable as well of moaning wails, and capable, too, of sweet, slow murmurings that mimic the human voice. Although the saxophone has been used in classical music, most notably by the French composer Georges Bizet (1838–75), its *timbre* is too complex, throaty, and (if you will) too impure for most classical sensibilities. But jazz *embraces* "impure" sound—from blue notes (which fall between "correct" tones) to syncopation (which emphasizes the "wrong" beats)—and the all-too-human qualities of the saxophone suit jazz perfectly.

As the saxophone rose in popularity, the clarinet declined; by the 1940s, it was regarded by many musicians and aficionados as old-fashioned—suitable mainly for playing old-timey Dixieland. By then, the sound of the saxophone had become the signature of jazz, much as, in later decades, the fuzz tone of electronic amplification would become the signature sound of rock 'n' roll.

Late 19th-century musicians display the full range of the saxophone family, from the straight soprano at left, to the alto, tenor, baritone, and bass. Image from arttoday.com.

A Little History

The saxophone is a fairly modern instrument, patented by one Antoine-Joseph Sax in Paris in 1846. Although Sax hoped that the instrument would find favor with concert orchestras as well as military bands, the classical world mainly shunned it. The French army embraced it, and the instrument enjoyed rapid popularity in marching bands worldwide, but not until the 20th century did it find its way into "social orchestras," dance bands, and, ultimately, into jazz.

Among the many great jazz saxophonists, the greatest are Coleman Hawkins (the first of the great soloists on the instrument), Sidney Bechet, Lester Young, Charlie Parker, Art Pepper, Sonny Rollins, Ornette Coleman, and John Coltrane, all of whom you'll meet later.

Meet the Family

In speaking of a jazz saxophonist, it is not sufficient to say that Charlie Parker played the saxophone. He played the alto saxophone. Hawkins, Young, and Rollins were "tenor men." Bechet played the soprano saxophone, and Coltrane played both tenor and soprano. It is customary to identify a soloist very specifically with the type of saxophone he plays.

The saxophone family is large, encompassing a very high-pitched sopranino instrument (in E-flat), the soprano (a B-flat instrument that sounds like a cross between a clarinet and a saxophone), the alto in E-flat, the tenor in B-flat (these two are the most popular), the baritone in E-flat (occasionally heard in jazz, especially in avant-garde works), the bass in B-flat, and the contrabass in B-flat.

Ivories and Ebonies

The piano would have been extremely important in jazz if for no other reason than it is extremely important in all Western music. Pianos are found everywhere—in the parlor, in the concert hall, in the church basement, in the school auditorium, and in the bordellos of 19th- and early 20th-century New Orleans.

But jazz took to the piano not just because it was available, but because it is capable of such a tremendous range of expression, from intimate and contemplative to bold, showy, and extroverted. The instruments we have mentioned so far are "melody instruments," capable of playing one tone at a time. In contrast, the piano is a "harmony instrument," capable of playing complex chords—capable, indeed, of playing one melody against another. It is a *polyphonic* instrument, and jazz is a very polyphonic music.

Talk the Talk

The word **polyphonic** refers to music with more than one melodic line sounded together; a polyphonic instrument, such as the piano, can play such music without accompaniment.

Ragtime Piano

Listen to the late, great Canadian classical pianist Glenn Gould (1932–82) play a Bach fugue, and you hear polyphonic music. Listen to a Scott Joplin rag, and you also hear polyphonic music—the material played by one hand working in intricately beautiful juxtaposition with that played by the other.

Dig This

Joplin himself recorded a number of player-piano rolls, which have been transferred to modern recordings. Thus we are able to hear the master's interpretations of his own works (from the year 1910!) on *The Elite Syncopations: Classic Ragtime* (Biograph).

The Piano Hits Its Stride

Ragtime composers and performers like Joplin often earned their bread and butter playing piano in "sporting houses" (the semi-polite name for bordellos), but ragtime piano also became popular in nightclubs and even in homes.

As ragtime made the transition to early jazz, the piano came right along. In ensembles, it was often part of the rhythm section, but the great early jazz pianists (most notably Jelly Roll Morton and Earl "Fatha" Hines) also brought the instrument front and center in groups and developed it as a formidable solo instrument as well.

Take Five

Ferdinand "Jelly Roll" Morton (1890–1941) was audacious enough to claim that he invented jazz. That's an exaggeration, but he was certainly in on its beginnings. You'll find some of his legendary piano work on *Jelly Roll Morton,* recordings from 1923–26 reissued on CD by Milestone.

Earl Hines (1903–83) was nicknamed "Fatha" in acknowledgment of the formative role he played in jazz piano. He transformed early stride piano into full-blown jazz. Want a sample? Listen to *Piano Man,* a Bluebird CD featuring recordings made in 1939–42.

Perhaps the most distinctive early development beyond ragtime piano is the exciting style known as *stride*. The name comes from the extremely athletic use of the left hand, "striding" up and down the bass keys. Stride pianists such as Willie "The Lion" Smith (check out *Willie "The Lion" Smith 1925–1937* on Classics), James P. Johnson (*Harlem Stride Piano* on Hot 'N Sweet), and Art Tatum (*Piano Starts Here* is the best of the best, from Columbia/Legacy) were great artists in their own right but (especially in the instance of Tatum) also formed a bridge between ragtime piano and mature jazz piano. We'll hear more from these gentlemen later in the book.

Talk the Talk

Stride is a style of jazz piano playing in which the left hand athletically "strides" the keys in aggressive accompaniment to the right hand's melodic line. The style was a bridge between ragtime and mature jazz.

Putting Them Together

We have seen that the first jazz ensembles were just marching bands or small dance orchestras. As jazz grew in popularity, however, jazz ensembles took on more distinctive identities.

James Reese Europe (1881–1919), an African-American composer and band leader, organized what might well be called the first "proto-jazz" band in 1910 in New York and toured the United States with it to great acclaim. During World War I, he served as leader of a U.S. Army band and also toured his proto-jazz ensemble in France. At the height of his success in 1919, he was stabbed to death in a nightclub brawl.

The Big Bands

Reese's success inspired many others to venture beyond the small ensemble. The most famous early jazz band was that of Paul "Pops" Whiteman (1890–1967), a symphony orchestra violist who organized a dance band in San Francisco in 1918 and achieved national success with his 1920 recordings of the songs "Whispering" and "Japanese Sandman." From the 1920s through 1958, Whiteman's orchestra produced some 600 recordings.

Dig This

Related to stride is "boogie-woogie," which shares stride's "walking bass"—the athletic lefthand rhythms—but is based more in blues traditions than in jazz. Boogie-woogie figured in jazz during the 1930s and 1940s, but reverted to its blues roots by the 1950s.

Many jazz aficionados put Whiteman down as someone who diluted the true character of jazz. Despite his having commissioned George Gershwin's *Rhapsody in Blue* (1924), the first successful wedding of classical and jazz traditions, it's true that Whiteman's music was more pop than jazz. However, the success of his 40-piece orchestra inspired more firmly jazz-oriented leaders to organize their own bands, and by the 1930s, the "big band" was born.

The typical *big band* had 10 to 15 instruments (though a few were as big as Whiteman's), and they came to dominate the jazz scene during the swing era (the 1930s through the middle '40s). We'll get into the history of the big bands in Chapter 12, but for now, take note that the distinctive sound of these ensembles came largely from the massed brass—especially trombones and trumpets—a saxophone choir (at least two altos and two tenors), and a clarinet or two.

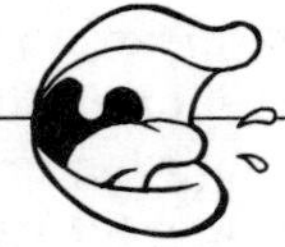

Talk the Talk

A **big band** is a jazz orchestra of 10 to 15 instruments or more. Typically, big bands are associated with music of the swing era.

The instruments were used together to create powerful, vibrant harmonies, but lead players on each instrument were also given solo turns, which added color, excitement, and individual creativity to the otherwise collaborative sound. Often, the bandleader was a key soloist: for example, Benny Goodman on clarinet, Duke Ellington on piano, Tommy Dorsey on trombone, Jimmy Dorsey on alto saxophone.

The Combo

The big band took jazz away from the small ensembles of the music's earliest period, and the public—as well as record producers—came to expect the sound of the larger group. That's why Benny Goodman met with protests when in 1935, he started the Benny Goodman Trio with pianist Teddy Wilson and drummer Gene Krupa. Was jazz yet another victim of the Depression? Couldn't Goodman afford to pay a big band anymore?

The sheer genius of the Trio put all carping to rest and quickly won over audiences. The jazz *combo*—a small ensemble to play the jazz equivalent of what classical musicians call chamber music—was born.

Combo—short for "combination"—is a broad term used to cover any small jazz ensemble up to about nine players. Beyond this number, you're dealing with a band. There is no set instrumentation for a combo. Essentially, it's any small group of musicians who get together to play—though, typically, a combo includes a rhythm section or rhythm instrument (drums, piano, double bass, and so on) and a "melody" instrument or instruments (such as a clarinet, saxophone, trumpet, and so on).

Dig This

The recording debut of the Benny Goodman Trio (and a lot of other great Goodman music) is on *Complete Benny Goodman,* vol. 1 (RCA).

Amplified Sounds

Jazz has traditionally been an acoustic genre, in contrast to rock, which is primarily an amplified music. Nevertheless, many jazz musicians now play amplified instruments, including electric guitars and an array of electronic keyboards.

Talk the Talk

A **combo** is any small jazz ensemble up to about nine players; it plays the jazz equivalent of what classical musicians would call chamber music.

The Guitar Plugs In

The great Charlie Christian (1916–42) introduced the electric guitar to a wider audience when he played with the Goodman band from 1939 until his untimely death from tuberculosis in 1942. Amplification brought the guitar front and center in Goodman's big band, enabling Christian to showcase his phenomenal talent as a jazz improviser.

Other electric jazz guitarists followed Christian (most notably Les Paul), but the instrument did not figure big in jazz again until the 1950s through the 1970s, when such soloists as Wes Montgomery, Larry Coryell, Al DiMeola, and John McLaughlin helped create fusion, a combination of jazz and rock (See Chapter 20).

Dig This

The Genius of the Electric Guitar (Columbia) presents great Charlie Christian performances with the Goodman band from 1939 to 1941.

Keyboards and Synthesizers

Fusion and avant-garde jazz (see Chapter 19) brought to the music an array of electronic keyboards, beginning with the Moog (rhymes with "rogue") synthesizer in the 1960s and developing in sophistication as microchip technology exploded during the 1980s and '90s.

Today, it's common to hear synthesizers in jazz, capable of creating the sound of virtually any instrument. Because synthesizer sound is digital, synthesizers can also create sounds that no acoustic instrument can make, including combining the tonal qualities of several instruments.

Dig This

Joe Zawinul (1932–) is a master of synthesizer keyboards. Check out his classic synthesizer work with Weather Report on *I Sing the Body* Electric (1971–72, Columbia).

By the Way

While electronic amplification and synthesizers may alienate some jazz traditionalists (just as Bob Dylan picking up an electric guitar stunned his folk fans in 1965), the fact is that jazz has always embraced new sounds—especially sounds that "break" the rules. The adventurous jazz listener will encounter in this piece or that an array of ethnic instruments—traditional African percussion instruments, as well as instruments from Asia. For jazz, probably the two most significant instruments off the beaten track are the vibraphone and the harmonica.

Good Vibes

The vibraphone—also called a vibraharp or just vibes—looks like a xylophone and, like that instrument, has a keyboard of tuned metal bars that are struck with felt or wool beaters. The major difference between the vibraphone and the xylophone is that a tubular tuned resonator is suspended below each aluminum bar. The resonators sustain the tone of the struck bars, and electric fans between the resonators and the bars create vibrato. The speed of the fans can be controlled by the player.

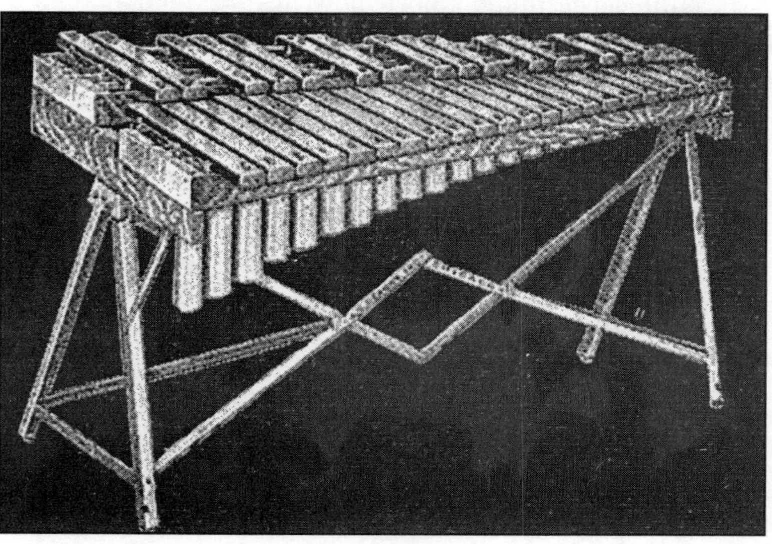

An early vibraphone. Image from arttoday.com.

The vibraphone was invented in about 1920, but not until drummer Lionel Hampton (1909–) took up the instrument in 1930, at the urging of Louis Armstrong, did vibes become a jazz instrument—and Hampton a leading figure in jazz.

Dig This

Red Norvo (1908–) played vibes in the late 1920s, but Hampton put the instrument on the map. Hampton's swing-era work is available on the *Hot Mallets* CD series from Bluebird. Want bop Hampton? Check out *Midnight Sun* on GRP. Cool school? Then it's *Hamp and Getz* from 1955 (Verve).

Harmonica

That the harmonica never made it big in jazz is curious, since it was and remains such an important instrument in the blues. Nevertheless, don't overlook the single great harmonica virtuoso in jazz, Toots Thielemans (1922–), whose *Man Bites Harmonica* (Jazz Original Classics) from 1957–58 is definitive and suggests that the instrument could have been much more important in jazz—if only more performers had chosen to play it.

While Toots Thielmans is the most important jazz harmonica player, Larry Adler (1914–) is probably better known—though he spent most of his career in the pop and classical fields (even commissioning harmonica concertos from major classical composers!) rather than jazz. He is pictured here, at left, in duet with a fiddling Jack Benny during a World War II USO tour in New Guinea.
Image from arttoday.com.

Strings Attached

If the harmonica failed to establish a deep niche in jazz, the role of most stringed instruments in the music has also been uncertain at best.

Jazz and Strings: Not Always a Blissful Marriage

The sound of bowed strings—violins, violas, cellos, and double basses—is so strongly identified with classical music and with pop orchestral music that, to most ears, it just doesn't sound right in a jazz context. For example, the quintessential bebop alto saxophonist Charlie Parker had a passion for the classics and was enthusiastic about recording with strings (*Bird with Strings*, recorded in 1950–52, is available on a Columbia two-CD set). Yet most jazz critics dislike these recordings.

If jazz and the symphonic string choir haven't mixed well, at least two symphonic string instruments have become very important in jazz.

Bass Assumptions

Second only to the saxophone as an icon of jazz is the double-bass or bass fiddle. The double bass was used in ragtime orchestras as early as the 1890s. From this time through the 1920s, it was played with the bow. By the 1930s, jazz bassists set down their bows and played pizzicato—that is, by plucking the strings.

Take Five

The cello is not a mainstream jazz instrument, but a number of double bass players also play jazz cello (Oscar Pettiford and Ron Carter, for example), and a few modern and avant-garde cellists have also made themselves heard. Harry Babasin pioneered the cello as a jazz instrument in the 1940s and can be heard (with Pettiford) on *Harry Babasin and the Jazz Pickers* (VSOP, 1957; available only on LP), which gives a good idea of the cello in traditional jazz. For a more modern sound, try Ron Carter's *Where?* from 1961 (Original Jazz Classics).

The deep sound of a plucked bass is difficult to hear over a large jazz ensemble, so it's no wonder the instrument came into its own in small combo work, especially during the bebop period (Chapter 13). Listen to Oscar Pettiford (*Deep Passion*, 1956–57, on Impulse) and Charles Mingus (*Pithecanthropus Erectus*, 1956, Atlantic) for an idea of what the instrument can do in a jazz setting.

The Jazz Violin

If any instrument seems an unlikely jazz vehicle, it's the violin—at home in the world of Brahms and Tchaikovsky, perhaps, or, as a country fiddle, in the mountains of Appalachia. But in jazz?

To be sure, the instrument has not fully entered the jazz mainstream, but three violinists nevertheless stand out as incredible jazz musicians: Joe Venuti (1903–78), Stephane Grappelli (1908–98), and Stuff Smith (1909–67).

Take Five

Joe Venuti recorded in Dixieland, swing, and classic jazz styles. *Fiddlesticks*, a collection from 1931-39 (Confier), includes Dixieland and classic jazz, while *Joe and Zoot* (Chiaroscuro) features swing—but (at this writing) has yet to be reissued on CD. Grappelli is more widely recorded than Venuti. Check out *Stephane Grappelli 1935-1940* (Classics) and *Live in London* from 1973 (Black Lion). The first recording includes some of his work with legendary guitarist Django Reihardt, with whom Grappelli frequently performed. Stuff Smith was another great swing violinist. Listen to *Stuff Smith and His Onyx Club Boys* from 1936-39 (Classics).

The violin has enjoyed exposure in recent jazz as well. Jean Luc Ponty has used it in his fusion jazz (Chapter 20) and as a supporting instrument in avant-garde works.

While no instrument is unique to jazz, jazz has found ways to use most familiar musical instruments in uniquely "jazz" ways. In the next chapter, we'll see how that most familiar of instruments, the human voice, has found its unique niche in the jazz tradition.

The Least You Need to Know

- Early jazz ensembles developed from marching bands and "social orchestras."
- The rhythm section includes more than drums; the piano and other melody instruments, including guitar, often are counted as rhythm instruments.
- The first great jazz soloists played trumpet (or cornet) and clarinet.
- By the 1930s, the standard larger jazz ensemble was the big band. Benny Goodman created the much more intimate combo with his 1935 Benny Goodman Trio.

Chapter 6

The Jazz Singer

In This Chapter

- Why some jazz fans don't listen to singers
- The difficult role of the jazz singer
- The categories of jazz singers
- A survey of male and female singers

Everyone who writes about jazz sooner or later points out how "conversational" the music is and how the great instrumental soloists aim to imitate the human voice through their horns. In the late 1920s, the public so closely identified jazz with song that when Warner Bros. released the first commercial talking picture in 1927, they called it *The Jazz Singer*.

Yet, strangely enough, most hardcore jazz fans show rather little interest in singers. Some even insist that jazz—"real jazz" or jazz "at its best"—is, by definition, instrumental, not vocal.

Why do they say such a thing? And is this opinion justified? Read on.

The Singer: A Jazz Orphan

Why do so many jazz buffs give singers such a hard time? Well, what's the big difference between music played on instruments and music sung?

Answer: the words. A singer is not only responsible for delivering a musical performance, but must also deliver the words and deliver them so that they make musical, emotional, and intellectual sense. This, according to some jazz commentators, prevents singers from freely improvising the way instrumentalists can. It ties them down—and if there's one thing that's incompatible with jazz, it's being tied down.

The Voice at the Root of This Music

Yet, as you read in Chapter 1, the human voice is undeniably at the root of jazz. The African and African-American traditions behind jazz are strongly verbal, conversational, and song-oriented. In jazz's close cousin, the blues, singing predominates over instrumental performance. And, as you've now seen more than once, instrumental performance in jazz is based on human song and even speech. Compared to classical music, jazz rhythms often seem quirky and irregular. Listened to as musical speech, however, they make perfect sense. The same may even be said for blue notes and the other liberties jazz takes with pitch and tonality: They sound like the accents and inflections of passionate, emotional speech.

Can Jazz Be Sung?

Yet what about improvisation? Emotion, conversational phrasing, and all the rest are important aspects of jazz, but, for many aficionados, the heart of this music is free invention and improvisation. For many, that's where the real excitement lies.

A jazz instrumentalist can freely depart from the written score—if she's even working from one—but a singer, whatever else he may do, has to stick with the words.

Can jazz be sung, then?

Here's one answer.

The American poet Robert Frost didn't like "free verse," poetry without regular meter and rhyme. He said that writing such poetry was like "playing tennis without a net." Think of the jazz singer's role in a similar way. The singer's responsibility to deliver the lyrics is his net. It doesn't stop him from playing the game. It just makes the game more challenging. For those listening, it also makes the game more exciting.

Classical Models and the Jazz Version

Classical singers, singers of opera and art songs, are divided into neat categories: soprano and contralto for the women, and tenor, baritone, and bass for the men. The soprano category is often divided further into coloratura soprano, who specializes in the high notes, and mezzo-soprano, whose vocal range is pitched between that of the soprano and the contralto.

In contrast to classical singers, jazz vocalists are not usually classed formally by vocal range. Instead, they are categorized by sex (gender, that is) and by the style of music that most suits them. For the men, the major categories are:

- Instrumentalists who also sang.
- Pop singers influential in jazz.

- Swing vocalists.
- Blues-influenced jazz singers.
- Practitioners of bop, scat, and vocalise.
- More recent generalists.

Male Call: Some "Name" Singers

The first great male jazz vocalist—and, many would argue, the first great jazz singer—was Louis Armstrong. His gravel-loaded voice was not only an instantly identifiable trademark, it made listeners really hear Satchmo's voice as a jazz instrument. That distinctive sound set his voice apart, compelling you to listen to the voice as much as to the words.

And what about the words? While traditional singers concentrated on delivering the lyrics straightforwardly, just the way they had been written, Armstrong played with lyrics, often trailing off into scat singing (the singing of nonsense syllables—an important subject you'll read about later in this chapter).

The jazz musicality of Armstrong's voice was not limited to its gravelly timbre. He played his voice as he played his trumpet, bending notes, hitting blue notes, and often purposely lagging behind the beat to heighten the jazz feel of the music.

If you want to hear the essence of jazz singing, Armstrong is your man. Several generations of jazz singers have done just that, poring over his recordings to hear how it is done.

Armstrong was very widely recorded. An excellent sampling of his vocal work is found on *From the Big Band to the All Stars (1946–56)*, an RCA two-CD set. Very special is *Porgy and Bess*, a unique version of songs (such as "Summertime" and "Bess, You Is My Woman") from George Gershwin's opera, sung in duet with perhaps the single greatest female jazz vocalist, Ella Fitzgerald.

Dig This

Some jazz buffs carp on Armstrong's embrace of pop material, including show tunes, in his later career. True, if you want Satch at his jazz best, listen to recordings from the mid-1950s and earlier. However, his pop recordings are well worth hearing. Check out any of his versions of tunes from the musical *Hello, Dolly!* (The best is on a Kapp LP and has yet to be issued on CD.)

Doubling on Vocals

While Armstrong was the most important of the instrumentalists who also sang, there were many others, including (for example) bandleader and trombonist Jack Teagarden (1905–64), trumpeter Henry "Red" Allen (1908–67), one-armed trumpet player Wingy Manone (1900–82), and bandleader, alto man, and clarinetist Woody Herman (1913–87).

Dig This

Chet Baker (1929–88) is a special case. A subtle, breathy trumpet player of the cool school (Chapter 14), he delivered vocals with a rare combination of intimacy, jazz feeling, and utter innocence. For a sweet taste of his singing, hear *The Best of Chet Baker Sings: Let's Get Lost* (Pacific Jazz), from 1953–56.

A few of the most distinctive instrumentalists who also sang were. . .

- **Fats Waller (1904–43)** A great pianist who sang with sly humor. *Fats Waller and His Buddies* (Bluebird) is a CD featuring some of his best vocal recordings from the 1920s.
- **Louis Prima(1911–78)** A fine trumpet player and jazz composer who was better known to the public as a jazz-influenced pop singer ("That Old Black Magic" was his biggest hit). Check out the *Capitol Collectors Series* (Capitol), which features recordings from 1956–62.
- **Nat King Cole (1919–65)** Jazz fans regard him as one of the great pianists of the 1940s, but his biggest success with the general public was as a suave pop vocalist during the 1950s and early 1960s. To hear this marvelous musician at his jazz-inflected vocal best, listen to *The Nat King Cole Story*, a double CD from Capitol.

Pop Goes: Pop Singers Influential in Jazz

Think of Bing Crosby (1913–93), and you probably think of a crooning rendition of Irving Berlin's "White Christmas." Hardly jazz. But before he became the ultimate laid-back crooner—and one of the most successful pop stars in the history of music—Crosby had been a jazz singer in the late 1920s (starting with the Paul Whiteman orchestra) and early 1930s. (His brother was Dixieland/swing bandleader Bob Crosby.) If you are a Crosby fan, you might want to invest in the four-CD collection *Bing! His Legendary Years, 1931 to 1957* (MCA), which features both jazz and pop work. After listening to Bing's early jazz singing, the jazz background of even his smoothest pop numbers becomes apparent in this collection.

Like Crosby, Frank Sinatra (1915–98) is a pop vocalist rather than a jazz singer. But he came of age vocally during the swing era, and a significant portion of his output was heavily influenced by jazz. *Songs for Swingin' Lovers,* recorded in 1955–56 and available on a Capitol CD, is a case in point. In turn, Sinatra's polished vocal technique influenced just about every American singer, pop or jazz, who's come along since.

Frank Sinatra—The Crooner—in 1943. Image from the Frank Driggs Collection.

Let's Swing

"Swing," you'll recall, is that indefinable something that makes jazz really *move*. The bands and singers of the swing era (discussed in Chapter 12) embodied this special motive quality in abundance.

While Sinatra's early years were spent performing with swing bands, the leading swing vocalists were Cab Calloway (1907–94) and Billy Eckstine (1914–93). Calloway was an all-round jazz-oriented entertainer, who became a household name by the 1930s and whose fame never greatly diminished. His specialty was scat singing, as in his classic "Minnie the Moocher," with its scat chorus, "Hi-di-hi-di-hi-di-ho!" Indeed, Calloway was so closely identified with this song that he was frequently billed as the "Hi-Di-Ho Man." For Cab at his best, sample *Cab Calloway (1930–1931)* on the Classics label.

Cab Calloway broadcasts from Harlem's Cotton Club, 1935. Image from the Frank Driggs Collection.

Eckstine was best known as a ballad singer with a rich baritone voice. His roots were in jazz, especially swing and bop, as evidenced by the magnificent *Mister B and the Band* (Savoy), a CD reissue of recordings from 1945–47.

A Shade of Blue

We know from Chapter 4 that jazz and blues are distinct from one another but still related, and jazz often shares an overall feel or mood with the blues tradition. It is no surprise, then, that the work of a number of blues singers often crosses over into jazz. The three best known are Jimmy Rushing (1903–72), Jimmy Witherspoon (1923–), and Joe Williams (1918–).

Rushing was short but of a girth so impressive that he was known as Mr. 5-by-5 ("five feet tall and five feet wide," as one of his favorite lyrics put it). His singing style was derived from the blues, yet rhythmically was very much in the jazz tradition. Thus he made his reputation not in blues venues but, beginning in 1935, as a singer with the Count Basie band. Rushing brought to Basie blues lyrics and the basics of blues structure, but he delivered it all in a swinging and sophisticated package that is a far cry from traditional rural blues. Vanguard has reissued *The Essential Jimmy Rushing* (1954–57) on CD.

Like Rushing, Jimmy Witherspoon marries swing to the blues. His approach is rather more aggressive than Rushing's and emphasizes blues *shouting* over jazz, but the jazz is certainly there. A good starting place is *Jimmy Witherspoon and Jay McShann*, recordings from 1947–49 reissued on CD by Black Lion.

Talk the Talk

Shouting is a style of blues singing in which a rough-voiced male performer shouts (shout-sings) the lyrics.

Joe Williams sang with a variety of big bands during the 1940s before joining Count Basie in 1954. One of the most popular jazz vocalists, his blues-inflected style forges straight ahead. Vintage work from the mid-1950s is on *Count Basie Swings/Joe Williams Sings* (Verve).

Scat! (and Bop)

Scat singing—improvising on a melody with nonsense syllables—may be traced to certain West African song traditions. In jazz, its lineage goes back to New Orleans in the early days of the music, when scat was a novelty gimmick—one that Louis Armstrong, New Orleans born and raised, took to remarkable heights. Armstrong's earliest recorded scat is "Heebie Jeebies" from 1926, and he kept scattin' until the end of his career.

Talk the Talk

Scat singing is improvising on a melody with nonsense syllables. At its best, it is a way of using the human voice as an instrument, eliminating the need for words entirely.

Scat has figured in early jazz, in swing, and, prominently, in bebop. In our discussion of bebop in Chapter 13, we'll see why. In a nutshell, bop is so fast and so heavily improvised that it is virtually impossible to sing "real" words and still sing bop. The bop master Dizzy Gillespie (1917–93), best known as a phenomenal trumpet player, was also a great scat singer, as can be heard on various cuts of *Dizzy Gillespie and His Big Band* (GNP) from 1948.

Now, I just said that putting real words to bop is "virtually impossible." The operative word here is "virtually," because two men stand out for their almost superhuman ability to accomplish just such a *virtually* impossible feat.

Eddie Jefferson (1918–79) was not only a bop scat singer but also a master of *vocalise,* a more sustained singing of meaningless syllables or even a single *fa* syllable. But he became even better known for putting "real" words to classic bop improvisations, emulating with his incredible vocal technique the flights of saxophonists Lester Young, Charlie Parker, Coleman Hawkins, and others. Jefferson's work is always dazzling and is at its most spectacular in *Letter from Home*, a 1961–62 recording reissued on CD by Original Jazz Classics. Jefferson's career ended violently when he was gunned down outside of a Detroit nightclub.

Talk the Talk

Vocalise (*vocal-eeze*) is a general term for singing meaningless syllables or a single syllable (usually fa). Scat is a form of *vocalise*.

As a 14-year-old, Jon Hendricks (1921–) sang with piano genius Art Tatum (Chapter 10) and later sang with such giants of bebop as Charlie Parker. Like Eddie Jefferson, he was a genius of vocalise, who also put words to "impossible-to-sing" bop classics. In the 1950s, he became part of a trio with singers Dave Lambert and Annie Ross—Lambert, Hendricks, and Ross—joining forces in bop vocalise and putting words to bop and swing. This group inspired the highly successful pop group of the 1970s, Manhattan Transfer. For Hendricks alone, listen to *Boppin' at the Blue Note* (Telarc, 1993). For great LH&R, try *Sing Along with Basie*, a CD reissue on Roulette from 1958.

Mixed Modern Bag

The more modern jazz vocalists don't yield to easy classification. They range from Mel Tormé (1925–98), whose nickname, "The Velvet Fog," accurately describes his muted vocal quality, and who is best known for his swing and pop work; to Dave Frishberg (1933–), who made his reputation singing his own quirky jazz songs; to Mose Allison (1927–), a pianist and singer, who specializes in hard bop (see Chapter 18) as well as what can only be described as folk jazz; and to Bobby McFerrin (1950–).

Dig This

Mel Tormé is featured at his jazz best on *Mel Tormé, Rob McConnell and the Boss Brass* (Concord Jazz, 1986). For Dave Frishberg, it's *Dave Frishberg Classics* (Concord Jazz, 1982); Frishberg is one of the great lyricists of jazz. Mose Allison can best be sampled on the outstanding *Allison Wonderland*, an anthology spanning 1957 to 1989 (Rhino/Atlantic).

McFerrin is a vocal phenomenon unto himself. He is a technician of superhuman power, having mastered "circular breathing," the ability to inhale *while continuing to sing*, as well as a technique of rapidly alternating falsetto with bass and sounding like a one-man trio. In addition, he provides his own rhythm section by "playing" his chest with his hands.

McFerrin might be described as a post-bop singer or perhaps as an avant-gardist, but truly, he defies categorization. A major jazz vocalist, he is also the conductor of a classical symphony orchestra, and he made what must have been a small fortune in 1988 with the fluke smash-hit pop song, "Don't Worry, Be Happy." The key McFerrin jazz album is from 1984, *The Voice* (Elektra).

Bobby McFerrin is best known as an avant-garde jazz vocalist, but has more recently conducted symphonic music.
Image from the author's collection.

Female Vocal: The Top Names

Every big band of the 1930s and 1940s had a "girl singer," typically chosen for her looks as much as for her ability to sell a tune. A few of the big bands of the swing era hired as singers extraordinary musicians of the caliber of Helen Ward, Maxine Sullivan, Ivie Anderson, Helen Forrest, Anita O'Day, and Helen Humes. The greatest innovators in this group were Ella Fitzgerald and Sarah Vaughan.

But the singers in front of the big bands were not the first women in jazz. Women played a big role in blues vocals beginning in the 1920s. Of this group, Alberta Hunter crossed over into jazz as well, joining such early giants as Ethel Waters.

The female vocalists in jazz are not as easily categorized as their male counterparts—it's best to group them chronologically rather than stylistically.

First Ladies

Alberta Hunter (1895–1984) began her professional musical life as a down-and-dirty blues vocalist in the 1920s, then became a sophisticated supper-club entertainer in the 1930s. She starred in the original production of Jerome Kern's *Showboat* with the great Paul Robeson during 1928–29 and, during World War II, worked tirelessly with the USO. She retired from singing in 1956 to become (at age 61) a registered nurse. She was forced to retire from this career in 1977, because her employer believed she was 65. In fact, she was 82.

And that's when she returned to jazz, singing at the Cookery, a club in New York City, until she was 89. *Amtrack Blues* (Columbia, 1978) is a jazz album, as are *Glory of Alberta Hunter* (CBS, 1981) and *Look for the Silver Lining* (CBS, 1982).

Ethel Waters (1896–1977) gained national fame after appearing in the 1943 all-African American musical film *Cabin in the Sky*. She was an artist in classic jazz (see Chapter 9). The must-have album is *Ethel Waters: 1925–1926* (Classics).

Lady Day: A New Jazz Voice

Billie Holiday (1915–59) may well be the most famous jazz singer of all time. Even people who don't know jazz know of her—and many of these folks even recognize her voice on such songs as "God Bless the Child" and "Them There Eyes."

Born Eleanora Fagan in a Baltimore slum, Holiday was the daughter of an itinerant guitarist. As a child, she ran errands for a brothel keeper, who allowed her to listen to her establishment's collection of recordings by Louis Armstrong and blues singer Bessie Smith. Much of Holiday's life was brutal, and she was frequently the victim of abusive lovers. She also suffered from a lifelong addiction to heroin. But she endured her pain, transforming it into exquisitely felt jazz recordings.

We will revisit Holiday in the context of swing in Chapter 12 and also in Chapter 21, but for now it's enough to know that to listen to her is to hear what can only be described as the essence of jazz expression.

A collectible original, Billie Holiday on the old Vocalion label, 1937. Image from the author's collection.

Holiday's voice is not conventionally beautiful. Nor is her vocal technique that of a virtuoso. But her ability to phrase a line in a way that perfectly blends jazz feeling with the emotion conveyed by the lyric is uncanny and unforgettable. Columbia has released nine CD volumes of *The Quintessential Billie Holiday*, all of which are extraordinary and central to the history of jazz. The first seven are superior to the last two—but only slightly. Choose any of these recordings or invest in them all.

Take Five

Vocalian, the record-manufacturing division of Aeolian, a New York piano maker, began production in 1916 and, the following year, issued a recording by the Original Dixieland Jazz Band, among the first-ever records by a jazz band. (ODJB's *Liver Stable Blues*, on Victor, was *the* first.) In 1926, Vocalion established a line of "race" records—records by African American performers intended primarily for a black audience—called the Vocalion 1000s. King Oliver, Jimmy Noone, and Duke Ellington all recorded for the series.

Warner Bros. took over the Vocalion label in 1930, selling it the following year to Consolidated Film Industries, which discontinued then restarted the race series and maintained the Vocalion brand. CBS took over the label in 1938, and in 1940 phased out the Vocalion brand, replacing it with the Okeh label, which specialized in jazz, blues, and country music.

The Women of Swing

The public expected every big band of the 1930s or 1940s to have a "girl singer," and the bandleader, in turn, expected a lot from her. She had to be capable of delivering jazzy, up-tempo numbers in the swinging and sassy way that characterizes much popular music of the era, but she also had to be able to sell a sweet, slow ballad as well. Moreover, the most successful swing singers combined a freshness and innocence with a certain wisecracking sophistication.

Let's take a closer look at a few of the names we mentioned earlier.

➤ **Lee Wiley (1915–75)** She combined crisp tone and an aura of sophistication with a frank sensuality. Her versions of standards by Gershwin, Rodgers and Hart, Harold Arlen, and Irving Berlin are jazz-inflected classics. Give a listen to *Lee Wiley Sings the Songs of Ira and George Gershwin* (Audiophile). Recorded in 1939–40, this was the first time a singer had devoted an entire album to the music of one composer.

➤ **Maxine Sullivan (1911–87)** Her first and biggest hit was a swinging 1937 recording of the traditional "Loch Lomond" ("You take the high road, and I'll take the low road...") as arranged by big band leader Claude Thornhill. Later, she sang with the Benny Carter band. Sullivan's approach to a song is light, airy, and always swings. Even late in her 50-year recording career, she managed to sound youthful, as if singing were effortless for her. Typical of her output are the 1940–41 recordings reissued on CD by Circle as *The Biggest Little Band in the Land.*

Billie Holiday in the 1940s.
Image from the Frank Driggs Collection.

- **Helen Humes (1913–81)** She was a singer's singer, totally versatile, at home with the blues and with swing standards. If you want to hear her do some jazz classics, listen to *Songs I Like to Sing*, from 1960 on the Original Jazz Classics label.

Queens of the Band

Two women who started in swing were innovative enough to take their vocalism into the bop era (Chapter 13). Anyone with even a casual interest in jazz song, American song, or song of any kind should listen to as much Ella Fitzgerald (1917–1998) and Sarah Vaughan (1924–90) as possible.

Perhaps judgments like this are meaningless, but people make them anyway, so here goes: Ella Fitzgerald was the greatest all-around female jazz singer in the history of the music. She combined a rich and beautiful voice with a sense of swing and absolutely perfect elocution. To listen to Fitzgerald sing is to hear every word of the lyric—yet also to be aware that you are listening to jazz. Fitzgerald never cut a disappointing record, which makes it particularly difficult to pick and choose. If you can afford the six-CD *Ella Fitzgerald* set on the Classics label, don't hesitate. If you can spring for a 16-CD set, *The Complete Ella Fitzgerald Song Books* (Verve), her renditions of the works of the great American song writers, is a treasure well worth owning. If you want a smaller sampling, the *75th Birthday Celebration* (GRP) is an excellent two-CD choice featuring recordings from 1938 to 1955.

Sarah Vaughan is very much in Fitzgerald's class but more thoroughly rooted in bebop. As such, her style was sassier than Fitzgerald's and lighter, earning her the affectionate nickname of Sassy. Like Fitzgerald, she was an outstanding scat singer. *Sarah Vaughan,* an EmArcy CD reissue from 1954, features Vaughan with bop trumpeter Clifford Brown. If you want to dig Sarah big time, invest in the first volume (that's six CDs) of *Complete Sarah Vaughan on Mercury* (1954–56, Mercury).

Jazz Goes Pop: Women of the '40s and '50s

The 1940s and '50s produced an impressive range of female pop vocalists who doubled in jazz. The most impressive of these include Dinah Washington and Carmen McRae. Annie Ross, whom we already met with Jon Hendricks, also came of age during this era but specialized in technically demanding bop vocals and vocalise, in contrast to the others, who focused on the standards, albeit with jazz inflection and feeling.

Dinah Washington (1924–63), whose life was cut short at 39 by an overdose of alcohol and pills, possessed a deliciously penetrating, high-pitched voice that she used to great effect on everything from blues to jazz to pop. A dose of Dinah geared up for jazz is on the EmArcy CD reissue of the 1954 *Dinah Jams.*

The voice of Carmen McRae (1920–94) did not equal that of Ella Fitzgerald or Dinah Washington—whose could?—but she made up for this with an acute rhythmic sense and an uncanny ability to phrase behind the beat, much as the great bebop instrumentalists did. McRae delivered a lyric with a sophistication, subtlety, and taste that never grew stale. Her mentor and musical idol was Billie Holiday, and the 1983 album she dedicated to her, *For Lady Day* (Novus/RCA), is a gem.

Annie Ross (1930–) was born Annabelle Lynch in England, where she became an actress. During the 1950s and early 1960s, she became famous as part of Lambert, Hendricks, and Ross, but she also cut some remarkable solo albums, including *Annie Ross Sings a Song of Mulligan* (Pacific Jazz), from 1958, with cool-school saxophonist Gerry Mulligan (see Chapter 14).

Pushing the Envelope

A cadre of female vocalists have been especially active in avant-garde jazz (Chapter 19), the most exciting of whom is Betty Carter (1930–98). She came of age among the beboppers, then went beyond them with singularly radical treatments of standard songs. Carter makes free use of tonal distortion and wildly ranging tempos, as on *Betty Carter at the Village Vanguard* (Verve), recorded in 1970.

Betty Carter is not to everyone's taste, but her music shows that the female vocalists of jazz were much more than ornaments to the band. Her work is also a great way of dipping a toe in the sometimes turbulent waters of avant-garde jazz—although Carter herself loathed the term "avant-garde."

With this chapter, we complete our survey of the basic ingredients of jazz. Beginning in the next part of the book, we explore the rich—and richly recorded!—history of the music.

The Least You Need to Know

- ➤ The singer has always occupied a backseat in jazz because many "purists" believe that jazz is first and foremost an instrumental medium. This seems a shortsighted view.
- ➤ Jazz singers must combine a free, jazz feel with the necessity of making intellectual and emotional sense of lyrics.
- ➤ Some jazz singers concentrate on scat and vocalise, using their voices quite literally as instruments.
- ➤ Each period and style of jazz has had its share of great singers.

Part 3

Backbeat

We begin with the music of West Africa and then the music of the West Africans transported to the New World as slaves. The "slave music" was in large part an expression of freedom and formed one of the central roots of jazz—along with influences from the music of Europe and of white America.

The major musical and cultural strains that produced jazz met and melded in the nation's most exotic city, New Orleans. Here is where early jazz was born, and from here it spread to Chicago, New York, and other cities. Outside of New Orleans, jazz evolved from a music of collective improvisation to individual improvisation, and beginning with Louis Armstrong, the star soloist emerged as a central fixture and feature of the music.

The "classic" jazz of the Roaring Twenties—the "Jazz Age"—gave way in the '30s and '40s to the big band sound of swing. By the end of the '40s, new styles emerged, bebop, and cool jazz.

Chapter 7

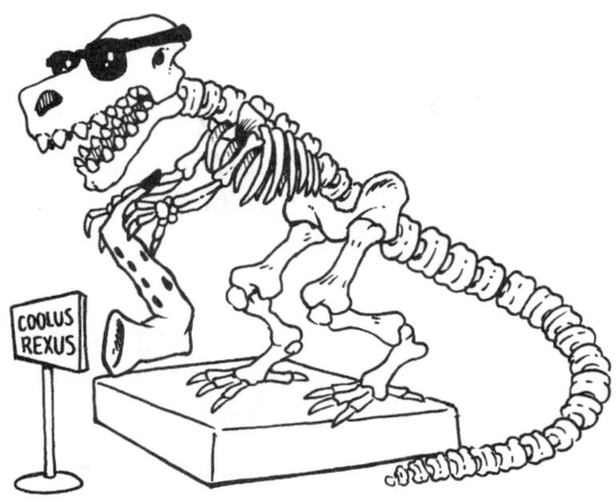

Lively Fossils: The Prehistory of Jazz

In This Chapter

- African roots and European influences
- New Orleans: cradle of jazz
- Influence of blues on jazz
- From dance band to jazz band
- Influence of ragtime on jazz

In Chapter 1 we glanced backwards to the origins of jazz. In this chapter, we will take a closer look at those beginnings. The African roots of jazz are so important to the music that it is difficult to overemphasize them. Nevertheless, this is precisely what many discussions do—defining jazz exclusively as a form of African-American music. African-American musicians have played central roles in creating and developing jazz at every step in the evolution of the music; however, jazz belongs exclusively to no single ethnic, racial, or even age group. If the music would not exist without African and African-American progenitors, neither would jazz be jazz without the contribution of various European and Euro-American traditions. The appeal of jazz is that it is flavored by the spices of many traditions—and by many individual musicians.

This chapter gives a broad view of the multiple roots of jazz.

Out of Africa

We have already mentioned (in Chapter 1) that jazz probably owes much of its immediacy—the sense listeners have that the music is woven of the very fabric of life—to its African roots. Among the peoples of the Gold Coast and Ivory Coast of West Africa, from whom the slaves were drawn, music played a functional role. In many ways an extension of speech, it accompanied all life activities. There were work songs, battle songs, songs of love and courtship, lullabies, spiritual songs, songs to coax fertility from land and people, and songs to heal.

Yet jazz is not "functional" music in this West African sense. While we don't think of it as being as formal as classical music and while the music does seem most at home in the nightclub rather than the concert hall, jazz is still *art*, the product of a creative process set at least somewhat apart from daily life.

Riffs

Sometimes they'd get a piece of tree trunk and hollow it out and stretch a goat's or sheep's skin over it for a drum.... They'd take the buffalo horn and scrape it out to make the flute.... Then they'd take a mule's jawbone and rattle the stick across its teeth.

—Former slave Wash Wilson in 1930, on how to make percussion instruments

The point is, jazz is something that happened when the basic African concept of music (as a life activity) met the basic European concept of music (as art). Both concepts, both traditions, are essential to jazz.

The Freedom of Slave Music

The perpetrators of slavery tried to take everything from their victims: names, possessions, family, and freedom itself. Yet, as was mentioned in Chapter 1, the slave owners, for the most part, let them keep their music. It seemed to make them more efficient workers.

If the slaves had been a different kind of people, they might have held onto their tribal music as a precious object in a museum dedicated to their consolation. Had they treated music this way, neither blues nor jazz would probably exist. African-American music today might just be a collection of sing-song chants and rhythmic patterns—interesting to anthropologists, but probably not the rest of us.

Talk the Talk

A **polyrhythm** is a complex musical structure in which one rhythmic pattern is superimposed on another.

Instead, the slaves used their musical tradition as a living thing. The music they created interacted with their new surroundings. Work songs picked up the speech rhythms of English as well as the West African languages. The hymns of white Christianity became the spirituals of African-American tradition. The slaves also absorbed and transformed the Euro-American folk music, popular music, and folk dance they encountered.

Yet there was always something eminently African in these interactions. Rhythms were complex *polyrhythms*, one rhythmic pattern superimposed on another in a way that was a marvel to white listeners. Most importantly, slave music was highly improvisatory, made up as they went along. Shackled in slavery, these musicians created, however fleetingly, freedom itself.

The traditions of the African-American work song survived long after slavery. This impromptu gathering took place on the wharves of Long Beach, California, in 1941. Image from arttoday.com.

Congo Square, New Orleans

For the most part, white masters looked on slave song as harmless, even productive. In a few places, however, the music was frowned upon or even feared—lest it induce rebellion. The "slave code" of 18th-century South Carolina banned drums for fear they might be used to communicate and coordinate a slave revolt. Colonial Georgia outlawed all instruments among slaves. Elsewhere, offended by the "African" music they heard, white civic leaders encouraged the distribution of such collections of church music as *Hymns and Spiritual Songs*, by Dr. Isaac Watts, in the hope that these would teach the slaves "proper" musical expression. (In fact, slaves transformed many of

"Dr. Watts's hymns" into classic African-American spirituals, today regarded as treasures of our cultural heritage, long after Dr. Watts has fallen by the wayside.)

One slaveholding community not only tolerated black music, it encouraged it. In 1817, the New Orleans city council established an official site for slave dances and song. Located where Louis Armstrong Park now stands, Congo Square became the focus of slave music, not in the context of labor or worship, but as entertainment.

It's no accident, then, that New Orleans is traditionally credited as the birthplace of jazz. Here the early African-American musical traditions were allowed to flourish and develop, and they were heard by blacks as well as whites. Nor is it a coincidence that Buddy Bolden (1868–1931), whom we shall meet in the next chapter as the legendary "inventor" of jazz, performed in the 1890s at Globe Hall within sight of Congo Square. The great New Orleans clarinetist and soprano saxophonist Sidney Bechet recalled that his grandfather would gather with other slaves on Sunday, "their free day," to "beat out rhythms on the drums at the square—Congo Square they called it."

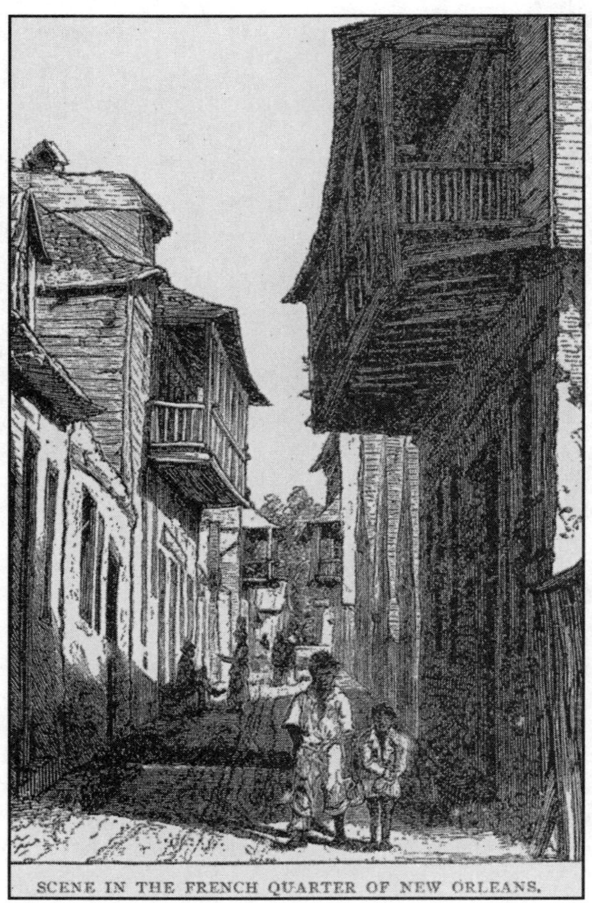

SCENE IN THE FRENCH QUARTER OF NEW ORLEANS.

New Orleans's French Quarter in the late 19th century.
Image from Ben Truman, From the Crescent City to the Golden Gate, *1886.*

It's also neither accident nor coincidence that New Orleans was not just a black city, but, during the long years of jazz prehistory, it was North America's most cosmopolitan metropolis. Among the many ethnic ingredients that make up the city's gumbo, the French and Spanish are as prominent as the African. When jazz emerged in the 1920s, no one outside of the United States embraced the music more enthusiastically than the French. And throughout this book, we will see that jazz has often been flavored by Hispanic traditions. New Orleans jazz pioneer Jelly Roll Morton went so far as to say that "if you can't manage to put tinges of Spanish into your tunes, you will never be able to get the right seasoning, I call it, for jazz."

Nothing but the Blues

It would simplify the task of anyone writing about the origins of jazz if it were possible to stop at Congo Square and post a sign: *Jazz Starts Here*. But the prehistory of jazz is much richer than that.

Blues Folk: Rural Roots

The music we call the blues is rooted in songs of lament from the days of slavery. While blues performance—in rural *juke joints* and on record—began in the 1920s, aged New Orleans blacks, some born in the 1860s, have reported to folklorists that "the blues was here when I come."

Talk the Talk

A **juke joint** was a roadhouse or tavern that played dance music, the blues, or even early jazz; the term connotes a rough place or dive.

Little is known of the sad non-religious songs of the slaves, since nobody wrote them down, and since this was one form of song that most slave owners actually discouraged. They figured that melancholy tunes would impede rather than promote production.

Nevertheless, musicologists believe that the blues was born in the plantation field, born of work songs and something called the *field holler*, which folklorist John W. Work described as a "fragmentary bit of a yodel, half sung, half yelled." The holler might be "sung," Work wrote, as a man approached "his house or that of his sweetheart in the evening, or sometimes out of sheer loneliness."

The contours of the blues were already apparent in the holler: *portamento* (a musical style in which the singer glides from one note to another rather than articulating each note separately), slow tempo, a tendency to flat the third (the "blue note" mentioned in Chapter 4), and the pervasive melancholy of the tune.

Talk the Talk

A **field holler,** one of the roots of the blues, is a song fragment, half sung, half yelled, that developed among African-American slaves and agricultural workers. **Portamento,** a characteristic of the blues and much jazz, is a musical technique or style in which the singer or instrumentalist glides from one note to another rather than articulating each note separately.

If the holler was the mother of blues, the work song was its father. Look at this example:

Oh, Captain, Captain, you better count yo' men;
Oh, Captain, you better count yo' men;
Oh, some gone to the bushes [escaped], *oh Lord, an' some gone in.*

Each verse begins with a long, drawn out cry, much like the holler. The words are slurred, and the end of each line trails off into grunts—typical of West African work songs. The cadence is that of hard, monotonous, heartbreaking labor. The cadence is also that of the classic blues heard in the early 20th century, still heard today, and also known as the "12-bar blues," in which each of the three lines of lyrics takes up four bars, or measures.

Classic blues is not the only kind of traditional blues. The "talking blues" harks back to the West African singsong style, in which speech and song are virtually one and the same. In 1961, folklorist Harry Oster recorded Smoky Babe (Robert Brown) of Scotlandville, Louisiana, in his improvised "Workin' Blues":

Spoken over guitar chords:

Well, I always get up every mornin'
'tween five an', oh, six o'clock,
Boy, I'm tellin' you it's a mess,
You know it's a mess, oh, you know it's a mess,
Well, if you ain't got yo' wife aroun',
you ain't got no woman,
She ain't at home, I'm tellin' you true,
yo' bed ain't made up.
Yo' floor ain't swept, an' everythin',
I'm tellin' you true,
It's rough, peoples, it's rough.
I gotta go out there an' feed my ole hogs,
An' fool aroun' ole cow an' everythin'...
You know out in the field, mean ole boss
an' everythin' in the mornin' time,
You know how you feel that mornin',
don't wanna get up,
But you gotta get up...
I'm talkin' about how I got to go out here
to work for my boss a while,
To get some money for Saturday night you know,
Have a good time then, hm...

Sung:

Well, I'm gonna find my little woman,
she lovin' somebody else.
You know how you gonna find her?
Yeah, how she done left you all alone, see,
She done quit you done gone to another house.
'Cause you ain't got nothin'
but the cotton pickin' blues...

Blues People: "Classic" Blues

By late in the 19th century, folk blacks were singing blues quite similar to the country blues of today. But the blues first reached beyond the rural South after August 10, 1920, when Mamie Smith cut Perry Bradford's "Crazy Blues," the first blues on disk.

Blues pioneer Mamie Smith, 1920s. Image from Lawrence Cohn.

Smith's record sold so well that record companies sought out performers in the country as well as the city. On April 1926, Paramount Records released "Booster Blues" and "Dry Southern Blues," its first sides by Blind Lemon Jefferson (1897–1929), destined to become the first "superstar" of the music.

Dig This

Sample the music of Blind Lemon Jefferson on *Blind Lemon Jefferson*, a Milestone CD.

Jefferson had an enormous impact on African-American country blues artists, and the tremendous popularity of his records hardened the blues into the classic 12-bar, three-line form—a sung line, followed by a guitar line repeating the sung line, then a new response from the instrument, and, finally, a concluding sung line. Over the following years, thousands of blues performers followed this pattern.

A record-company publicity photo of Blind Lemon Jefferson—autographed no less! (Like many blues artists, Jefferson was indeed blind.)
Image from Lawrence Cohn.

Despite its often rigid structure, the blues is almost infinite in its variety. Within the standard patterns, performers freely improvise instrumentally and inject intense emotion and varied styles into their singing. While the rigid structure keeps it very distinct from the more broadly improvisational jazz, blues laid the emotional and stylistic foundation on which jazz is built. Blues performance set the example for jazz, in which feeling and individual expression are paramount.

Real Square

Don't tell a blues fan that the music he loves was no more than a stepping stone to jazz. You're in for a fight if you do. Jazz did not replace the blues or make it obsolete. On the contrary, the blues developed along a path separate and independent from jazz and is still very much alive and well.

European Connections

Beginning in the 18th century, white Protestant missionaries set about preaching the gospel to slaves. They had their work cut out for them, since slavery is eminently unchristian, but no matter—African-Americans readily took to the new religion, making it very much their own. This included the music, as we have mentioned: the staid and austere Protestant hymns becoming the emotionally intense spirituals and, later, gospel music.

African-American musicians also transformed white, Euro-American popular music. Combine the feel of the blues with Euro-American popular dance and song forms, as well Euro-American bands and orchestra instruments, and you begin to have jazz.

Shall We Schottische?

Let's return to New Orleans at the end of the 19th century. A host of modest African-American "social orchestras" (typically consisting of violin, cornet, clarinet, trombone, drums, double bass, and guitar) made a living for their members by providing music for dances, parties, picnics, and funerals. The repertoire consisted mainly of the popular dance music of the day, waltzes, polkas, quadrilles, and schottische.

Pre-jazz and the earliest jazz bands were expert in playing music for the popular dances of the late 19th and early 20th centuries. These dances included…

- The *waltz,* most familiar as the rapid $^3/_4$-time Viennese ballroom dance, also a form of folk dance.
- The *polka,* originally a Bohemian folk dance associated with courtship, characterized by three quick steps and a hop danced in $^2/_4$ time and covering considerable space as couples whirl around the dance floor.
- The *quadrille,* which began as an aristocratic court dance in Europe during the 18th and 19th centuries, involving four couples moving in square formation and intertwining figures. Quadrilles were danced in the refined ballrooms of the United States during the 19th century and were also translated into rustic social dances.

- The *schottische*, which is probably Scottish or German (or imported from Scotland through German sources) and was popular in American as well as European ballrooms during much of the middle to late 19th century. The step is typically a variation on a basic three rapid steps and a hop. Dancing couples circle the room, promenade forward, and turn round each other. The dance has many variations.

All of these popular European dance forms were imported into America. Often, the black orchestras played this music straight, emulating their white counterparts. But, increasingly during the early years of the 20th century, they brought a blues—as well as ragtime—feel to these danceable Euro-American forms. It was from this hybridization that jazz emerged.

Funeral Marches in New Orleans

The early New Orleans dance orchestras did not confine themselves to the ballroom or social hall. They officiated at funerals as well. Sometimes, they would ride in the procession in a wagon—violin, double bass, and guitar included. Sometimes, they would drop the strings and change instrumentation to that of a marching band, proceeding on foot.

Dig This

Want a taste of the New Orleans brass band tradition? Try *New Orleans Brass Bands: Down Yonder*, a 1989 CD release from Rounder Records, which includes traditional as well as modern music.

On the way to the cemetery, the music was a spiritual played as a solemn dirge, albeit with touches of something very like jazz: portamento notes, rubato rhythm, an occasional blue note. But on the return trip, it was the band's task to lift the gloom with tunes that may have been built on spirituals or even marches, but were transformed by all the elements of jazz in primitive form: wild syncopation, flatted notes, heavy portamento, and the general exuberance created by *polyphony* (simultaneous melodies and counter-melodies) and *heterophony* (as many as a dozen winds playing roughly harmonized, approximately parallel musical lines). The effect was riotous. Enthusiasts started calling it "hot music."

Talk the Talk

Polyphony involves instruments playing simultaneous melodies and countermelodies, whereas **heterophony** is the playing of roughly harmonized and only approximately parallel musical lines.

From Missouri

The hot music played by the parade bands is exhilarating, but it is rough and ready rather than disciplined. It's close to jazz, but it's not jazz. Blue notes, bent notes, slurred notes, growls, and the loosening of the melodic line from the underlying beat all create a jazz feeling, but it would take the influence of another musical style to transform hot music into jazz.

Music in "Ragged Time"

While the musical gumbo was bubbling in New Orleans, by the end of the 19th century much of the nation was becoming intrigued by music coming not from the Gulf, but from the Midwest, especially in and around Missouri.

It started in the rough honky-tonks of towns along the Mississippi and Missouri rivers—piano music mainly, characterized by headlong, syncopated rhythms. In contrast to the New Orleans hot musicians, the practitioners of ragged time—or ragtime—weren't influenced by hollers or the blues, but by traditions more distantly inspired by plantation life: minstrel-show songs and African-American syncopated banjo-picking styles. If hot music was in part built on dances like the polka and schottische, ragtime took inspiration from the highly syncopated beat of the *cakewalk,* originally a strutting, high-stepping dance popular among slaves and performed in the presence of their masters—though it was, in fact, a mocking parody of white ballroom dances.

A 1904 illustration from the British humor magazine Punch *showing men doing the cakewalk. Image from arttoday.com.*

Mr. Scott Joplin

By the start of the 20th century, ragtime had risen from honky-tonks and bordellos to become the predominant form of American popular music. It would remain so for almost two decades.

In a just society, the immense popularity of ragtime should have brought riches to the greatest ragtime composer, Scott Joplin (1868–1917), but for a young black musician, turn-of-the-century America was hardly a just society. Joplin studied piano with local teachers near his Bowie County, Texas home and then toured the Midwest from the mid-1880s, performing to acclaim at Chicago's Columbian Exposition in 1893. He settled in Sedalia, Missouri in 1895 and formally studied music at the George R. Smith College for Negroes.

Joplin's dream was to become a classical concert pianist. For a black American at the end of the 19th century, this was an impossible dream—the first of many crushing disappointments the pianist would suffer.

Now we could stop here with an observation that life in a racist society can be heartbreaking, if not worse. But there is more to Joplin's passion for classical music. He took that passion and infused it into his ragtime pieces, elevating them far above the level of mere popular novelties. The jazz composer and scholar Gunther Schuller has called Joplin the "American Chopin," and it is true that many of Joplin's beautiful rags, such as "The Maple Leaf Rag," "The Entertainer," and "Solace (A Mexican Serenade)," exhibit a classical lyricism, complexity, and clarity. They are unmistakably the work of an academically trained composer (who also happened to be a genius).

Talk the Talk

Originally a strutting, high-stepping dance popular among slaves and performed in the presence of their masters, the **cakewalk** (which got its name much later) was actually a sly parody of white ballroom dances. By the end of the 19th century, the cakewalk had become a stage dance for couples and was subsequently adapted as a ballroom dance. It played an evolutionary role in dance steps accompanying ragtime and jazz.

Ragtime brought to embryonic jazz more of the classical European tradition, but it also introduced an especially propulsive form of syncopation. Finally, ragtime masters like Joplin raised the bar of formal musicianship for popular music generally and for jazz in particular. In large part thanks to Joplin and other ragtime musicians, jazz moved further from its folk roots and became more sophisticated and professional.

As for Joplin, his first published songs did bring him fame and a degree of financial reward. In 1900, he moved to St. Louis to be near his publisher, John Stark. But he had aspirations beyond composing for ragtime piano. He wrote a ballet suite based on ragtime and two rag-influenced operas, the second of which, *Treemonisha*, wasn't recorded or performed until long after the composer's death. After Joplin moved to New York City in 1907, he published *The School of Ragtime*, an instruction book outlining the complex elements of ragtime. It proved highly influential not only for rag pianists but, later, for jazz musicians as well.

Joplin broke his heart and health trying to get *Treemonisha* produced. He suffered a total nervous collapse in 1911 and was ultimately confined to an asylum in 1916. A year later, he was dead.

Putting Two into Four

Ragtime all but died with Joplin before the beginning of the 1920s, although a few later practitioners (notably Max Morath) both revived the tradition and kept it alive. Hollywood composer Marvin Hamlisch adapted a number of Joplin rags (including "The Entertainer" and "Solace") for the score of the 1972 hit film *The Sting*, which launched a nationwide ragtime recording revival.

Take Five

Ragtime makes for wonderful listening. Pianists Max Morath and Joshua Rifkin have done much to introduce the style to contemporary audiences. Morath's *World of Scott Joplin* (Vanguard) and Joshua Rifkin's *Scott Joplin Piano Rags* (Nonesuch), both available on CD, are great recordings. Joplin recorded player-piano rolls, so you can also hear the master playing his own works on *The Entertainer: Classic Ragtime from Rare Piano Rolls* (Biograph). Joplin's opera *Treemonisha* has been splendidly recorded by Gunther Schuller and the Houston Grand Opera Orchestra and Chorus for Deutsche Grammophon (DGG).

While Scott Joplin overshadows other ragtime composers, many are worth hearing. Biograph's *The Greatest Ragtime of the Century* features performances (transcribed from original piano rolls) by Jelly Roll Morton, Fats Waller, James P. Johnson, Eubie Blake, and Jimmy Blythe. Max Morath's *World of Scott Joplin* (Vanguard) features performances of Joplin and his contemporaries.

Composers such as William Bolcom and Reginald Robinson still compose in the ragtime medium, and the traditional rags are still performed; however, for all practical purposes, ragtime has ceased to be an *active* creative style and has been wholly replaced by jazz. The principal transformation from ragtime to jazz was rhythmic. Most rags were based on two-beat march rhythms. Early in the century, some musicians began playing ragtime in four-quarter time, in effect undergirding the two-beat rag with a four-beat ground rhythm. The effect was greater speed and greater flexibility—the scope for rhythmic variation that is so essential to jazz.

W.C. Handy's Triumph

Jelly Roll Morton claimed to have invented jazz in 1902 when he played ragtime while stomping his foot in $^4/_4$ time. Maybe so. Exactly *who* "invented" jazz is open to endless speculation and fruitless dispute. What is clear is that an Alabama-born musician, William Christopher Handy (1873–1958), combined blues with ragtime and created what many Americans started calling jazz.

Handy's "Memphis Blues" (1911) and, even more, his still-popular "St. Louis Blues" (1914) swept the country and began a rapid transition from ragtime to jazz. While Handy by no means single-handedly invented jazz, he introduced the concept of blues as a harmonic framework in which to improvise, continued the rhythmic updating of ragtime, and delivered it all in a popularly orchestrated package. No rough New Orleans street music for W.C. Handy. His orchestrations were sophisticated, and his musicians were formally trained. Moreover, Handy's fate stood in happy contrast to that of Scott Joplin. Handy was a skilled and tireless self-promoter, who very profitably conducted his own orchestra from 1903 to 1921, and started and managed his own music-publishing house.

In a strictly musical sense, W.C. Handy did not complete the transition from blues and ragtime to jazz. He did, however, popularize that transition, putting jazz on the national map by professionalizing it and making it palatable to a large audience, both white and black.

Within a half-dozen years of the publication of "St. Louis Blues," the Jazz Age began in earnest, and American popular music would become celebrated around the world.

The Least You Need to Know

- The role of African-American music and musicians is central to jazz, but the music is a product of African-American *and* Euro-American musical traditions.
- Bringing together black, Spanish, French, and other ethnic and popular-music traditions, turn-of-the-century New Orleans was the ideal cradle and nursery of jazz.
- Unique personal expression is central to jazz, but part of the framework for that expression comes from traditional popular dance music.
- Both the blues and ragtime influenced and shaped early jazz. While jazz supplanted ragtime as a style, the blues continued to develop on its own path and is still a rich and important musical style today.
- No one person "invented" jazz, but W.C. Handy broadened the appeal of blues and ragtime from black to white audiences, thereby launching jazz as popular *commercial* music.

Chapter 8

Down in the Big Easy: Jazz Is Born

In This Chapter

- Storyville: hotbed of jazz
- Buddy Bolden: legendary "king of jazz"
- Dixieland: white New Orleans Jazz
- Jelly Roll Morton: self-proclaimed inventor of jazz
- The music moves north
- Early Louis Armstrong

We've called New Orleans a gumbo. In the 19th and early 20th century, the city they call the "Big Easy" was musically just that: a melange of sounds and traditions. Socially, however, it was something else. Blacks and whites were separated, but so were "African" blacks and Creoles—people of Euro-African ancestry. New Orleans Creoles loved music as much as the African blacks, but they were typically literate and could read music. Creole musicians took pride in their formal training, and Jelly Roll Morton, a Creole, spoke disparagingly of "black Negroes" who couldn't read "those little black dots."

But in 1894, the white New Orleans government enacted Code No. 111, which, invoking white supremacy, sent Creoles packing out of white neighborhoods. This gradually led to a lowering of self-imposed barriers between African blacks and the Euro-African Creoles. It also meant a lively musical exchange between formally trained Creole musicians and untutored "black Negroes." While the exchange may have generally raised musical literacy among New Orleans African Americans, it more importantly freed Creole musicians from adherence to printed scores. Black and Creole traditions met and mingled in the tenderloin district along Canal Street called Storyville, and many jazz historians consider it the birthplace of jazz. That's where this chapter begins.

The Storyville Story

New Orleans treated prostitution with much the same tempered tolerance as it had the singing and dancing of slaves. Just as it had set aside Congo Square for slave music in 1817, so in 1896 did crusading Crescent City politician Sidney Story push through the city council an ordinance confining prostitution to a 38-block area centered on Canal and Basin streets. The neighborhood had no particular name, and Story could not have been pleased that, after the passage of the ordinance, this latter-day little Gomorrah was unofficially but universally named in his honor: Storyville.

Storyville became a showcase of vice—sex, gambling, drugs—but it also became a showcase for "hot music." A host of the earliest jazz musicians made their living as "professors" (piano players") in "mansions" (brothels). The money was good, and the environment, to say the least, stimulating. Here, in this dividing-line district, black and Creole musical traditions and practices cross-fertilized. As the folklorist Alan Lomax put it, Storyville was the realization of the "master formula of jazz—mulatto (Creole) knowingness ripened by black sorrow."

Riffs

People have got an idea that the music started in whorehouses. Well, there was district here, you know, and the houses in it, they'd all have someone playing a guitar or mandolin, or a piano...someone singing, maybe; but they didn't have orchestras, and the musicianers... would go to those houses just whenever they didn't have a regular engagement.

—New Orleans soprano saxophonist Sidney Bechet clarifies the role of "the district"

Buddy Bolden's Blues

Black sorrow. Charles Joseph "Buddy" Bolden was born in New Orleans in 1877, the son of a domestic servant. Four years after his birth, his five-year-old sister died of encephalitis. Two years after that, his 32-year-old father succumbed to pneumonia. Such was life and death in black New Orleans.

Buddy managed to survive and took cornet lessons from a neighbor. He joined a social orchestra in the 1890s, playing the rough and raucous "hot music" that soon took Storyville by storm, at first to the dismay of more conservative Creole musicians, who only reluctantly joined in later.

Bolden played dives and honky tonks, though not the brothels. His music was not only "hot" in strictly musical terms, it was daring in social terms as well. Songs like "Buddy Bolden's Blues" included lyrics lambasting a local judge and other white authority figures. As Sidney Bechet recalled, "The police put you in jail if they heard you singing that song. I was just starting out on clarinet, six or seven years old, ...Bolden started his theme song, people started singing, policemen began whipping heads."

Musically, Bolden wowed contemporary musicians with the power of his tone, his rhythmic drive, and the emotional eloquence of his slow blues. Within the first few years of the 20th century, he had blown away the more genteel Creole bands. Those Creoles who didn't embrace the hot new music found themselves without employment in and around Storyville.

Dig This

There are no known recordings by Buddy Bolden.

Bolden was not a great improviser, although he is said to have been a master of impressive ornamentation. Nevertheless, the sheer intensity of his music earned him nearly legendary status as the father of jazz—at least among the next generation of New Orleans musicians.

And like all truly enduring legendary figures, Bolden is shrouded in mystery. By 1905, his star had risen, and he played not only in Storyville, but in dance halls elsewhere in the city, in parks, and on outings. The very next year, he was being hailed as the "King of New Orleans Jazz." He was fabled not for his music alone, but for his supernatural "way with women" and his capacity for drink.

Yet in the year of his greatest triumph, 1906, he began suffering from headaches accompanied by psychotic delusions. He attacked his mother and was arrested and released, only to fall into repeated fits of rage and depression. Arrested a second time, in September 1906, he was soon committed to the Insane Asylum of Louisiana. There he died, unheralded and unrecorded, in 1931.

Riffs

Buddy Bolden's legend was enduring. In the 1950s when Duke Ellington wanted a certain sound from trumpeter Clark Terry, he told Terry to play like Buddy Bolden. Terry protested that he didn't know who Buddy Bolden was. Ellington explained. "Buddy Bolden was suave, handsome, and a debonair cat who the ladies loved. Aw, he was so fantastic! He was fabulous! He was always sought after. He had the biggest, fattest trumpet sound in town. He bent notes to the nth degree. He used to tune up in New Orleans and break glasses in Algiers!"

ODJB: Jazz Enters the Mainstream

The world of Buddy Bolden was dangerous, delicious, and ultimately depressing. Bolden's music was likewise dangerous and daring, but ultimately forgotten—if only because Bolden's career came and went like a shooting star. In contrast was ODJB, the

Original Dixieland Jass Band: five dapper white musicians (Nick LaRocca, leader on cornet; Larry Shields, clarinet; Eddie Edwards, trombone; Tony Sbarbaro, drums; and Henry Ragas, piano) who started out in the Crescent City but made their national reputation in Chicago (1916) and New York (beginning in 1917).

Talk the Talk

Dixieland is traditional New Orleans jazz as played by white musicians. (New Orleans jazz played by African Americans is called simply that: "New Orleans jazz.")

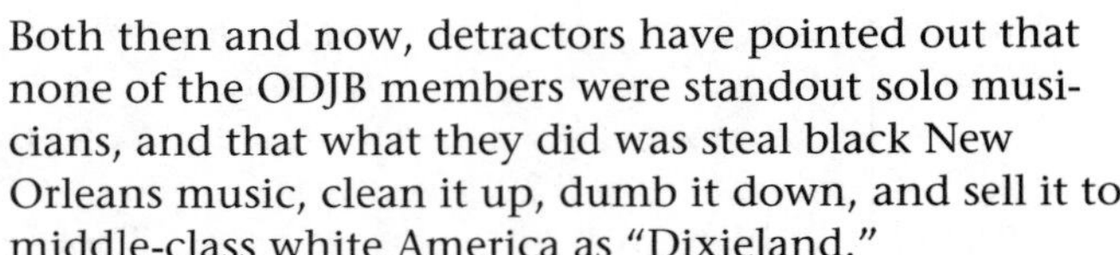

Both then and now, detractors have pointed out that none of the ODJB members were standout solo musicians, and that what they did was steal black New Orleans music, clean it up, dumb it down, and sell it to middle-class white America as "Dixieland."

Maybe. But without the ODJB, who knows when jazz would have entered the American mainstream? The group was the first to cut a jazz record ("Livery Stable Blues" in 1917 and the celebrated "Tiger Rag" the following year), and, through the 1920s, they did much to sell jazz to the American public.

Dig This

In Chapter 5, I recommended the *75th Anniversary* CD on Bluebird. Fans will also want *ODJB in England* (EMI Pathe/Jazztime), recordings made during a 1919–20 visit to Britain. Interestingly enough, ODJB recorded some of their most attractive material abroad.

Mister Jelly Roll

ODJB always had and always will have its critics. But its most passionate advocate was none other than cornetist and leader Nick LaRocca, who repeatedly claimed to have been one of the inventors of jazz. In this, he can get in line with Buddy Bolden and one Jelly Roll Morton.

Born Ferdinand LaMothe in New Orleans in 1890, he called himself LaMenthe, only to abandon the name for Morton because (he said) of racial prejudices directed against the French. His family were strict, fairly well-to-do Creoles, who held themselves aloof from African-American culture. Yet when he was 12 years old—just two years after having learned to play the piano—he found work as a ragtime pianist in a Storyville brothel.

Red Light Entrepreneur

Morton's family disowned him when he strayed into Storyville, but Jelly Roll (the nickname has nothing to do with pastry but is a slang reference to sex and to the female genitalia) embraced the life of the infamous district. He was not only a pianist in Storyville (and in many cities in Louisiana, Mississippi, Alabama, and Florida), but a professional gambler, a pool hustler, and a pimp. He was also a composer—and yes, he claimed to have invented jazz, in Storyville, in about 1902 when he played $^2/_4$-time ragtime while stomping out a jazzy $^4/_4$-time beat.

The truth is Morton was a blowhard (though a genius at the piano), and few jazz historians give him credit for inventing the music—in 1902 (at age 12, no less) or later. Nevertheless, it is also a fact that from 1904 to 1922, he played nationwide, from New York to Los Angeles, introducing "hot music" to a wide audience. In the process, he certainly combined many disparate elements of black music—ragtime, blues, minstrel show tunes, spirituals, and even field hollers—with Latin music from the Carribean and popular music in the Euro-American vein. If this wasn't exactly inventing jazz, it came fairly close.

Red Hot Peppers

Morton arrived in Los Angeles in 1917, enjoying such acclaim there that he stayed until 1922 when he moved to Chicago. He was not alone in this move. The Windy City had become the nation's new jazz mecca, as both black and white New Orleans musicians moved north.

Dig This

Ever the ostentatious self-promoter, Morton always dressed with impeccable flash. His wardrobe included such trademark accessories as diamond-studded garters to hold up his socks and a diamond filling in a front tooth.

Between 1923 and 1926, Morton recorded many of his best piano solos, which are available on *Jelly Roll Morton*, a Milestone CD essential for anyone interested in early jazz. Morton compositions such as "King Porter Stomp," "Black Bottom Stomp," and "The Chant" are breathtaking. Less well known is "Grandpa's Spells," a study in contrast and texture that is always propelled by an unerring sense of swing.

As wonderful as the first three Chicago years were, Morton's truly epoch-making year was 1926, when he headed up the Red Hot Peppers, a group formed to record for the Victor company. Over the next several years, until 1930, the band consisted of seven or eight of the greatest names in early jazz, most notably cornetist George Mitchell, trombonist Kid Ory, clarinetists Omer Simeon and Johnny Dodds, banjo players Johnny St. Cyr and Bud Scott, double bassist John Lindsay, and drummers Andrew Hillaire and Baby Dodds (brother of Johnny). From the piano, Morton led the Peppers in brilliant arrangements of his own compositions, including "Black Bottom Stomp," "Smoke-House Blues," "Doctor Jazz," and many others.

Dig This

An investment in the moderately priced five-CD *Jelly Roll Morton Centennial: His Complete Victor Recordings* (1926–39) is money wisely spent; for Morton's work with the Peppers set *the* standard for jazz arranging and performance. And a high standard it is. Morton had a genius for exploiting texture, color, and timbre, yet doing so within the tight confines of his well-structured compositions.

For much of the '20s, Chicago was a hotbed of jazz evolution. New Orleans musicians such as bandleader King Oliver, cornetist Louis Armstrong, clarinetist Jimmy Noone, and clarinetist and soprano saxophonist Sidney Bechet were just some of the luminaries who left the Crescent City for the Windy City and earned their national fame there.

Two views of Chicago in the mid 1920s: the elegance of Michigan Avenue's Wrigley Building (top left) and Tribune Tower (top right), and the South Side ghetto (bottom). Both scenes became well known to the African-American musicians who trekked north from New Orleans. Images from arttoday.com.

Inspired by the New Orleans exodus, Chicago also developed homegrown versions of the New Orleans style. Among the most notable of the native Chicago musicians who started in the 1920s were the so-called Austin High School Gang: Jimmy McPartland (cornet), Dave Tough (drums), Frank Teschemacher (clarinet, alto saxophone), Joe Sullivan (piano), and Bud Freeman (tenor saxophone).

The New Orleans musicians also inspired such giants as clarinetist Benny Goodman, drummer Gene Krupa, and cornetist Muggsy Spanier, all Chicago natives who got their start in the '20s. Non-natives Eddie Condon (banjo and guitar), Pee Wee Russell (clarinet), and Red McKenzie (vocals) moved to the city early on and launched their careers here.

While Chicago was geographically and climatologically a long way from New Orleans, it shared much of the southern town's anything goes attitude, at least in the Roaring '20s. In Chicago, sex, booze, and music were all for sale in an abundance that more than equaled what Storyville and the French Quarter had to offer.

Dig This

For a taste of the Austin High style, try Bud Freeman's *Jammin' at Commodore* (Commodore).

Take Five

The United States' entry into World War I in 1917 brought the U.S. Navy into New Orleans to protect the Gulf of Mexico and the mouth of the Mississippi from possible attack. Sailors turned loose on Storyville were understandably overjoyed, but Secretary of the Navy Josephus Daniels was not. On November 14, 1917, he issued an order prohibiting prostitution within five miles of any U.S. Navy base. And that was the end of Storyville. The district never recovered financially. The exodus of jazz musicians (and, doubtless, other professionals) began.

On to the Apple

Chicago was as important to jazz in the 1920s as New Orleans had been in the teens and earlier. But as the torch had passed from New Orleans to Chicago, so it would leave the Windy City, too, by the end of the '20s. Jelly Roll saw this coming, and in 1928, he moved to New York City, the new capital of jazz in America.

Morton continued his performing and recording career in the Big Apple, but he gradually discovered that, in New York, jazz was maturing beyond him. Morton was able to make superficial changes in orchestration and even harmony in an effort to get his music in step with the times, but he couldn't entirely change his New Orleans spots.

Morton had grown up musically in an environment of *collective improvisation*, in which each member of the group contributes a musical line of equal importance. This is an essential quality of New Orleans jazz. And it is one reason why this music, once so *hot*, sounds old-fashioned to us today. Whether we realize it or not, we are accustomed to jazz that is orchestrally sophisticated beyond collective improvisation and that features *individual improvisation*. Indeed, individual improvisation we now take for granted in jazz, but it wasn't always a part of the music. It developed, for the most part, in New York, beginning in the late '20s and early '30s.

Talk the Talk

Collective improvisation is a musical style in which each member of an ensemble contributes a musical line of equal importance. Characteristic of traditional New Orleans jazz, it was supplanted by **individual improvisation** (improvisation focusing on soloists) during the late 1920s.

The new jazz of New Yorkers Don Redman, Fletcher Henderson, and others left the elegant Morton in the dust. Eclipsed in New York, he moved to Washington, D.C., where he managed a nightclub and had the good fortune, in 1938, to be "discovered" by folklorist Alan Lomax, who recorded from him an oral history of early jazz for the Library of Congress, which included many piano performances. (The musical portions of the Library of Congress recordings are available on four CDs from Rounder Records.) The efforts of Lomax rekindled public interest in Jelly Roll Morton, but years of the high life caught up with him in 1941, when he died at age 51.

More Jazz Towns

Jazz histories give the impression that everything of importance in the music happened in New Orleans, then Chicago, and then New York. While it is true that these cities enjoyed a concentration of activity, jazz was pervasive coast to coast by the 1920s.

Detroit, Miami, Memphis, and Los Angeles all had active jazz scenes in the '20s, and so did the likes of Milwaukee, Cincinnati, Omaha, as well as many of the towns and cities of Texas, which came to be celebrated for "Texas piano," a combination of honky-tonk, boogie-woogie, and the blues.

Most important of the "secondary" cities of early jazz was Kansas City. Like New Orleans and Chicago, KC was wide open in the 1920s. As one newspaper columnist put it, "If you want to see some sin, forget Paris and go to Kansas City."

Talk the Talk

A **riff** is a short melodic ostinato (constantly repeated) phrase, usually two to four bars long. Born in Kansas City jazz, the riff became a mainstay of large-ensemble jazz.

The jazz that developed early on in Kansas City combined the blues feel of the Southwest, the emerging big band sound of the Northeast, and the improvisational freedom of New York's Harlem. Kansas City jazz is short on elaborate arrangements but celebrates individual invention and great solo work. Early on, the Kansans exploited the possibilities of the *riff*, a short melodic phrase that became a trademark of Kansas City jazz and, ultimately, of jazz in general. KC players were noted for their ability to improvise endlessly on simple riffs.

A view of Kansas City, Missouri, in the late 1920s.
Image from arttoday.com.

Kansas City is sometimes cited as the birthplace of swing—destined to be the dominant style of the 1930s and much of the '40s. By far the most important Kansas City band was the hard-swinging Bennie Moten Orchestra, active from the early '20s into the early '30s. Many jazz histories give the nod to Moten only because his group was the nucleus of the first of Count Basie's orchestras; however, the "Moten Swing" is important and fun enough to enjoy in its own right. *Basie Beginnings*, a Bluebird CD, features the orchestra from 1929 to 1932 and is probably the best of Moten on record. If you want to hear very early KC swing, *Bennie Moten (1923–1927)*, on the Classics label, is a fine collection.

King Oliver's Ambassadors

Born in New Orleans in 1885, Joe Oliver learned trombone and later cornet. By 1907, he was playing with brass bands, dance bands, and other New Orleans groups. He did not make it big until he moved to Chicago in 1918 and acquired the nickname "King" Oliver. Within two years he was leading his own band, and at various times during the 1920s, he could count among his personnel the most important of the young New Orleans musicians who had moved to Chicago.

What does "most important" mean? In this case, it means the New Orleans musicians who would play major roles in the future of jazz: Sidney Bechet, Kid Ory, the Dodds brothers (Baby and Johnny), and, above all, Louis Armstrong.

Dig This

Why doesn't Moten get all the credit he deserves in jazz histories? Well, he was not only overshadowed by his own second pianist, Count Basie, but he had the terrible misfortune to die young in 1935 at age 41 after a botched tonsillectomy.

Except, perhaps, in his ability to attract tremendous talent, Oliver was not a great musician. Listen to *Sugar Foot Stomp*, a CD reissue on GRP of 1926–28 recordings by Oliver's most important band, the Dixie Syncopaters. The music is exuberant, joyous, extraordinarily skillful but also four-square compared to the jazz that was about to emerge from New York. Listen to Oliver's cornet solo on "Dippermouth Blues," his most famous composition, and you will hear a piece that generations of jazz trumpeters have learned by heart. It is undeniably brilliant, but it is also distinctly old fashioned. Clipped and staccato, it stands in stark contrast to the much looser and more expressive cornet work of Oliver's famous alumnus, Louis Armstrong.

Yet it is a fact that Oliver's succession of orchestras produced the second generation of early jazz stars. If Oliver was king, these men were his ambassadors—musicians who helped make jazz the dominant sound of the 1920s and, beyond this, a compelling and enduring element of American popular culture.

Sidney Bechet

While it is generally agreed that Louis Armstrong was the first great jazz soloist, Sidney Joseph Bechet (1897–1959) beat him onto a recording by a few months in 1923. On clarinet or, even more, on soprano saxophone, Bechet's tone and style are unmistakable. Both lyrical and loud, he played with a fat, exaggerated vibrato that listeners either love or hate. In any case, it is a style so singularly assertive that even brass players found it difficult to compete with him.

Sidney Bechet playing soprano with Fats Waller, piano, and James P. Johnson, bass, 1930s. Image from the author's collection.

Bechet was born into a cultured New Orleans Creole family, which was filled with music. He studied clarinet with local musicians Lorenzo Tio, Jr., Big Eye Nelson, and George Baquet, but progressed so quickly that he largely taught himself. As a child of seven or eight, he was already playing in bands and even teaching clarinet. (Jimmy Noone, two years Bechet's senior, was one of his most brilliant students.)

Bechet came to Chicago in 1917, then, after World War I, toured Europe and the States. By the early '20s, Bechet had developed a sense of swing second only to that of Louis Armstrong, and he joined the youthful Duke Ellington Orchestra in 1923. At the time, the Ellington ensemble was a popular dance orchestra rather than a jazz ensemble, and it was largely through Bechet's example that the band made the transition to jazz. Bechet was an especially strong influence on alto and soprano saxophonist Johnny Hodges, one of the most important members of the Ellington organization.

Dig This

Few soloists choose the soprano saxophone as their instrument, but it suited Bechet's personality perfectly, because its sound is much more piercing and assertive than the more retiring clarinet. Bechet is strong medicine.

During the Roaring Twenties, Bechet enjoyed sufficient financial success to open his own nightclub in Harlem, but he fell on hard times during the Depression and supported himself by opening a little tailor shop. Despite a hit recording of Gershwin's "Summertime" in 1938, Bechet drifted into obscurity until he was invited to play at the Salle Pleyel Jazz Festival in Paris in 1949. Bechet's career was reborn, and he spent the last decade of his life touring and performing with the same operatic gusto and authority that had characterized him in the high-flying 1920s.

The Chronological Sidney Bechet is a four-volume CD series issued on the Classics label. If you want to buy a single CD, start with the first volume, 1923–1936, which features Bechet on clarinet as well as soprano saxophone. This CD includes a legendary 1932 session with the New Orleans Feetwarmers—steamy, torrid music from the end of the New Orleans era.

Talk the Talk

Tailgate trombone is a style of trombone playing that uses the slide frequently and with gusto to draw attention to an instrument typically "trapped" between the trumpet and clarinet. The name is derived from the way early bands played crowded into advertising wagons with the slide trombonist standing out on the tailgate so that he'd have room to play his instrument.

Kid Ory

Ory (1886–1973) was a New Orleans trombonist who developed what came to be called the *tailgate* style. The name derived from the way early bands crowded onto advertising wagons with the slide trombonist out on the tailgate so that he'd have room to play his instrument. Playing tailgate trombone came to mean using the instrument the way it was frequently used in marching bands, as the ensemble's inner voice, behind the trumpet and clarinet. Ory called attention to this often unrewarding role by broad use of the slide.

The effect of Ory's tailgate style is both raucous and exciting, albeit quite dated. But tunes like "Ory's Creole Trombone," "Society Blues," and "Muskrat Ramble" are still marvels of early jazz.

Kid Ory is best heard not on the older historical recordings, but on two disks originally cut in the fifties and reissued on CD by Good Time Jazz: *Kid Ory's Creole Jazz Band* (1954)—which features warhorses like "That's a Plenty" and "When the Saints Go Marching In"—and *Legendary Kid* (1955). Both of these are uncomplicated examples of New Orleans jazz at its best.

Less of a pioneer of the instrument than Kid Ory, Jack Teagarden (1905–64) ultimately became even more famous and successful, straddling the worlds of Dixieland and (later in his career) swing. (Listen to The Indispensible Jack Teagarden, *a retrospective RCA CD.)*
Image from Lawrence Cohn.

Dodds: Baby and Johnny

Brothers Baby (Warren) and Johnny Dodds were New Orleans-born musicians who stood out as unadulterated examples of the New Orleans style. Baby (1898–1959) was a drummer who introduced equipment and techniques that became standards of jazz practice. Many young drummers learned from him, most notably the outstanding popular percussionist of the swing era, Gene Krupa. Indeed, Baby Dodds was a determined teacher, who took the extraordinary step of recording a series of extended drum solos with spoken explanatory commentary.

Baby Dodds may be heard on King Oliver's early recordings, including those reissued as *Okeh Sessions* (an EMI LP that has yet to be released as a CD) from 1923. What sets Dodds apart from other early drummers is his extreme precision and his ability to improvise at great length. These are qualities taken for granted in later jazz percussionists, but it was Dodds who set the standard.

Brother Johnny (1892–1940) played clarinet, and some authorities consider him not only the most significant clarinetist of the twenties, but the ideal exemplar of the early New Orleans style. His tone in the instrument's upper as well as lower registers is beautiful, and he proved a worthy foil in solos with Louis Armstrong in the Hot Five and Hot Seven sessions, which are very hot indeed.

The Classics label has released *Johnny Dodds: 1926*, which presents truly classic New Orleans sides.

Riffs

The only advertising they had would be to get the band on a wagon and put a couple of posters on the side. We would sit there and go from block to block or corner to corner, and play.

When some other outfit was also advertising and we met each other... the guys would put the wheels together and tie them.... That made us stay right there and [musically] *fight it out. The band that got outplayed could not run away.*

—Drummer Baby Dodds

Louis Armstrong

We will meet Louis Armstrong (1901–1971) as a mature player in the next chapter. A great trumpeter and vocalist, he was arguably the most influential musician in the history of jazz. Some would even insist that Armstrong was the single most important musician in jazz—period.

It is pointless to debate such superlatives, but it is undeniable that Louis "Satchmo" Armstrong introduced jazz to untold multitudes and that he compelled them to listen by virtue of the stunning brilliance of his solo work. By any measure, Armstrong was a great musician.

This much was apparent in his early work with King Oliver when the young cornetist quickly eclipsed the older musician. (*Louis Armstrong and King Oliver*, recordings from 1923–24, is available on CD from Milestone.) Armstrong's genius shines through even more powerfully in his recordings with the Hot Fives and Hot Sevens.

Check out the Columbia CD, *Hot Fives and Sevens*, vol. 3. Must-hear numbers on this CD include "Potato Head," "Struttin' with Some Barbecue,"

Dig This

Armstrong's nickname, "Satchmo," was itself short for another nickname, "Satchel Mouth."

and "Hotter Than That." These make it clear that Armstrong delivers everything a jazz genius can possibly deliver: Sweetly sustained notes alternating with machine-gun jabs; an ability to play in the highest register of the instrument, where other early cornetists wouldn't venture; a deliciously loose approach to rhythm, consistently coming in a little behind the beat, so as to increase the feeling of swing even in the slow passages; and a seemingly inexhaustible reservoir of invention.

Even after he left New Orleans, Armstrong never forgot his roots. This 1931 photograph shows him (in the stylish suit jacket and striped trousers, leaning on a bat) with Armstrong's Secret 9, a New Orleans baseball team he sponsored.
Image from Lawrence Cohn.

Armstrong's greatness is the more remarkable when we consider his background, raised fatherless in the most wretched and violent of New Orleans neighborhoods, clothed in rags, often forced to scavenge garbage for a meal. Early brushes with the law landed him in the Home for Colored Waifs, where he was first presented with a cornet. After two years in the orphan home/reform school, he emerged no longer a boy bent on crime, but a young man determined to become a musician.

In King Oliver, Louis Armstrong found the strong, strict, but caring father he had lacked. Scholars debate whether Oliver really influenced Armstrong musically—their styles were actually worlds apart, Oliver backward-looking, Armstrong ready to take jazz into the future—but the older man sponsored and watched out for the youthful cornetist, giving him the discipline required to go beyond mere genius and become a *professional* genius.

Riffs

No doubt Armstrong was a genius, but he was also a canny showman. When trumpeter Erskine Hawkins told Armstrong that hitting the high notes was easy for him and that he "didn't like to puff and act like it was hard for me," Armstrong replied:

Now, you made your point. Now, let them think it's a little hard for you to do it. ...You're making it look too easy.

Whatever it may have been musically, the relationship between King Oliver and Louis Armstrong is jazz at its best. Faced with hardship, pain, and adversity, Armstrong found a man willing to communicate the tradition of the music he loved. On this foundation, Armstrong not only built a life, but was able to create works of beauty and excitement that have dazzled and delighted untold millions.

Through such musicians as Buddy Bolden, Sidney Bechet, King Oliver, and Louis Armstrong, the multi-cultural popular music heard in New Orleans evolved into music the nation would embrace, as we begin to see in the next chapter.

The Least You Need to Know

- Early in the 20th century, New Orleans' freewheeling Storyville district, separating the white from black neighborhoods, became the hotbed in which jazz took root and grew.
- Buddy Bolden, a shadowy New Orleans musician, was legendary for his musical as well as sexual prowess and is often identified as the "father" of jazz. Many others also claimed credit for having "invented" the music—most notably Jelly Roll Morton.
- By the early 1920s, most of the great New Orleans jazz musicians migrated north, many settling in Chicago, which became the nation's jazz mecca during much of the 1920s. Kansas City and New York were other important jazz centers during this period.
- Young Louis Armstrong emerged from New Orleans as the most important and influential jazz musician of the 1920s.

Chapter 9

Toddlin' Town and Harlem Renaissance: Classic Jazz

In This Chapter

- New popularity after the Great War
- Humor: an important ingredient in jazz
- Jazz on record: the early years
- Armstrong moves up north
- Fletcher Henderson: genius arranger
- New ambitions for jazz: Whiteman and Gershwin

The jazz that migrated north from New Orleans evolved in its new environment in ways that matured the music. The exuberant, spontaneous, but typically down-and-dirty standards of the Crescent City parade bands no longer cut it in the speakeasies of the urban North. Nor did this unpolished approach appeal to the major record producers. Bands and individual performers either became professionals or they found themselves cast adrift. Even more important, performers like Louis Armstrong dramatically raised the bar on improvisation. The catch-as-catch-can collective improvisation of the New Orleans tradition gave way to improvisation born of individual genius. It was more varied, more daring, and a great deal more demanding.

Between about 1920 and 1930, jazz came to focus increasingly on individual players. The greatest thrill in hearing the music came with the solos. What would Satchmo do now? How would *he* play that line? This chapter takes jazz through the first phase of its maturity.

From Bawdy House to Speakeasy

The musical exodus from New Orleans was part of a much larger migration of African Americans from the rural South to the urban North. For many American blacks, service in World War I during 1917–18 was an eye-opening experience. True, the American military was segregated. But Europe wasn't, and black doughboys learned there was a world beyond the cotton field and the small town. True, African Americans were compelled to settle separately from whites up North, too, in neighborhoods that came to be called ghettoes, but the degree of cultural interchange between white and black was much greater than it had been in the South. Greater, too, were economic prospects—not only for musicians, but for their audiences as well. In ghettoes like Chicago's South Side and New York's Harlem, African-American musicians played for black as well as white audiences.

The North offered a market for jazz. Whereas many of the early New Orleans musicians had been sideshow attractions amid the sex and sin of Storyville and the Quarter, in cities like Chicago and New York they became the principal attractions. To be sure, this transformation took place in clubs that existed for the purpose of dispensing illegal booze, but plenty of people came for the drink and stayed for the music.

Transplanted: New Orleans Rhythm Kings

In the last chapter, we saw how King Oliver took the Windy City by storm and gave the next generation of jazz greats their start in the city. From our historical perspective, this seems a profound step, and when we listen to early Armstrong, for example, we can't help but marvel at the power of emerging genius.

True enough. But we'd better lighten up. Oliver, Armstrong, and the other musicians of this period thought of themselves less as artists than as entertainers. Whatever else jazz was and would become, most of its early Chicago audience regarded it as feel-good music for high times and raucous crowds. The 1920s may have produced a generation of profound American writers (including Hemingway, Faulkner, and Fitzgerald), it may have seen the further development of the work of Einstein and Freud, it may have spawned some of Igor Stravinsky's most important compositions—but it also was the era of flagpole-sitting and fraternity brothers proving who could swallow the most live goldfish.

Some of the most popular bands of early Chicago jazz were comic. Today, we tend to take our jazz seriously, even to the point of pretension. Back in the '20s, most jazz performance included a liberal helping of laughs, because the public craved novelty. It would be a pity if we forgot some of the better novelty bands; for jazz, which so many think of as intense and brooding, is one of the few musical styles that readily lends itself to laughs. Remember, jazz is a music born of everyday life, and sometimes life is funny.

Some say jazz was born in a bawdy house. That's not quite true. But it's a fact that jazz grew up in a speakeasy. The prohibition poster is from 1926, and the sketch of high times in a speakeasy from a 1929 book titled New York Is Like This.
Images from arttoday.com.

Certainly, this was the attitude of the New Orleans Rhythm Kings, whose fans called them NORK. Like the Original Dixieland Jass Band, the (usually) eight members of the band were white, but no one could accuse them of dumbing down New Orleans jazz the way ODJB did. This was because the band's principal players included three outstanding soloists, bandleader Paul Mares on trumpet, Leon Rappolo on clarinet, and George Brunies on trombone.

All three had distinctive instrumental voices, and Rappolo (whose career was cut short by mental breakdown and confinement to an asylum) and Brunies were truly brilliant soloists. As if this weren't enough, the band was funny. Brunies (1902–74), whose Dixieland career extended into the early 1970s, played with a big, vibrant tone and went for extra laughs by working his trombone slide with his foot.

Most memorable today are the sides NORK cut with Jelly Roll Morton in 1923, including "Farewell Blues," "That's a Plenty," and "Tin Roof Blues," all destined to become enduring jazz standards.

Dig This

George Brunies had a passion for numerology. Told by one numerologist he consulted that his name added up to an unlucky number of letters, Brunies dropped an "e" from his first and last names, becoming Georg Brunis.

Bow Wow Blues and Skeleton Jangle

Brunies was hardly alone as an early virtuoso jazz comedian. Songs with titles like "Bow Wow Blues" and "Skeleton Jangle" abounded during the '20s, as did performers like bandleader and clarinetist Ted Lewis (1892–1971), who delighted audiences with his "laughing clarinet" and "crying trombone" effects.

Recordings of Lewis are hard to come by these days, but another early master with a comic touch, Chicago-born cornetist Muggsy Spanier (1906–67), a Ted Lewis alumnus, is still well represented. Bluebird's *The Ragtime Band Sessions* presents definitive 1939 recordings of sixteen Dixieland standards (plus eight more) that are hard to resist and impossible not to smile at. What keeps the performances of such classics as "Dinah" and "Big Butter and Egg Man" from coming off as simply corny is the panache and virtuoso skill of Spanier (cornet), Brunies (trombone), and Joe Bushkin (piano). It's perfectly all right to say that this music is good for a laugh, as long as you underscore the word *good*.

Dig This

New Orleans Rhythm Kings and Jelly Roll Morton, recordings from 1922–23, is available on a Milestone CD.

Jazz Recording Capital of the World: Richmond, Indiana

Not everyone, even in the major cities, could afford to go regularly to clubs to hear jazz, and not all fans of the music were inclined to go. Jazz made it onto records very early in its history, and perhaps the most aggressive and important of the early labels was not a major firm out of New York, but a small company owned by Starr Piano of Richmond, Indiana and named after Starr's three most important managers, brothers Harry, Fred, and Clarence Gennett.

*A Gennett record label from 1929. Barely visible to the right, below the company's name is the classification of this selection (*Mandy *as performed by Zack Whyte's Chocolate Beau Brummels: "Race Record—Dance."*
Image from the author's collection.

Take Five

Gennett Record Company was owned by the Starr Piano Company of Richmond, Indiana, and issued its first release in 1917. By 1919, the company was recording New Orleans-style jazz, and in 1923, it began to produce "race records"—recordings by African-American artists intended primarily for black audiences.

Gennett recorded a great deal of early jazz, ranging from King Oliver and Jelly Roll Morton to the Gene Goldkette Orchestra—which numbered the great Bix Beiderbecke among its members.

The Gennett label was discontinued in 1930, though it continued to issue jazz recordings on the subsidiary Champion and Superior labels. In 1934, many of Gennett's copyrights were sold to Decca.

The importance of Gennett was not just its willingness to record and issue jazz, but to record African-American performers at a time when major recording companies would think of doing no such thing. Gennett's first issues came as early as 1917, and by 1919 the company was recording such groups as the New Orleans Jazz Band. Gennett dipped a toe into what was then called the "race market" by recording African-American New Orleans jazz using white performers. One group, recorded in 1921, was the Original

Memphis Five, white musicians who performed for the label under the pseudonym Ladds Black Aces. However, beginning in 1923, Gennett started recording many African-American musicians, including King Oliver and Jelly Roll Morton and many other African Americans as well as white jazz artists through about 1930. By this time, all of the major record labels were recording and selling jazz, and the music was being sold throughout the country.

Dig This

Beginning in 1924, Gennett printed the labels of recordings by black artists with the legend "race record."

Jazz in the Apple

While the midwestern heartland served as the cradle of the jazz recording industry in the 1920s, the music continued to evolve most dramatically in Chicago and New York, which vied with one another during the '20s for status as the nation's jazz capital. By the end of the decade, the balance had clearly shifted to New York.

Riffs

[H]e said to Louis, "Boy, let me have your trumpet." So Louis looked at me and I bowed my head, so Louis gave him the trumpet. So, Freddie, he blew—oh, he blew and blew and then the people gave him a nice hand. Then he handed the trumpet back to Louis. And I said, "Now, get him, get him!" Oooh, never in my life have I heard such trumpet playing! If you want to hear Louis play, just hear him play when he's angry. Boy, he blew and people started standing up on top of tables and chairs screaming, and Freddie eased out real slowly.

—Armstrong's wife, Lil Hardin, on trumpet rival Freddie Keppard coming to hear Armstrong

Satchmo: Hot Fives and Sevens

King Oliver had brought Louis Armstrong to Chicago in 1922, and in 1924, Armstrong married his second wife, Lil Hardin, the Oliver band's pianist. She persuaded Armstrong to break with his mentor and join Fletcher Henderson in New York. Mrs. Armstrong recognized that King Oliver and Chicago represented the past, while the brilliant Henderson and New York City were the future of jazz.

A year with Henderson—whom we shall discuss in a moment—not only exposed Armstrong to modern sounds better suited to his genius for improvisation, it made him famous with the public and fellow musicians alike. *Fletcher Henderson and Louis Armstrong* is a valuable CD on the Timeless label, which features many Armstrong solos from 1924–25. You hear Armstrong's rapid evolution as a modern artist, veering away from four-square New Orleans-style melody and into pure jazz invention. Moreover, his exciting approach to rhythm unfolds on this CD: We hear Armstrong literally play with time, coming in fractionally before or after the beat in a manner that virtually defined *swing* for the next generation of musicians.

But Armstrong's important time with Henderson was only a prelude to his recordings with two groups, the Hot Five and the Hot Seven. He returned to Chicago late in 1925 and, through 1928, cut more than 60 "sides" (tunes that fit on one side of a 78-rpm record) that changed jazz forever.

The original Hot Fives were Armstrong on cornet, Kid Ory on trombone, Johnny Dodds on clarinet, Johnny St. Cyr on banjo, and Lil Hardin Armstrong on piano; in 1927, Pete Briggs on tuba and Baby Dodds on drums joined to make the group the Hot Seven. Musicologists and jazz historians have stumbled all over one another analyzing the Hot Fives and Sevens recordings. It is enough to say here that, with such cuts as "Struttin' with Some Barbecue," "Hotter Than That," and especially "West End Blues," Armstrong suddenly revealed the full range of possibilities for the jazz soloist. After the Hot Fives and Sevens, jazz was no longer an ensemble-oriented, folk-derived music, but was now and forever after a popular art form defined by virtuoso solists.

Take Five

The complete Hot Fives and Sevens have been reissued on three Columbia CDs. *Hot Fives,* volume 1, spans 1925–26, *Hot Fives and Sevens,* volume 2, encompasses 1926–27, and *Hot Fives and Sevens,* volume 3, 1927–28. If you can afford only one of these, make it volume 3, which includes perhaps the three most exciting performances ever recorded by a jazz artist: "Struttin' with Some Barbecue," "Hotter Than That," and "West End Blues." To invest in all three volumes, however, is to purchase the jazz equivalent of holy scripture. Jazz is about individual taste, whim, and desire. Don't let anyone tell you what to like and what not to. These recordings may or may not turn out to be among your favorites (they *probably* will!), but it is beyond dispute that this music is among the most important in the history of jazz.

The Genius of Fletcher Henderson

Folks who are really into jazz know Fletcher Henderson (1898–1952) as a brilliant jazz *arranger,* who was the first orchestrator to use written scores that did not impede improvisation. This was important because it made it possible for jazz to become a sophisticated orchestral music while still retaining its spirit of free invention. It made the era of the big band possible. Henderson did for jazz what Franz Joseph Haydn did for classical music when he invented the symphony. He extended the music's expressive range.

Talk the Talk

An **arranger** does not compose music but orchestrates an existing composition to make the most expressive use of a particular ensemble.

But if Henderson is known to aficionados, he does not have the general name recognition of an Armstrong, Ellington, or Basie. This was because he lacked the personality—not the genius!—of a great bandleader. He was not a self-promoter, he was a poor businessman, and he often lost control of chronically unruly band members. Indeed, unlike the other early jazz greats we have discussed, he did not start out as a professional musician at all. Despite his musical talent, he decided to take a degree in chemistry and mathematics at the all-black Atlanta University. After graduation in 1920, he came to New York City for graduate work, but by 1923, his musical side got the better of him, and he found himself working as a bandleader.

Whatever his shortcomings as a leader, he not only was a brilliant arranger but also had an unerring ear for major talent. Between 1923 and 1939 when he left bandleading for a time to write some of the most important arrangements in jazz history for Benny Goodman, Henderson hired (and ultimately lost) the likes of Coleman Hawkins, Lester Young, Ben Webster, Chu Berry, and Benny Carter—collectively the greatest saxophonists of their day—and Louis Armstrong, Roy Eldridge, Henry "Red" Allen, Rex Stewart, Tommy Ladnier, Dickie Wells, J.C. Higginbotham, Joe Smith, Benny Morton, and Jimmy Harrison, the greatest brass players.

He attracted the best because they all recognized that his sophisticated arrangements were the future of jazz. He provided the framework within which individual genius could blossom into great music. Audition for yourself the curiously titled *A Study in Frustration/Thesaurus of Classic Jazz,* a three-CD Columbia set featuring Henderson from 1923 to 1938. You'll hear the top performers who put in time with Henderson, and you'll hear Henderson create the big band sound of the 1930s.

Gershwin and Whiteman: Making a Lady Out of Jazz

Fletcher Henderson was not the only New York figure of the 1920s who had what may be called symphonic ambitions for jazz. Paul "Pops" Whiteman, whom we met in Chapter 2, was a classically trained white musician (he had been a violist with two major symphony orchestras) who had a taste for popular music. He recognized the appeal of jazz, but he felt that, until the music shed its identification with the seamier side of life—bordellos and speakeasies—it would never reach its broadest possible audience. Whiteman wanted, as he often said, "to make a lady out of jazz." To this end, in 1924, he commissioned George Gershwin to write a concerto-like work for piano and orchestra, which would capture the feeling of jazz, yet in the context of a more formal, classical-music setting.

Take Five

Whiteman was frequently billed as the "King of Jazz," a title that continues to outrage jazz buffs who would agree with jazz scholar Wilder Hobson that "Whiteman drew very little from the jazz language except some of the simpler rhythmic patterns.... There was little more than a trace of the personal expression, improvisation, counterpoint, or rhythmic subtlety of natural jazz." Nevertheless, the Whiteman orchestra attracted very significant jazz talent, including (at various times) legendary trumpeter Bix Beiderbecke, saxophonist Frankie "Tram" Trumbauer, vibraharpist Red Norvo, saxophonist Jimmy and trombonist Tommy Dorsey, guitarist Eddie Lang, and jazz violinist Joe Venuti.

Famed as a songwriter, Gershwin (1898–1937) was not a jazz composer but did inject his tunes with an unmistakable jazz feel. He responded to Whiteman's commission with *Rhapsody in Blue*, which became one of his most popular works. Gershwin originally scored it for two pianos, and it was Whiteman's arranger, Ferde Grofé (best known today as the composer of the *Grand Canyon Suite*) who orchestrated it first for piano and large jazz band, then for piano and symphony orchestra.

Rhapsody in Blue is not jazz (it really is closer to a classical piano concerto), but like all of Gershwin's extraordinarily beautiful works, it owes a lot to harmonies and rhythmic devices introduced by jazz. The same is true of the composer's most ambitious work, the "folk opera" (as he called it) *Porgy and Bess* (1935). Like *Rhapsody in Blue*, it demonstrates how key elements of jazz can be used to write what is essentially classical (or "light classical") music. This is important because, for many listeners and critics of the '20s and '30s inclined to dismiss jazz as popular trash or downright disreputable music, Gershwin's works gave the music legitimacy.

Dig This

Wander into any record store, and you will have no trouble finding an array of recordings of *Rhapsody in Blue*. Everyone has their favorite. Mine features Leonard Bernstein conducting the New York Philharmonic from the piano on *George Gershwin: Rhapsody in Blue and An American in Paris* (CBS Great Performances). Thanks to piano rolls, you can hear Gershwin play the music himself on *George Gershwin Plays Rhapsody in Blue* (Pro Arte).

George Gershwin
Image from arttoday.com.

Dig This

A great modern recording of *Porgy and Bess* features the Houston Grand Opera and is available on RCA Red Seal. The recent performance conducted by Simon Rattle, on EMI, is also a standout.

Indeed, at the height of his fame, Gershwin traveled to Paris and sought out the great French classical master Maurice Ravel (1875–1937). When Gershwin asked to study with him, Ravel replied that he could teach him nothing and asked, in turn, if Gershwin could teach *him* about jazz! Listen to such Ravel masterpieces as the *Piano Concerto in G*, and you will hear Gershwin's unmistakable influence. As we'll see in Chapter 16, beginning in the 1920s, a number of classical composers, including Darius Milhaud and Igor Stravinsky in addition to Ravel, drew upon the jazz idiom in creating their works. Gershwin, tragically, would not be among them. He succumbed to a brain tumor shortly before his 39th birthday.

Borrowed Clothes

Today, many jazz snobs look down their noses at these efforts to "elevate" jazz to the status of high culture. It's not real jazz, they say, and efforts to dress the music in borrowed clothes are all misguided.

It's true that neither *Rhapsody in Blue* nor *Porgy and Bess* nor, for that matter, Ravel's *Piano Concerto in G* is jazz. So what? These are good pieces of music that wouldn't have come into existence *without* the influence of jazz. And jazz suffered no affront as a result of the efforts of Whiteman, Gershwin, and others. It is a measure of the essential strength of jazz that it was enriched by whatever other musical styles it came into contact with, even as it, in turn, enriched those styles.

The Least You Need to Know

- Humor, an element too often overlooked by jazz fans, was especially important in popularizing early jazz.
- Louis Armstrong revolutionized jazz with his Hot Five and Hot Seven recordings, launching a new era of solo improvisation.
- Fletcher Henderson made the arranger a supremely important figure in jazz, laying the foundation for the big bands of the 1930s.
- Popular bandleader Paul Whiteman wanted to "make a lady out of jazz" and commissioned George Gershwin to write *Rhapsody in Blue,* beginning a rich, if controversial, relationship between jazz and classical music.

Chapter 10

Limelight and Legends: The Soloist Takes Center Stage

In This Chapter

- Armstrong's Hot Fives and Sevens
- Bix Beiderbecke: tragic genius of jazz
- Harlem: black jazz, white audiences
- Fats Waller: taking humor in stride
- Art Tatum: taking stride to new heights

If jazz was being "legitimated" during the 1920s as an ensemble music, like a classical symphony or concerto, it was far more importantly emerging as a soloist's medium, a showcase for bold, dazzling, and innovative genius. Louis Armstrong is universally recognized as the first great jazz soloist—not just by the public, but by other musicians as well. Fellow trumpet players frequently demanded to see Armstrong's horn, thinking he had somehow rigged it to play higher notes than any of them could. But Armstrong didn't just blow away the competition. He encouraged it. A small, elite army of great jazz soloists followed in Satchmo's footsteps. This chapter looks at the first wave of important solo stars.

Dig This

While frankly less important to the history of jazz than the music of the Hot Fives and Sevens, Armstrong's later work is still outstanding and highly enjoyable. A good sampling is on this two-CD set from RCA: *From the Big Band to the All Stars (1946–56).*

More Armstrong

With the Hot Fives and Sevens, Armstrong had inaugurated the era of the soloist. He not only used his trumpet brilliantly, but also developed the vocal style for which he quickly became famous. In 1929, after the Hot Fives and Sevens, Armstrong's style became simpler, less dense, more spare. Musically, this is often less interesting, but audiences loved it. By the mid-1930s, Armstrong was clearly identifying himself more as a popular entertainer than as a cutting-edge jazz musician, and this evolution (some hardcore jazz fans would call it a *devolution*) continued through the end of his career.

Louis Armstrong later in his career, broadcasting over Radio Liberation, *a U.S. government-sponsored service beamed at the Soviet Union during the early 1950s.*
Image from Lawrence Cohn.

Young Man with a Horn: The Beiderbecke Phenomenon

Louis Armstrong was a poor black kid who overcame the desolation of his childhood to achieve recognition as one of the greatest figures of jazz, earning enduring fame and considerable fortune. Leon "Bix" Beiderbecke was a middle-class white kid, born in 1903 and raised in Davenport, Iowa, who went on to achieve legendary status as a lyrical cornet player and as *the* archetypal jazz musician: possessed by his genius as if by a demon, driven to music as well as to drink, dissipation, despair, and an early death.

Bix was an unruly, rebellious child whose frustrated parents sent him in 1921 to Lake Forest Academy, a military school in north suburban Chicago. Bix often cut class and took the commuter train into the city to hear the hot jazz of King Oliver, Jimmy Noone, and others. Ultimately expelled, he joined the Chicago-based Wolverines as cornetist in 1923. He recorded with them the following year, but it was clear that his talents far outstripped the rest of this student group, and, in 1924, he joined the Jean Goldkette Orchestra, a professionally competent if blandly commercial group.

Dig This

Beiderbecke's greatness is commemorated annually in Davenport, Iowa's Bix Beiderbecke Jazz Festival. Attend, and you can purchase a "Bix Lives!" T-shirt.

Beiderbecke was an undisciplined prodigy who had never bothered to learn to read music. This soon cost him his job with Goldkette, but under the tutelage of saxophonist Frankie "Tram" Trumbauer (who became his best friend), Beiderbecke learned how to read. He played with Trumbauer's orchestra, then returned to Goldkette, and, finally, joined the Paul Whiteman Orchestra.

Those who heard Beiderbecke play were overwhelmed by the sheer beauty of his tone—there has never been anything like it again in jazz—and with the striking originality of his improvisational style. Unfortunately, in his recorded work with the larger ensembles, these qualities are only fleetingly apparent, since the Goldkette and Whiteman orchestras were essentially pop rather than jazz organizations. A fuller impression of his extraordinary skills comes through in his performances with small ensembles, especially when paired with Trumbauer, as on *Bix Beiderbecke, Volume 1: Singin' the Blues*, recordings from 1927 reissued on a Columbia CD. (The second volume, *At the Jazz Band Ball*, is also well worth acquiring.)

Riffs

[Bix lived] in the apartment of a bass player named George Kraslow, out in Sunnyside, Queens. Kraslow recalls that many times through that period Bix would pick up his cornet, no matter what time it was, and play.... The tenants in the building would mention to Kraslow that they had been awakened at two or three in the morning by the lovely music.... They would also make a point to add, "Please don't mention we said any-thing as we don't want him reprimanded and would hate for him to stop."

—Jazz writer George Hoefer (1909–67) on Beiderbecke's last weeks

Tragically, the music is only part of the Beiderbecke legend. A self-destructive alcoholic, he drank himself out of his career and, ultimately, out of his life, dying in 1930 at 28. As with many musicians and artists cut off in—or before—their prime, a cult developed around Beiderbecke's memory, and he even became the subject of a best-selling 1938 novel, *Young Man with a Horn*, by Dorothy Baker. Musically he influenced the likes of trumpeters Jimmy McPartland, Bobby Hackett, and a host of others.

Up in Harlem

To think of Harlem today is mainly to think of a troubled New York neighborhood, but in the 1920s, it was filled with at least as much hope as despair. While oppression was still a fact of African-American life during the 1920s, white intellectuals became intensely interested in the literature, art, and music of blacks. African-American artists and writers were drawn to Harlem in a cultural and creative movement that came to be called the Harlem Renaissance. Black political leader W.E.B. Du Bois (1868–1963) edited *The Crisis*, the magazine of the National Association for the Advancement of Colored People, and poet Countee Cullen (1903–46), novelist Rudolph Fisher (1897–1934), poet-essayist Langston Hughes (1902–67), folklorist Zora Neale Hurston (1901–60), poet James Weldon Johnson (1871–1938), and novelist Jean Toomer (1894–1967) wrote works that drew the attention of the world.

The revitalized Harlem became a popular spot not just for curious white intellectuals, but for white nightclubbers seeking first-class jazz from the likes of Fletcher Henderson, Louis Armstrong, and others.

Among the many great black jazz musicians who played the Harlem clubs—mainly to white audiences—Duke Ellington and Count Basie stand out most immediately, but because their greatest fame came during the swing era, we'll discuss them in the next chapter. Two major—and very different—artists achieved their first enduring fame during the Harlem Renaissance: pianists Fats Waller and Art Tatum.

Virtuoso and buffoon: Thomas "Fats" Waller strikes a characteristic pose in a 1940s performance. Image from the Frank Driggs Collection.

Fats Waller: Virtuoso and Buffoon

Thomas Wright Waller (1904–1943) acquired his nickname "Fats" because of his impressive girth and ebullient public persona. He was one of the jazz comedians of the 1920s, but that comic facade belied a core of great virtuosity as a pianist and true genius as a composer.

He rebelled against his father, a Harlem clergyman, by becoming a professional pianist at age 15, working clubs and theaters. Early in the '20s, he met James P. Johnson (1894–1955), the great pianist and composer who is often called the father of *stride*, which transformed and reinvigorated the moribund ragtime piano tradition. Stride pitted a so-called "walking bass" pattern played by the left hand against syncopated melody in the right. Tempos were breakneck, and wide octave leaps the norm. It was a style at once athletic and dazzling.

Dig This

James P. Johnson's brand of stride is best heard on *Harlem Stride Piano,* music spanning 1921–29 and reissued as a CD on the Hot 'N Sweet label.

Inspired by Johnson, Waller became a great stride pianist, and some of his most popular performance pieces were tunes he had composed, which became instant standards: "Ain't Misbehavin'," "Honeysuckle Rose," "Squeeze Me," and others. His broad humor and willingness to play the buffoon won him the widest possible audience and even landed him roles in such films as *Stormy Weather* (1943), but his recorded legacy marks him as one of the most accomplished of jazz pianists. Pick up *Piano Masterworks*, volume 1, a CD from EPM offering solo piano performances from 1922 to 1929, and get set to be blown away by a master. Nor should you neglect Waller's work with his bands. *Fats Waller and His Buddies*, recordings from 1927–29, is available on a Bluebird CD. A special treat on this album is Waller playing the organ (he was the first jazz musician to do so) while his mentor Johnson plays piano.

Talk the Talk

Stride is a style of jazz piano playing in which the left hand athletically "strides" the keys in aggressive accompaniment to the right hand's melodic line. The style was a bridge between ragtime and mature jazz.

Riffs

Pop kept two bottles of gin on a table during rehearsals. One bottle was for himself or anyone who happened to be visiting. The other bottle was the "encourager," as he called it. When one of the band excelled in an improvisational section, Dad would stop the rehearsal, pour him a healthy shot of gin, and the two of them would toast each other. If you wanted to drink at rehearsal, you had to shine.

—Son Maurice Waller recalls how Waller encouraged improvisation in his band members

Strivers and Striders: The Piano of Art Tatum

For all its power and dazzle, the stride piano style strikes most modern ears as a bit dated. The demands of keeping up that incessant, insistent "walking bass" ultimately limit the expressive range of the music.

Except in one case.

Art Tatum (1910–56), all but totally blind from an early age, took up the violin as a child, but, by 13, had switched to piano. A prodigy, he performed on local Toledo radio, and, after listening to recordings by Fats Waller, began teaching himself stride piano. By the time he was 21, he had developed a style that can only be described as pyrotechnic. To hear a Tatum solo is to shake your head in disbelief that a *single* pianist could play so many notes so fast so well. Built on a stride foundation, it takes the style to a level that defies any description other than perhaps the vague term "modern piano."

Art Tatum at New York's Café Society, about 1941. Image from the Frank Driggs Collection.

He moved at this time to New York and embarked on a brilliant recording and performing career, specializing in solo as well as trio work—with guitarist Tiny Grimes and bassist Slam Stewart.

What sets Tatum apart from more traditional and readily classifiable stride pianists, no matter how brilliant, is not his prodigious technique alone. He introduced to the stride idiom an unheard-of range of improvisation. The rhythmic drive and regularity of stride tended to cramp improvisation, but Tatum took to inserting entirely new chord progressions into the fleeting space of a measure or two; that is, he would take the music in an entirely new direction by playing a new chord on each rapid-fire beat, then return to his original course.

Dig This

Don't neglect another, more traditional, strider, Willie "The Lion" Smith (1897–1973), usually considered the third member in the stride trinity that included James P. Johnson and Fats Waller. *Pork and Beans* on Black Lion features solos from 1966.

To have heard Tatum in live performance must have been extraordinarily exciting, but his speed-of-light style was such that, if your attention lapsed for more than a second or two, you missed a lot of the music. For this reason, hearing Tatum on CD provides the great advantage of being able to play a piece over and over. Each repetition is a revelation. *Piano Starts Here*, recordings from 1933 and 1949 rereleased on CD by Columbia/Legacy, is a dazzling starting place. The danger in purchasing this CD is that it will compel you to spend your hard-earned cash on the many, many other Tatum recordings available—a good number of them multi-CD boxed sets.

Riffs

I wish I could play like Tatum's right hand.

—Charlie Parker

Fats [Waller] was playin' pool and Fletcher [Henderson] and them was playin' cards. All of a sudden, boom, we all dropped out and let Art go. Boy, you could hear a rat piss on cotton! That sumbitch tore that Rhythm Club up! I laugh at these cats that say, "Well, I finally got a decent piano." He played any of those pianos: He'd play it if it only had four keys on it!

—Trumpet genius Roy Eldridge recalling the first time Tatum played at New York's Rhythm Club, a musicians' hangout

Well, there are a lot worse ways to blow your bankroll. For Art Tatum, whose music is endlessly fascinating in itself (and something that's fun to dazzle your non-jazz friends with!) is also a link joining classic jazz rooted in the New Orleans heritage with the music that would develop not only during the swing era (Chapter 11), but that would evolve into the stratospheric sounds of bebop (Chapter 13).

The Least You Need to Know

- Armstrong's Hot Five and Hot Seven recordings are considered not only his breakthrough works, but monuments of improvisational genius.
- Bix Beiderbecke is one of the early tragic archetypes of jazz, a genius who knew how to bring a wistful, lyrical, melodic beauty to jazz, but who didn't know how to survive the trap of drink and drugs.
- By the late 1920s, jazz became a lively medium in which "mainstream" white culture met black creativity.
- Fats Waller and Art Tatum were two great early soloists in the stride style; Tatum may well have been the most influential pianist in jazz history.

Chapter 11

...If It Ain't Got That Swing: The First Big Bands

In This Chapter

- The big band: what it is and how it came to be
- Big band prototype: the Fletcher Henderson group
- Coleman Hawkins shows how saxophone is done
- Creating the sound of the swing era
- Ellington's eloquence

By the end of the 1920s, jazz was developing in two complementary directions. It was becoming a music of individual stars, who took listeners on daring flights of solo improvisation and who possessed stylistic signatures the public instantly recognized. At the same time, jazz was also becoming a genuinely orchestral medium. The early New Orleans bands had been collaborative efforts—collections of musicians who happened to play together. This gave the music a large helping of spontaneous energy, but it was also limiting. The collaborative approach meant that the music had to be structurally simple and essentially tune-oriented.

In contrast, by the end of the 1920s, written arrangements were increasingly common. The collaborative model had given way to the symphonic: A single mind and imagination—the arranger's—conceived of how the instruments should sound together. With a fully thought-out arrangement, pieces could be longer, more varied, and more complex. And if playing arranged music eliminated collaborative improvisation, it still provided plenty of room for individual improvisation. Thus the big bands became sound machines that were also showcases for star solo talent.

And nothing—but nothing—could *swing* like a big band. As the lyrics to one Duke Ellington hit declare, "It don't mean a thing if it ain't got that swing."

Big Band Background

The big band—an ensemble of at least 10 instruments and typically 15 or more—didn't materialize out of thin air. It had a background.

Europe and Castles

In Chapter 7, we briefly met James Reese Europe, who introduced the nation and the world to an early version of orchestral jazz just before and after World War I. The sensation Europe made with what one contemporary critic called a "gorgeous racket of syncopation and jazzing" inspired the formation of other jazz bands after the orchestra leader's untimely death in 1919, the result of a knife wound sustained in barroom brawl.

Between 1914 and 1917, Europe had led the Society Orchestra, best known for accompanying the enormously popular ballroom dance team of Irene and Vernon Castle. Backed by Europe's music, which combined traditional dance tunes with ragtime and even elements of African-American folk tradition, the Castles developed an elegant dance style that was also distinctly jazzy. The jazz-inspired dance created a greater demand for jazz orchestral music, even as this music produced more jazz-oriented popular dances.

Tin Pan Alley, Broadway, and Ballroom

By the 1920s, the feeling of jazz had penetrated *Tin Pan Alley*, as the New York-centered popular music industry was dubbed. Songsmiths turned out a string of tunes that begged to be backed by ensembles capable of playing jazz. Broadway composers like Jerome Kern and George Gershwin were creating musicals that embodied elements of jazz, further popularizing the music by taking it out of the speakeasies and putting it on stage.

Finally, the 1920s was a decade, in part, defined by popular dance crazes. The most famous of these was the Charleston, but just about all the dances people did called for a hot orchestra, a band that could swing.

Talk the Talk

Tin Pan Alley refers to the popular music industry during the early 20th century. Tin Pan Alley was a New York City neighborhood on Seventh Avenue between 48th and 52nd streets, which housed most of the major publishers. The phrase is derived from 19th-century musician's slang for a cheap, tinny piano.

Club Alabam and the Henderson Line-Up

In January 1924, Fletcher Henderson began leading a dance band at the Club Alabam on Broadway. Later in the year, he and his group played the Roseland Ballroom, New York's premier dance hall. For the next 10 years, Roseland served as the platform from which Henderson and his band rose to national fame.

In the very beginning, there was nothing particularly special about the Henderson organization. There were probably thousands of similar groups coming together across the nation at the time. Moreover, Henderson had come to jazz late and was neither a brilliant pianist nor a forceful bandleader. But he had two undeniable gifts. He could identify major talent, and he could write great arrangements.

His importing Louis Armstrong to the Roseland band in 1924–25 not only put his group on the musical map, it transformed the big band concept. Armstrong impressed not only audiences, but fellow band members as well, who emulated Satchmo's solo style, even after Armstrong left the band in 1925.

We had a glimpse of Henderson's line-up in the preceding chapter: giants including most of the era's great reed and brass players, among other high-caliber musicians. Put that talent together with Henderson's ability to write terrific arrangements showcasing the massed forces of the band as well as the talents of individual stars, and you had the prototype of the big band.

Riffs

The Fletcher Henderson and Chick Webb bands were frequently booked opposite each other in a "battle of bands." Fletcher's problem was that his brother Horace would copy his arrangements and sell them to Chick. Fletcher, preparing to amaze Chick with something he hadn't heard, would find that Chick had gone on ahead of him and was playing it first.

—Trumpeter and singer Harman Autrey

Enter Hawkins, with Axe

Coleman Hawkins (1904–69) started piano lessons in his native St. Joseph, Missouri, when he was five, switched to cello at seven, then took up the tenor saxophone at nine. It was not a promising instrument for a child of Hawkins's manifest ability and was regarded as a novelty item at best, something a band might use if a trombone wasn't available. In Hawkins's hands, however, the tenor saxophone became one of the great instruments of jazz.

Hawkins began his career playing in a Kansas City theater orchestra, then, in 1921, he joined the Jazz Hounds, the band that backed blues great Mamie Smith. In 1923, he began his association with Fletcher Henderson. To say that Hawkins was the number one tenorman in jazz at this time is no great compliment. The pickin's were slim. Doubtless, though, he was a fine player. What elevated Hawkins to a greatness that lasted some 40 years was the example of Armstrong. Working with Satch in the Henderson band, Hawkins abandoned the

Talk the Talk

To a jazz musician, an **axe** (or *ax*) is any instrument, but especially a saxophone.

Talk the Talk

To play **staccato** is to sharply attack and articulate each note, separating one from the next. To play **legato** is to connect the notes, moving seamlessly from one to another.

sharp, staccato style he had favored (a style that sounds very dated today) for the more musically enduring legato style Armstrong demonstrated on cornet.

Hawkins played with the Henderson organization until 1934, then moved to Europe, returning to the States only on the eve of World War II. You can hear the sound with which Hawkins helped define the swing era on *The Great Swing Saxophones*, a Bluebird CD featuring performances from 1929 to 1946. Hawk's European period is well represented by the three-CD *In Europe 1934/39* set from Jazz Up, and his later work back in the States, during the height of the swing era, may be heard on *Body and Soul* from Bluebird.

Take Five

In a profession where all too many died young, Hawkins enjoyed a long career and took much ribbing on account of it. Late in the 1950s, someone pointed out that he used to play with Mamie Smith. "That was somebody else using my name," Hawk replied.

"I can remember you, a grown man, playing with Fletcher Henderson when I was still a child," a swing-era musician remarked. Hawk replied: "I don't think that I ever was a child."

Prelude to a Duke

Hawkins's rich, warm, throaty tenor was the perfect sound for the emerging swing era, which combined swinging, up-tempo arrangements with an often unabashedly sentimental streak. At its best—and Hawkins is among the very best—the swing sound is both exciting and just plain gorgeous.

Don Redman: A Neat Arrangement

But it wasn't the soloists alone who defined the big band swing sound. It was the way instruments were used together. It was orchestration. Henderson made the first big leaps in swing orchestration, and his music director, Don Redman (1900–1964), took the sound even further. Redman was a child prodigy from a musical family who graduated from Storer College, in Harpers Ferry, West Virginia, with a degree in music. He joined the Henderson orchestra in 1923, playing clarinet, alto saxophone, and writing some of the band's arrangements. Like Hawkins, he was profoundly influenced by Louis Armstrong. He turned from a focus on ballroom dance music to jazz, creating works of increasing harmonic and rhythmic sophistication and setting the standard against which many other arrangers would be measured.

Redman's influence was felt first in the Henderson band, but he went on to arrange for many of the big bands, including those of Count Basie and Jimmy Dorsey, so the Redman sound greatly defined the era.

What was this sound? Most important was the ongoing dialogue between brass and reeds, sometimes in question-and-answer or call-and-response fashion, and sometimes one on top of the other, with reeds playing riffs under the brass or the brass riffing under the reeds. The treatment of reeds and brass as distinct choirs gave the big band its forceful yet mellow appeal.

While the sophistication of Redman's arrangements demanded precise ensemble playing, he also wrote in a way that provided many opportunities for extended improvised solo passages.

The First Benny—Carter

No discussion of the creation of the swing era would be complete without a look at Benny Carter. Born in New York in 1907, Carter is still active today as a major jazz performer and composer! As an instrumentalist, he was primarily an alto saxophonist, but he also mastered the trumpet, clarinet, piano, and even turned in a vocal or two. Like Redman, however, his greatest genius lay in arranging and, beyond this, in composition. Whereas Redman and other swing-era arrangers emphasized the music's "hot" aspects, Carter explored the lyrical qualities of jazz, creating moody, expansive, contemplative compositions that lent a singing quality to much of the swing sound.

All of Me, a Bluebird CD featuring a sampling of Benny Carter classics spanning 1934 to 1959, presents the more thoughtful aspects of the swing sound. If you can, sample arrangements by Henderson, Redman, and Carter from the 1930s. To do so reveals the full breadth of the early swing style.

Edward Kennedy Ellington

In part, the swing era was about translating good feelings to music; however, Benny Carter extended swing's vocabulary well beyond that, paving the way for another musician who would take swing even further. In fact, by the 1930s, the music of Duke Ellington sounded so elegant, so *right*, that one is tempted to look back from Ellington and conclude that everything in swing up to this point was a prelude to Duke.

He was born Edward Kennedy Ellington on April 29, 1899, in Washington, D.C. Beginning piano at age seven, he was playing professionally by 17 and had already acquired such a reputation for elegance that he was universally called "Duke."

He led a small group at New York's Kentucky Club in 1923, consisting of baritone saxophonist Harry Carney, drummer Sonny Greer, trumpeter Bubber Miley, and trombonist Tricky Sam Nanton. These men became the core of later, larger Ellington ensembles, and their coming together was the product of Ellington's genius for recruiting instrumental individualists who nevertheless worked almost magically with one another. Together, this core of musicians developed what came to be called the "jungle style," a highly colorful, exotic style characterized by piercing sonorities that conjure up images of primitive times and exotic places. "Black and Tan Fantasy" and "Creole Love Call," both composed in 1927, are typical of the style, which greatly extended the expressive range of jazz in general and swing in particular.

Ellington is a true giant of American music, who created more than a thousand orchestrations, and he composed not only standard songs of the swing era (including "Satin Doll," "Sophisticated Lady," "Don't Get Around Much Anymore," "Do Nothin' Til You Hear from Me," and "In a Sentimental Mood"), but large-scale works, among them film scores, operas, ballets, Broadway shows, and even sacred music.

In contrast to Fletcher Henderson, Ellington retained a great many of the musicians he worked with. They built their entire careers with him, and he, in turn, used them—not just their instruments—as the colors of his orchestral palette. Ellington was on intimate terms with the unique sounds of the stars of his band, such as trumpeter Cootie Williams, alto saxophonist Johnny Hodges, and bassist Jimmy Blanton.

Moreover, while Ellington thoroughly assimilated the signature sound of the era as defined by Henderson and Redman, he frequently violated this pattern to write more symphonically. Instead of consistently treating each group of instruments—brass, woodwinds, and so on—as a unit, he would combine *different* instruments into fresh orchestral units, achieving a richly exotic sound. No other arranger or composer of the swing era could have created the cool seduction of Ellington's subtly orchestrated "Mood Indigo," for example, which brings together the timbres of bass clarinet, muted trumpet, and trombone.

Take Five

The three-decade collaboration of composer-arranger Billy Strayhorn (1915–67) and Duke Ellington was unique—so close that it is often impossible to tell where the work of one man begins and the other ends. Ellington's fans typically refer to Strayhorn as the maestro's "alter ego."

Strayhorn began working with Ellington in 1938 and didn't stop until he died in 1967. The pair collaborated on something like 200 compositions, including such standards as "Take the 'A' Train" (the Ellington band's theme song) and "Satin Doll." Strayhorn was a master ballad writer, creating for Ellington such songs as "Lush Life" and "Chelsea Bridge."

Nor should we forget in all this that Ellington was also an elegant pianist, who used the instrument to provide very special touches of orchestral color. Although he had modeled his piano technique on the striders, he stripped down, streamlined, and generally minimalized that sound, transforming its athletic energy into delicate filigree and ornamentation.

The music of Duke Ellington first came of age in the swing era, an era Ellington helped to create. A good place to sample Ellington from early in this period is the aptly titled *Early Ellington (1926–1931)*, a three-CD package from Decca. To hear Ellington at his best a decade later, during the height of swing, listen to a live recording made in Fargo, North Dakota (that's right, Fargo), *Fargo ND, November 7, 1940*, and reissued as a two-CD set on Vintage Jazz Classics. Also not to be missed from the high swing era is *The Carnegie Hall Concerts (January 1943)*, a two-CD Prestige set.

A Victor label for a recording of Duke Ellington's Ebony Rhapsody, *1934.*
Image from the author's collection.

Yet for all that he contributed to swing and that swing gave to him, Duke Ellington transcended the period. He was a part of it, but he stood above it as one of the towering figures not only of jazz, but of American music—period. Some critics have gone as far as to declare him the greatest American composer of his time—quite a mouthful, when you consider that Ellington's time included the likes of Gershwin, Aaron Copland, and a host of other extraordinary composers.

Both as a composer and a performer, Ellington survived long beyond the end of the swing era, working to great acclaim right up to the end of his life in 1974. We will return to the Duke in Chapter 15. But we must first return to the swing era itself, because, great as the Duke was, there's a lot more swing to hear. This is the subject of the next chapter.

Take Five

Founded in 1901 as the Victor Talking Machine Company, this label was not only among the earliest of all recording companies, but among the widest ranging, recording virtually every kind and style of music. Its "dog and gramophone" logo with the slogan "His Master's Voice" is one of the most famous trademarks of all time.

In 1917, Victor recorded the very first true jazz performance, *Livery Stable Blues* by the Original Dixieland Jazz Band, but as early as 1913–14, the company had recorded the "proto-jazz" music of James Reese Europe's Society Orchestra. This pioneering momentum was not sustained, however; it was smaller labels, such as Gennett, rather than Victor, that entered the "race" (black music) market, and through the early '20s, Victor confined its jazz output to the polite music of such white orchestra leaders as Paul Whiteman.

This changed in 1926, when Nat Shilkret replaced Edward T. King as the label's A&R (artists and repertory) man. Jelly Roll Morton, Bennie Moten, Duke Ellington, and King Oliver were recorded, and the company even ventured out into the field to record rural blues. After RCA took the label over (as RCA Victor) in 1929, the company aggressively recorded jazz greats such as Fats Waller, Lionel Hampton, and Benny Goodman, expanding to many others during the 1940s and to the present.

RCA Victor started a number of important subsidiary jazz labels in the '30s, including Timely Tunes, Sunrise, and Bluebird. Beginning in the 1960s, French RCA has been in the forefront of historical jazz reissues, on such series as Treasury of Jazz, Black & White, and Jazz Tribune. Domestic RCA created the Camden label in 1950, the Flying Dutchman label in 1976, and revived the Novus label (originally issued by Arista) in 1980—all dedicated to jazz.

The Least You Need to Know

- While the term "big band" may be applied to any jazz ensemble with at least 10 instruments, it is most often associated with the large (15 instruments or more) ensembles of the swing era.
- Big bands developed out of dance orchestras; Fletcher Henderson's big band was the first to really swing, due in part to Henderson's brilliant arrangements and also to his battery of great jazz soloists.
- In the swing era, Coleman Hawkins did for the tenor saxophone what Louis Armstrong had done for the trumpet in the era of classic jazz: He elevated it to the status of a great vehicle for solo expression.
- Duke Ellington, one of the greatest musicians in the history of American music, helped to create the sound of the swing era, but produced a wealth of music that transcended any particular musical style or historical period.

Chapter 12

Long Live the Kings of Swing

In This Chapter

- The Goodman reign
- This king was a count: the Basie bands
- More great bands
- Swinging off to war

The big band concept of the swing era made a Duke Ellington possible, giving him an ample vehicle of expression, yet because many of his works are more symphonic in scope, his music transcends swing, and the name Duke Ellington doesn't leap to mind when you think of the swing era.

Who, then, do we think of?

Well, Benny Goodman was the original "king of swing"—and there were plenty of worthy pretenders to the throne as well. This chapter looks at Goodman and the rest.

From Synagogue to the Austin High School Gang

Benjamin David Goodman was born in Chicago in 1909 and took his first clarinet lessons at the local synagogue in 1919 before joining a boy's band at Hull House, the community settlement house established by social reformer Jane Addams. He also took lessons from a classical clarinetist, Franz Schoepp. Goodman's professional debut took place in 1921, and the following year he began playing with members of the Dixieland-oriented Austin High School Gang, absorbing from them key elements of the New Orleans tradition. A chance meeting with trumpet legend Bix Beiderbecke on a lake excursion was also formative, probably inspiring Goodman's lyricism and careful choice of notes.

Benny Goodman plays the Panther Room of Chicago's Hotel Sherman, 1941.
Image from the Frank Driggs Collection.

Goodman was only 16 when he joined the Ben Pollack jazz band in 1925. He made his first recording with Pollack the next year, and in 1929 moved to New York City, where he worked with Red Nichols's Five Pennies and as a general studio musician before organizing his first big band in 1933–34.

Despite a complement of some of the greatest musicians of swing—including trumpeter Harry James, drummer Gene Krupa, vibraphonist Lionel Hampton, and pianist Teddy Wilson—the band struggled until an August 21, 1935, performance at the Palomar Ballroom in Los Angeles. The teenaged audience went crazy, nearly starting a riot, the likes of which would not be seen until the era of Elvis Presley and the Beatles. Unknown to Goodman, the national radio broadcasts of his *Let's Dance* program, which enjoyed a modest audience on the East Coast, created a sensation on the West Coast. Goodman's audience there was more than ready for him.

King of Swing

From 1935 on, Goodman's star rose on the wings of swing—with assistance from extraordinary orchestrations by Fletcher Henderson and (after 1940) by Eddie Sauter. Goodman's popularity was such that he was able to break the color barrier that had kept bands segregated. For the first time in a major group, white and black musicians played together. This was true in the Benny Goodman big band, as well as in the trio (Chapter 5) and other small ensembles he pioneered.

What it means to swing. The jitterbug, an exuberant and athletic improvisational couple dance, swept the nation and reached the height of its popularity in the 1940s. These dancers were photographed in 1946. Image from arttoday.com.

Take Five

Goodman's perfectionism was legendary. Contrasting the Goodman band with that of the easy-going Bob Crosby, pianist Jess Stacy commented that "Goodman was really a taskmaster. With Benny, perfection was just around the corner. He was hell on intonation [playing in tune], too. Between each set he had me pounding A's on the piano so the saxes and trumpets could be perfectly in tune. When I went with the Bob Crosby band I had that habit of pounding A's between sets. Bob looked at me and said, 'If you keep pounding that A, I'm going to give you your five years' notice'."

Carnegie Concert

If Goodman's band crossed color barriers, so did the appeal of his music. Indeed, it crossed barriers of all kinds, impressing the most committed jazz enthusiasts, black and white, as well as those otherwise indifferent to jazz. It was, in the fullest sense, *popular* music.

Perhaps the most formidable barrier Goodman shattered was the one separating classical music from jazz. While New York's Carnegie Hall, the nation's capitol of classical performance, had hosted jazz before, it never before saw the wild acclaim that Goodman's January 16, 1938, concert drew. Goodman hadn't just proven jazz to be "as good as" classical music, he had demonstrated beyond all doubt that jazz was good music—period.

Dig This

The Carnegie concert is available on a Columbia CD, *Benny Goodman Carnegie Hall Concert.* The tapes on which this momentous live 1938 concert were preserved had been stored away in a closet until 1950, when they were discovered by accident.

Classicists as well as fans in general were drawn to the way in which Goodman's ensemble combined the precision and clarity of classical music with a propulsive swing as irresistible as an onrushing train. As for Goodman, he was arguably the greatest jazz clarinetist ever. Certainly, he was the most popular. Like his ensemble, his solo technique had a classical purity (he even played and recorded classical works—see Chapter 16), grounded in the early Chicago-New Orleans clarinet style and flavored as well with the *klezmer* tradition from Goodman's Jewish heritage.

It is simply impossible to purchase a disappointing Benny Goodman recording, and if you don't like Goodman, well, better just steer clear of swing entirely. A must-have set is the three-CD *The Birth of Swing,* recordings from 1935–36 reissued on the Bluebird label. *On the Air 1937–1938* is double-CD set from Columbia/ Legacy, which features broadcasts of the big band, trio, and quartet: a very exciting set.

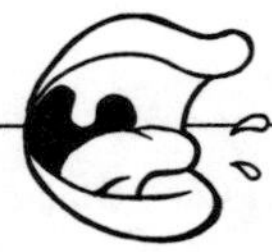

Talk the Talk

Klezmer (*klets-mare,* derived from the Hebrew *kele zemir,* "instuments of song") music developed late in the Middle Ages among the Jews of eastern Europe. Jewish folk musicians (*klezmorim* in the plural) played in ensembles consisting of a violin, flute, bass viol (a small string bass), and cymbals. Later, the clarinet was featured. They played at family festivals, such as weddings, and on certain special festival occasions.

And Now, the Count

William Basie was born in Red Bank, New Jersey, in 1904 and studied piano first with his mother and then learned all he could from James P. Johnson and Fats Waller (who gave him jazz organ lessons, too). He went to work as a theater musician on the precarious black vaudeville circuit, and, finding himself marooned in Kansas City in 1927, he settled there and eventually won a place in the important Bennie Moten band (see Chapter 10). In 1935, following the untimely death of Moten, Basie organized a nine-piece band consisting of former members of the Walter Page and Bennie Moten orchestras. It was a radio announcer who, during an early Basie broadcast, spontaneously dubbed the bandleader "Count" Basie in order to elevate him to the status of "Duke" Ellington.

Count Basie in the studios of Mercury Records, New York, 1952.
Photo by "Popsie" Randolph.
Image from the Frank Driggs Collection.

Kansas City jazz was gaining a national reputation during the mid-1930s, and when the influential jazz critic and producer John Hammond heard the Basie broadcasts on his car radio, he brought the Count to Chicago. During the '30s and '40s, Basie recruited such great soloists as the incredible tenorman Lester Young, trumpeters Buck Clayton and Harry "Sweets" Edison, trombonist Dickie Wells, and Mister 5 by 5, the great jazz-blues shouter, Jimmy Rushing.

Take Five

It was Lester Young who gave Billie Holiday the nickname "Lady Day" (she called Young "Prez," declaring him president of saxophonists). But then, Young called a lot of people "Lady," male or female. In fact, he invented his own language, pinning idiosyncratic labels on a great many things. A white person he might call a "gray," and a black would be an "Oxford gray." When his saxophone keys got bent, he took the instrument to fellow tenor saxophonist and amateur repairman Flip Phillips: "Lady Flip, my people won't play!"

Young called policemen "Bob Crosbys," marijuana was "ettuce," and the bridge section of a tune became a "George Washington." If something was a bore or a pain, he'd call it a "von Hangman." If someone slighted him (or he encountered racial discrimination), he'd declare that he was "feeling a draft." And when the Basie band would hit a town that was home to an old girlfriend, he'd excuse himself, saying that he was "going to see a wayback."

Basie's arrangements were never as elaborately sophisticated as Ellington's nor as airy and clear as Goodman's. Instead, they embodied the driving, straight-ahead Kansas City style—but with plenty of room for solo genius and for the elegant punctuation of Basie's piano playing. Like Ellington, Basie had learned piano from the great striders, and like Ellington, too, he had refined and streamlined the style. But Basie minimalized it even more than Ellington had, so that the piano became his delicately witty signature that served to make each note and musical gesture important.

GRP has reissued *The Complete Decca Recordings (1937–1939)* on a three-CD set, but Basie is also one of the relatively few swing musicians who survived and prospered into the 1950s. The Verve CD reissue of *Count Basie Swings, Joe Williams Sings* is an outstanding 1955 recording.

Take Five

Established in 1938 by New York music shop owner Milt Gabler, the Commodore label specialized in Chicago classic jazz and swing, recording such groups as the Kansas City Six (and Five), Coleman Hawkins, and trumpeter and vocalist Hot Lips Page, as well as classic sides from Billie Holiday.

While Commodore was an important jazz label, its output dwindled by the 1940s and ceased altogether in the 1950s, Gabler having joined the Decca record company as A&R (artists and repertory) man. When Gabler retired from Decca, he revived Commodore in the late 1970s, reissuing classic material and issuing for the first time previously unreleased recordings. Many original Commodore releases are available today on the Mosaic label.

In Full Swing

The 1930s were chock full of really wonderful swing bands. Political historians may credit the economic policies and programs of Franklin Delano Roosevelt for successfully bringing the nation through the ravages of the Great Depression, but the life-affirming sound of the swing bands probably played just as important a role. More than a handful of bands are remembered as standouts and are, fortunately, well represented on record.

Jimmy Lunceford

Lunceford (1902–47) put together a big band that contemporaries rated with those of Ellington and Basie, but which emphasized ensemble work over soloists. Unfortunately, few Lunceford recordings fully capture the magic—though *Jimmie Lunceford*, a Masters of Jazz CD, comes close.

Cab Calloway

Cab Calloway (1907–97) sported a trademark yellow *zoot suit* that announced him as the good-time master entertainer that he was. As was true of Fats Waller, Calloway's buffoonery—typically slyly sexual—obscured the excellence of his music making. As we saw in Chapter 9, Calloway was known as the "Hi-De-Ho Man" because of the runaway success of his song "Minnie the Moocher" (with its "hi-de-hi-de-hi-de-ho" chorus), but his band, which included such luminaries as trumpeter Doc Cheatham, string bass player Milt Hinton, tenor saxophonist Chu Berry, and trumpet master Dizzy Gillespie (in his pre-bop days), was capable of much more. *Cab Calloway (1930–31)*, reissued on a Classics CD, is an ideal sampler of Calloway at his best—and, yes, you'll find "Minnie the Moocher" here, too, in its original version, no less.

Talk the Talk

The **zoot suit** was the uniform of the late '30s/early '40s swing hipster. Typically of gaudy color, it featured full-legged, tight-cuffed (pegged) trousers and a very long coat with exaggerated lapels and padded shoulders. Knobby-toed shoes, a broad-brimmed fedora, and a long watch chain completed the zoot-suit look.

Chick Webb

Life dealt this Baltimore-born drummer and bandleader a lot of dirt. A dwarfish hunchback, he was plagued by ill health and, at age 30 in 1939, succumbed to TB. As if he knew that he wasn't long for this world, Webb drummed and drove his band with a demonic energy that so awed Gene Krupa (destined to become perhaps the most famous jazz drummer of his era) that he spoke of Webb in what have been described as "shell-shocked" tones.

Webb came to New York in 1924 and formed a band two years later, but it wasn't until 1935, when he hired a youthful, inexperienced Ella Fitzgerald, that the band really took off. With her, the Chick Webb ensemble was at the height of its power and fame when Webb died, uttering his final words: "I'm sorry, I've got to go."

To hear some of the Webb magic—and the early Ella that helped him get there—listen to *Chick Webb (1935–1938)*, a CD reissue from Classics.

Teddy Wilson

Wilson (1912–86) is best remembered today for his trio and quartet work with Benny Goodman, Gene Krupa, and Lionel Hampton. And that is not a bad thing to be remembered for. But he was also the definitive swing pianist, whose style was skilled, brilliant, and also genial—less elaborate and, therefore, more immediately accessible than the pianism of Earl "Fatha" Hines or Art Tatum.

Dig This

Listen to Wilson on the Benny Goodman trio and quartet recordings. A two-CD RCA set, *The Complete Small Combinations,* is a great way to hear this music.

Wilson briefly led his own big band in 1939–40 and a sextet at Manhattan's Cafè Society during 1940–44. He was so highly respected that he was appointed to the summer faculty of Juilliard during 1945–52.

As of this writing, *Teddy Wilson and His All-Stars* has yet to be released on CD. If you have a turntable, look for a copy of this extraordinary Columbia LP, which features Wilson as pianist and bandleader with sublime vocals by Billie Holiday. You can also hear him to advantage as a pianist and a bandleader on *Central Avenue Blues,* recordings from 1944–45, which are available on CD from Vintage Jazz Classics.

Drummer Gene Krupa (1909–73) was perhaps the first soloist on the instrument to gain the spotlight with extended (and incredibly strenuous) solos. Uptown, *1941–42 recordings reissued on Columbia, offers a fine taste of the Krupa style. Image from Lawrence Cohn.*

The Dorsey Brothers

Jazz historians speak of the bands of Basie or Goodman or even Chick Webb as *the* quintessential swing ensembles, but many fans who actually lived through the period would point to the Dorsey brothers as the ideal embodiment of the period.

Jimmy (1904–57) and Tommy Dorsey (1905–56) were the sons of a music teacher. The two freelanced in white jazz circles during the '20s, Jimmy on clarinet and alto saxophone (ultimately his preferred instrument) and Tommy on trumpet and then exclusively on trombone. Although they recorded together as early as 1928, it wasn't until 1933 that they formed an orchestra together, and by 1935, they were enjoying great success, propelled in no small measure by Bob Crosby vocals and Glenn Miller arrangements.

That success was short lived. In 1935, the brothers argued over the tempo of "I'll Never Say Never Again" during a ballroom gig. They split up instantly, each creating his own orchestra—and each enjoying popular success, reconciling and reuniting in 1953.

Dig This

Frank Sinatra launched his phenomenal career as a vocalist with Tommy Dorsey's band. *All-Time Greatest Dorsey/Sinatra Hits,* Volume 1, an RCA CD, will take you back to the early days of "The Voice," 1940–42.

Take Five

Tommy Dorsey was uncompromising in the demands he made on his musicians. In need of a trumpet player, he asked for candidates. "How about so-and-so," a band member offered. "He's a nice guy."

"Nice guys are a dime a dozen," Dorsey replied. "Get me a prick that can play!"

Both together and apart, the Dorsey bands played wonderful popular music rather than authentic jazz, but it was highly representative of the big band era nonetheless. *Best of the Big Bands,* a Columbia CD offering the brothers' band from 1932–34, is more strongly jazz-oriented than later recordings by either Tommy or Jimmy alone.

Bunny Berigan

During the 1930s, Bunny (his given name was Rowland Bernart) Berigan was acclaimed as a trumpeter who might well be the equal of Louis Armstrong. Certainly, bandleaders respected him as much as the public loved him. Berigan played with Whiteman, the Dorsey Brothers, Benny Goodman, and with Tommy Dorsey, and also briefly led his own quite successful big band.

Bunny Berrigan swings, about 1940. Image from Lawrence Cohn.

Berigan is not as well remembered today as he should be; for his tone is richly beautiful—qualities that greatly enhance such pretty tunes as "Marie," which was a Tommy Dorsey favorite. He was also a daring soloist, who never took the safe route and who wasn't afraid to fall down. Unfortunately, like Bix Beiderbecke, to whom he was often favorably compared, Berigan put a bottle to his lips as often as he did a trumpet. He died in 1942 at age 34. Bluebird has reissued *The Pied Piper*, recordings from 1935–40, which includes "Marie" and "Nothin' But the Blues"—considered by many to be Berigan's most magnificent solo—as well as Berigan's "theme song," "I Can't Get Started."

Woody Herman

Herman (1913–87) got his start in swing but also made the transition to bop, hard bop, and rhythm and blues, performing with a series of Thundering Herds (as he called each of his big bands) through the 1980s. Herman's straight-ahead, aggressive approach to swing can best be heard on *Thundering Herds 1945–47*, a Columbia CD, which includes Herman's signature "Woodchopper's Ball."

Artie Shaw

Born in 1910 in New York, Shaw started out playing alto saxophone in a dance band in the '20s, but became famous as a great swing clarinetist, composer, and arranger. His brand of swing was always tempered by a certain classical influence (he loved the music of Claude Debussy and Igor Stravinsky), and while he was probably Benny Goodman's technical equal on clarinet, he lacked BG's fire.

Shaw's matinee-idol good looks and extramusical life—eight marriages, including one to Ava Gardner and another to Lana Turner—tended to draw attention away from his prodigious musical accomplishments. These are best heard on *Begin the Beguine*, 1938–41 recordings reissued on a Bluebird CD, and *The Complete Gramercy Five Sessions*, another Bluebird reissue, featuring small group sessions form 1940–45.

Take Five

Shaw was an intellectual who spent whatever time he had between gigs (and marriages) reading. When he and Goodman were working as studio musicians in the early 1930s, Goodman asked him what he was reading. "Thorstein Veblen's *The Theory of the Leisure Class*," Shaw replied. Thereafter, Benny always greeted him with "How ya doin', J.B.?" Shaw tried to resist asking what he meant by that, but, finally, he gave in. "All right, Benny, what does J.B. stand for?"

"George Bernard," Goodman replied.

Charlie Barnet

Depending on who you believe, Charlie Barnet fell just short of Artie Shaw in wives—or eclipsed him. Some say he was wed a half-dozen times, others as many as 11. Born in 1913 in New York to wealthy parents, he rebelled against their ambition for him to become a corporate lawyer and led a shipboard band on a liner when he was only 16. In 1932, he became leader of the Paramount Hotel (Manhattan) band and subsequently formed a number of his own ensembles. In 1939, he hit it big with a song called "Cherokee," which became his trademark.

Like Goodman and Artie Shaw, Barnet pioneered the integration of white and black musicians, and his bands included the likes of Roy Eldridge and Charlie Shavers on trumpets and Benny Carter on alto saxophone. His featured vocalist was Lena Horne.

During 1939–42, Barnet's was among the most popular swing bands in the nation, combining much of the exotic orchestral textures of Duke Ellington (whom Barnet deeply admired) with a simpler, more accessible approach. *Drop Me Off in Harlem,* recordings from 1942–46, is a fine representation of Barnet on a Bluebird CD reissue.

The Sounds of War

Watch any movie depicting the events of World War II, and you are almost certain to hear the strains of swing on at least some part of the soundtrack. To be sure, army bands played "The Star-Spangled Banner" and "The Stars and Stripes Forever," but the real American anthems of the war were set to the rhythms and expressed in the massed harmonies of swing.

Most of the big bands we have mentioned pitched in during the war, entertaining troops on USO tours and the like, but two popular bands stand out for their wartime popularity.

Captain Glenn Miller, USAAF

Alton Glenn Miller (1904–44) was born in Clarinda, Iowa, and was educated briefly at the University of Colorado, but became a professional musician, joining Ben Pollack's band in 1926. His skill as a trombonist earned him great success as a freelance player in New York, and his talent for leadership landed him jobs organizing the bands of others, including the Dorsey brothers (1934). He tried and failed to start his own orchestra in 1937, but succeeded at last in 1939 and rapidly achieved widespread fame.

Glenn Miller at the Municipal Auditorium, Kansas City, 1939. Photo by John Randozzo. Image from the Frank Driggs Collection.

Miller included jazz in his orchestra's repertoire, but, actually, his was a dance ensemble that played a wide variety of phenomenally popular music, including his theme song, "Moonlight Serenade" and more swinging numbers, such as "In the Mood," "Tuxedo Junction," "Chattanooga Choo Choo," "A String of Pearls," and "Pennsylvania 6-5000."

A patriot, Miller enlisted in the U.S. Army Air Force, organizing a great military *jazz* band. That Miller was given this assignment is a testament to how important military leaders thought swing was to boosting and maintaining the morale of the American soldier. To hear Miller's rendition of "St. Louis Blues March"—an arrangement of the venerable W. C. Handy standard that transforms it into a swing-time march—is a genuinely stirring experience.

The Hollywood Canteen was a World War II USO haven for Pacific-bound troops. It was filled with the sounds of swing. Here starlet Martha O'Driscoll jitterbugs with a PFC. Image from arttoday.com.

On December 15, 1944, Miller was flying across the English Channel to set up engagements on the continent, when his plane was lost, apparently the victim of friendly (British) fire. The bandleader achieved posthumous war-hero status, and his recordings became more popular than ever. The *Complete Glenn Miller* is available on 13 CDs from Bluebird, but you can get a good one-CD sampling on *Spirit Is Willing* (Bluebird).

Harry James: A Swing Gabriel

Today, few jazz historians would accord Harry James (1916–83) the accolades he received during the 1940s, when he was not only the most famous trumpet player in the nation, but leader of one of the country's most successful big bands. Like Miller, he specialized in the sweeter side of swing, including sentimental ballads such as "You Made Me Love You" and "I'll Get By."

At its best, Harry James's music is a nostalgic evocation of an emotionally intense era. It is also an example of the mainstreaming of jazz in general and of swing in particular. James fans can do no better than *Bandstand Memories 1938 to 1948*, a three-CD set on the Hindsight label.

The swing era, as many see it, was a golden age for jazz, not just because so much of the music is so wonderful, but because it was so popular, so pervasive—the sound that moved America for more than a decade.

The Least You Need to Know

- Combining impeccable musicianship with great improvisational skill and a self-propelled sense of swing, the Benny Goodman Orchestra was the matchless embodiment of the swing era.
- The best swing musicians were accomplished technicians on a par with major classical virtuosos.
- Count Basie brought a simpler, more streamlined approach to swing in a hard-driving style born in Kansas City.
- Literally thousands of big bands flourished in the 1930s and early 1940s, creating a kind of soundtrack for the era. Swing helped the nation through the Great Depression and was an invaluable morale booster during World War II.
- Swing-era jazz was the dominant popular music of its time.

Chapter 13

Being Bop: Life After Swing

In This Chapter

- Bebop: a musical and social rebellion
- How a dance tax helped create bebop
- Charlie Parker and Dizzy Gillespie: bebop pioneers
- Boppers versus the moldy figs
- A tale of two pianists: Monk and Powell
- Bop fades into the mainstream

Swing turned out to be one of the most durable styles of popular music. Only rock, first heard in the mid-1950s and still going strong, has proven longer lived. Yet, by the 1940s, many musicians, if not the public, were growing tired of the swing sound.

They felt the music had gone stale. In fact, the musical rebels of the 1940s—called rebobbers, beboppers, or just plain boppers—referred to swing-oriented musicians and other traditionalists as "moldy figs." But the rebellion against swing went deeper than the music. Young African-American musicians heard in this sometimes superficially pleasant music uncomfortable echoes of the minstrel show, born of a tradition in which blacks were caricatured as happy-go-lucky "darkies" who delighted in nothing more than the amusement of white masters. Black swing musicians, the boppers came to believe, were minstrel-like entertainers, and they wanted to break with them. They wanted to reclaim jazz as essentially African-American music, not merely entertaining tunes for mostly white audiences to dance to.

Thus bop emerged, musically radical and politically charged. The combination made it controversial as well as intensely energetic. Unlike genial swing, bop can be frenetic and even angry. Musically and socially, it makes certain demands on listeners. Those willing to give the music a chance may find that bebop is the most exciting direction jazz has ever taken. Here's the story.

Revolution or Evolution?

Historians of jazz like to see it this way: The swing music of the 1930s had a propulsive, irresistible, but ultimately naive or innocent energy behind it. The onset of World War II gave swing a more nostalgic, sentimental turn. Then bebop emerged—suddenly—after a horrendous war that put an end to innocence and sentimentality. Into the brave new postwar world, a new, hard-edged, frenetic, even frantic and angry jazz had been born.

That's a neat story, but it wasn't quite so simple. Jazz writers and critics, eager to spread the gospel to a broad audience, often seek simple explanations. Some, for example, tell us that jazz is "really" nothing more than a form of African-American folk music. But folk music is by definition conservative rather than innovative, and while jazz is indisputably rooted in black traditional music, it is also driven by a progressive, modernist urge. This is one of the unique qualities of this remarkable music: It is "root music" at the same time that it is progressive, restless, radical, innovative music.

This innovative urge has always been a part of jazz; it didn't suddenly emerge after World War II. Even in the 1930s, in the heyday of the swing era, some musicians began to tire of the simple riffs and easygoing vocals that appealed to the masses. Some became impatient with dance music and being bound to the invariably thick textures of big band orchestration, the brass and reed sections always interlocked, the sound always big and meaty.

Yet looking back—or listening back—on the war years and the postwar years, the change from populist swing to the rebellious and insistent sound of bop does seem sudden.

Why?

The answer lies in the course of history.

The Dance Tax and a Strike

Of the many terrible hardships World War II imposed on Americans and others, the rationing of the raw materials used to manufacture phonograph records and a federal "cabaret tax" imposed on dance halls were trivial. Unless you happened to be a jazz musician. Recording dates dried up, and many club owners booked smaller, cheaper ensembles instead of the big bands. To make matters worse, wartime audiences demanded nostalgia and sentimentality, elevating crooners above instrumentalists, and pretty tunes over jazz.

The leading musicians' union, the American Federation of Musicians, blamed the music-industry crisis on radio. With clubs expensive and bands small, people stayed home and listened to the radio. The AFM called for broadcasters to pay musicians royalties, and when they refused, the union called a ban on instrumental recording. The silence endured for about two years, from 1942 to 1944, until a royalty agreement was concluded. But by this time, the combined effects of the cabaret tax and the recording ban had dealt many big bands blows from which they could not recover.

Dig This

The **cabaret tax** was a devastating 30 percent (later reduced to 20 percent) charge tacked onto customers' bills.

Bebop was another story. Beboppers shunned the big band sound in favor of smaller ensembles. That suited the club owners, who were desperate to save money. The fewer musicians to pay, the better. Moreover, the cabaret tax was really a *dance* tax. Venues that didn't offer dancing could identify themselves as restaurants or saloons rather than cabarets, nightclubs, or dancehalls and thereby avoid the tax. What they needed, however, was music that could *not* be danced to. The bebop musicians, eager to break out of the dance band mold, were happy to oblige. Bebop is for listening, not dancing.

Dig This

You can hear "Anthropology," "Ornithology," and other Parker gems (such as "Ko Ko," "Donna Lee," and "Parker's Mood") on *Complete Savoy Sessions,* a three-CD set from Savoy, covering 1944–48. Stash offers two CDs from Parker's earliest years: *The Complete "Birth of Bebop"* and *"Early Bird."*

With the AFM recording ban, the evolutionary emergence of bebop has not been documented. It happened, but it happened live rather than on record. Thus, from our perspective in time, the emergence of bebop seems very sudden.

New Wine, Old Bottles

Fellow musicians called him Bird or Yardbird, but Charles Christopher Parker, Jr. (1920–55) was best known as Charlie Parker, alto saxophonist, composer, bandleader, and, with trumpeter Dizzy Gillespie, one of the founding fathers of bebop. To listen to "Anthropology" or "Ornithology," two early monuments of bop, is to understand why Parker is considered by many the greatest improviser in jazz history.

These are wild, intense, heated excursions into musical territory that seems light years' distant from the airy rhythms of a Benny Goodman or the debonaire piano fills of a Count Basie. Yet Parker's "Anthropology," wild as it sounds, is built on the underlying chord structure (the "changes") of the Gershwin standard "I Got Rhythm." "Ornithology" reworks "How High the Moon"—another standard, which was to prove a favorite harmonic foundation on which beboppers would build.

Take Five

Where did Parker get the nicknames "Yardbird" and "Bird?" Bandleader Jay McShann explains that Parker was in a car on his way to a gig at the University of Nebraska when they hit a chicken. "Charlie told the driver, 'Man, go back, you hit that yardbird.' They went back, and Charlie jumped out and got the chicken. When they got to Lincoln, he asked the lady who ran the boarding house where we were staying to cook it for dinner." From then on, Parker was "Yardbird," "Yard," or just plain "Bird."

Similarly, while the move away from big bands to small combos may seem revolutionary, it was merely a reduction in size. The instruments remained the same: A rhythm section of piano, drums, and double bass accompanied the "melody" instruments—brass and woodwinds.

So what makes songs like "Anthropology" and "Ornithology" so *new*?

Bebop began by almost completely reinventing two basic jazz elements. First, rhythm: The syncopated patterns that had long characterized jazz now gave way to long phrases played *on* the beat, only to be punctuated by bursts of incredibly fast notes and sharply intoned phrases suddenly played *off* the beat. Moreover, the basic rhythm was now 4/4 time rather than 2/4 time, which greatly increased the range of rhythmic possibilities. Beboppers delighted in beginning musical phrases on the weak beats—not on beat one in a bar, but beat two. And they ended phrases similarly, on beat four rather than beat three of a four-beat measure. To keep the listener off balance—propelling him forward—they often began and ended phrases *between* beats.

Earlier, we compared jazz to conversation, questions and answers. Bebop put the emphasis on the questions rather than the answers. The result is that the music never sounds *settled* or *finished*. It is querulous, restless, nervous, keyed up—anything but "easy-listening."

The second reinvention was improvisation. This had always been important in jazz, but it now took on a new dominance and daring. In big band music, improvisation consisted of solos sandwiched neatly between stretches of fully written-out orchestral music. Beboppers, in contrast, invested everything in complex, prolonged, and intense improvisation, letting the ensemble recede well into the background.

Take Five

The AFM allowed a single exception to its recording ban. In 1943, the U.S. War Department authorized a series of recordings called "V-discs" ("V" for victory) to be distributed exclusively to U.S. military installations and personnel worldwide. Between 1943 and 1948, some 8 million V-discs were distributed. Hearing familiar American swing music on the European front or in a Pacific jungle was a great boost to morale. The content of V-discs was predominantly swing—beboppers need not apply—and in effect, these wartime recordings provide a glimpse of jazz frozen in time. There is no hint of the (unrecorded) revolution under way at this time.

Diz and Bird

If the innovative Parker recycled familiar tunes, he also learned technique from some of the most advanced swing-era musicians, especially tenor saxophonist Lester Young. In contrast to the prevailing swing saxophone style, Young had developed a light, precise, even machine-like technique, which Parker absorbed before he moved from Kansas City to New York City in 1939. Here he played in the Earl Hines and Billy Eckstine bands with trumpeter Dizzy Gillespie.

The Giants Meet

John Birks "Dizzy" Gillespie (1917–93) was born in South Carolina and took formal classes in music theory at the Laurinburg Institute in North Carolina. He composed, arranged, and played with major swing bands, including those of Cab Calloway and Benny Carter in addition to Earl Hines and Billy Eckstine.

The Minton's Playhouse Sessions

In Parker, he found a kindred musical spirit, and the pair would jam at Harlem's Minton's Playhouse during the '40s with pianist Thelonious Monk and drummer Kenny Clarke. These musicians—Parker, Gillespie, Monk, and Clarke, with the addition of bassist Oscar Pettiford—formed the core of the bebop movement. In the Eckstine's band, in 1944, Parker and Gillespie showcased bebop in a big band setting, and the next year, they formed their own quintet.

Eckstine's Big Bop Band

Although he would enjoy his greatest financial and popular success as a pop singer, Billy Eckstine (1914–93) was also a pioneering bop bandleader, who hired Parker and Gillespie, then gave them all the room they needed to create a new sound. While Parker took improvisation to new heights, Gillespie reinvented the trumpet, modeling his technique on that of Roy Eldridge, who coaxed from his horn the rapid-fire lines that others blew from a saxophone. Gillespie explored the highest register of his instrument, creating complex and jagged phrases and exploring new concepts in harmony. He shared with Parker the soul of a high-wire artist, unafraid to perform feats of daring that threatened to send him hurtling to the ground. Yet always, somehow, his music made sense.

Dig This

Parker and Gillespie can be heard in abundance in the *Charlie Parker and Dizzy Gillespie: The Complete Dial Sessions,* a four-CD set from Stash.

Nor was Gillespie a mere stuntman. He brought a new element into modern jazz: the Afro-Cuban sound, dubbed "Cubop" and kicked along by the exciting conga (traditional Cuban drums) player Chano Pozo, a Cuban emigre whose career was cut short when he was murdered in 1948.

Dig This

Gillespie and Miles Davis are the two best-known trumpeters to emerge from the bebop period, but Roy Eldridge (1911–89) may have been the most exciting. Where Gillespie was witty and Davis cool, Eldridge was combative. Yet he was at heart a swing musician forcibly transplanted into bebop. Try *After You've Gone,* on the GRP label, featuring swing and early bop from 1936–46.

Men of Influence

Gillespie introduced a number of the elements that define modern jazz, including the augmented eleventh (flat fifth) chord interval. His intensity, musical ideas, and presence influenced the next generation of jazz greats, among them Miles Davis, John Coltrane, Dexter Gordon, and James Moody. He also composed some of the great standards of modern jazz, such as "Night in Tunisia," "Manteca," "Con Alma," and "Birks Works."

As for Parker, his prowess as a soloist became legendary—as did his self-destructive addiction to drink and drugs. During his lifetime as well as after his death, aspiring jazz performers pored over recordings and transcriptions of each and every Parker solo. His influence was widespread, not only among such saxophonists as Sonny Rollins, John Coltrane, and Ornette Coleman, but among all jazz players.

Charlie "Bird" Parker playing in the New York club named in his honor, "Birdland," about 1949. Photo by "Popsie" Randolph. Image from the Frank Driggs Collection.

Hawkins Goes Bop

Perhaps the greatest testament to the compelling power of Parker and Gillespie is that Coleman Hawkins (1904–69) embraced bop. Hawkins had started his professional career back in 1922–23, playing with the Jazz Hounds, a group led by blues great Mamie Smith, and he made his first records with Fletcher Henderson in June 1923. His full-bodied, even lush tone established the tenor saxophone as a popular jazz instrument, and by the late 1940s, Hawkins could have been considered one of the music's elder statesmen. But he was no moldy fig. It was Hawkins who, in February 1944, assembled an all-star band (which included Gillespie and bop drummer Max Roach) to make what are generally considered the first bop recordings.

'Round Midnight

Bop deeply divided jazz in the postwar years as figs and boppers sniped at one another in such public forums as the pages of the popular jazz magazine *down beat*. Remember, the boppers were (in part) rebelling against the racially charged role of "happy-go-lucky entertainer," and the otherwise good-natured Dizzy Gillespie accused Louis Armstrong of having become a "plantation character." In turn, Armstrong called bebop not modern music, but "modern malice."

Dig This

You can hear the "first bop record"—a truly landmark 1944 session featuring Hawkins, Gillespie, Roach, and bassist Oscar Pettiford—on *Rainbow Mist*, a Coleman Hawkins reissue from Delmark. This CD belongs in every serious jazz collection.

Take Five

Hawkins "never liked to look back at things," reed man Eddie Barefield observed. "Hawk," Barefield once asked him, "why don't you play one of them old Fletcher Henderson slap-tongue solos that you used to play?"

He says, "I never played like that. I never played anything like that." I said, "Okay, I'll bring you a record tomorrow." And I brought "Dicty Blues," where he was slap-tonguing. He said, "No, man, that wasn't me. I don't want to hear that."

The intense world of bop spawned many legends. Bop guitarist Tal Farlow (1921–) became one not only for his phenomenal virtuosity, but because he performed so rarely, virtually retiring in his prime in 1958. For rare bop guitar, listen to The Tal Farlow Album, *recordings from 1954–55, reissued on a Verve CD.*
Image from Lawrence Cohn.

Perhaps Armstrong's remark was mistaking intensity for anger, but it is also true that the boppers' attitude toward their audience was "take it or leave it." Despite this defiance, bop did catch on among a sizable minority of jazz fans, and by the late 1940s, the major bop stars were Gillespie, Parker, and drummers Kenny Clarke and Max Roach. Clarke had introduced the "bomb" into bop, using the bass drum not to keep time, but to supply loud, unexpected accents. A young piano player named Bud Powell burst onto the scene as a virtuoso sensation whose like had not been heard since Art Tatum. And, at this time, just emerging from the shadows, was another pianist, Powell's friend and mentor, Thelonious Monk.

Talk the Talk

A **bomb** is a loud, unexpected accent on the bass drum. "Dropping bombs" became a trademark of bebop drummers.

Sphere Was No Square

He had been born Thelious Monk, Jr. in Rocky Mount, North Carolina, moved with his family to New York when he was four, began performing as a *sideman* (supporting player) with various groups in the early '40s, and worked as a pianist at Minton's Playhouse. Later, he also changed his first name to Thelonious and inserted as a middle name *Sphere*: Thelonious Sphere Monk.

Talk the Talk

A **sideman** is a supporting player in a small jazz ensemble.

Monk met and played with all the early greats of bebop, and it was he who encouraged and guided fellow pianist Bud Powell. But whereas Powell's piano style, flowing, dazzling, and chock full of cascading notes, catapulted him to fame within the small but widening circle of bop fans, Monk's style—quirky, curiously loping, choppy, full of dissonances (not *blue* notes, but *wrong* notes), harmonically strange—left most listeners bewildered.

Riffs

[I]n about three months Monk said maybe two words. I mean, literally, maybe two words. He didn't say, "Good morning," "Goodnight," "What time?" Nothing. Why, I don't know. He sent word back after the tour was over that the reason he couldn't communicate or play was that Art Blakey and I were so ugly.

—Bassist Al McKibbon recalling a tour with Monk, an introvert's introvert

From roughly 1945 to 1954, when bop was generally gaining ground and verging on entry into the mainstream, Thelonious Monk was a largely neglected figure. Indeed, even some bop musicians (but not Gillespie or the other majors) thought his music was unplayable and Monk himself crazy.

At last, in 1955, recording contracts came—but also went. Then, beginning in 1957, Monk recorded for the Riverside label a series of albums that made him an "overnight" sensation. *Brilliant Corners, Thelonious Himself,* and *Thelonious Monk with John Coltrane* (we'll have much more to say about

Coltrane in Chapter 19) were immediately acclaimed, with many listeners calling Monk the most important improviser and composer of the era.

Not that he won everybody over. Those who liked their composers and performers neatly pigeonholed found Monk simply annoying. But the greatness of his music is that it defies categorization. He is historically linked to the boppers, because he performed with them. Yet his music sounds nothing like that of Parker, Gillespie, or even his friend Powell. It is angular, craggy, and architectural. Yet, in contrast to much avant-garde music, it is eminently enjoyable, always interesting, often wry and witty, and sometimes intensely beautiful. No jazz composition is more utterly gorgeous than "'Round Midnight," composed in the 1940s, and this most challenging musician also wrote a string of popular jazz standards, including "Straight No Chaser," "52nd Street Theme," "Blue Monk," "Ruby My Dear," "In Walked Bud," "Brilliant Corners," "Rhythm-a-Ning," and many others.

Take Five

Thelonious Monk was not only a great jazz musician, he was one of the most important of American composers in any field. No Monk recording is without interest, so the listener new to Monk can joyously dive in anywhere. However, if you want to dip a toe first, you can do no better than *Brilliant Corners,* the classic 1956 LP re-released on CD by Original Jazz Classics. If you want to take the plunge with both feet, pull out your charge card and invest in the 15-CD *Complete Riverside Recordings,* which span 1955–61 and have been re-released on the Riverside label.

Among jazz fans, the legendary status of tenor saxophonist John Coltrane (Chapter 19) is second only to that of Monk himself, so even if you expect a great deal from *Thelonious with John Coltrane* (1957–58 recordings from Original Jazz Classics), you won't be disappointed.

The Tatum Legacy: Bud Powell

Earl "Bud" Powell (1924–66) had been born into a musical family headed by a father who played stride piano. The stride style of Fats Waller and, even more, the super-charged stride-inspired music of Art Tatum appealed to Powell from early childhood. By age 15, he had dropped out of school to become a professional musician. Within a few years, Powell discovered Minton's Playhouse, the Harlem club where the early beboppers played. While other musicians shooed the youthful Powell from the bandstand, Thelonious Monk, Minton's house pianist, welcomed and encouraged him.

From the example of Tatum, Powell absorbed prodigious technique. If Tatum is stride on steroids, Powell's brand of bop piano often resembles Tatum taken to warp speed. It is hard to believe that human fingers could fit so many notes into such brief spans of time. Yet prodigious technique was not the be-all, end-all of Bud Powell. He brought to bop piano an intensely melodic quality as well, always tempered by a spare, even brittle touch in the slow passages. He was, in short, a pianist of tremendous technical, musical, and emotional range, and his example was an elusive benchmark for the pianists who followed him.

Dig This

Both Powell and Monk were renowned as shy, reclusive men of few words. What was their friendship like? Probably not highly verbal. However, it was marked by intense loyalty. As Monk had encouraged the young Powell, so Powell, after earning a reputation as *the* bop pianist, championed Monk's music. By persuading trumpeter-bandleader Cootie Williams to record "'Round Midnight," Powell helped launch his long-struggling friend's career.

Powell's pianism has a vulnerability about it, the demonstrations of technical prowess alternating with tenderness that never verges on sentimentality. Perhaps this fragility reflects Powell's own tortured life. Plagued by mental instability, he was frequently confined in institutions. Some believe his precarious mental health was the result of a beating dealt him by the Philadelphia police when he was arrested for disorderly conduct in 1944. Perhaps we are fortunate to have any music from this seemingly cursed genius, who died at 41 of a combination of alcoholism, tuberculosis, and malnutrition. The 1986 film, *'Round Midnight*, starring tenor legend Dexter Gordon, is loosely based on the life of Bud Powell.

Dig This

The Amazing Bud Powell, Volumes 1 and 2, a pair of Blue Note CDs, are a great introduction to this awesome pianist. If you're looking for something more comprehensive, the four-CD *Complete Blue Note and Roost Recordings*, on Blue Note, is a fine investment.

The Parker-Gillespie Sets

While Bud Powell is considered *the* quintessential bop pianist, the collaboration of Charlie Parker and Dizzy Gillespie is deemed the quintessence of bop. To hear the best of these recorded collaborations, try *The Complete "Birth of Bebop"* (Stash), recordings from 1940–45. If you've got the cash, *Bird: Complete on Verve* (Verve), a 10-CD reissue set spanning 1946–54, is a great investment. If you can pop for four CDs, *The Complete Dial Sessions* (Stash), from 1946–47, is also a standout.

Cover art from the Bud Powell: Complete Blue Note and Roost Recordings, *one of the most important reissues of bebop-era music. Image from* Blue Note.

Gillespie Rising

Of all the major bop artists, Dizzy Gillespie was the most outgoing. He had the personal integrity and strength of personality necessary for organizing a short-lived bop big band in 1945, then a quintet and sextet, and, in the late '40s, another big band. This group included Chano Pozo, the Cuban conga player, and thus bop was invigorated by a dash of Cuban heat. Although the band dissolved in 1950—a victim of the general decline of big bands, which, ironically, bop had helped cause—Gillespie enjoyed a long and rewarding career until his death in 1993.

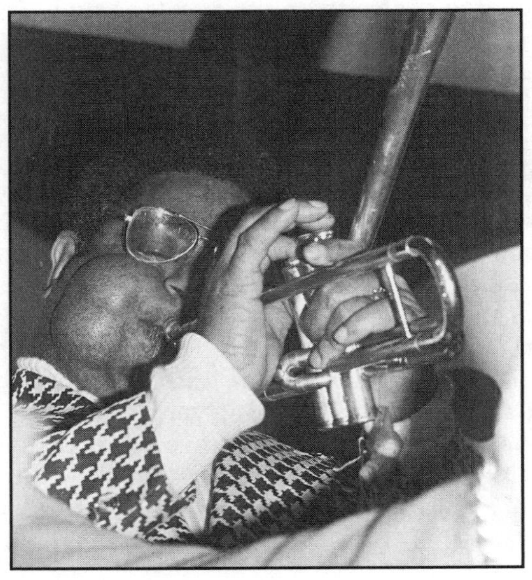

Close-up of Dizzy Gillespie and his unmistakable trademarks: the trumpet with upswept bell and the balloon-like cheeks (a condition the medical books now call "Gillespie pouches"). Photo by Gerry Bahl. Image from the Frank Driggs Collection.

Take Five

Three things made Dizzy Gillespie instantly recognizable. Beginning in 1954, he blew a trumpet with a distinctively upswept bell. The prototype of this misshapen instrument was not custom made in any factory, but was the result of an accident while Gillespie was on a world tour for the U.S. State Department. A dance team knocked Diz's trumpet offstage. When he saw what had been done to his horn, Gillespie was furious—until he played it and discovered he could hear himself better. He ordered a new horn—bent just like the damaged one.

Then there was the trademark beret and goatee, which certified Diz as a real-live beatnik—a stereotype both the public and press understood and accepted in the 1950s.

Finally, Gillespie's face was a sight to see when he played. His cheeks would balloon out, calling to mind a blowfish or some exotic frog in the throes of a mating ritual. Late in his career, Gillespie was contacted by a physician, who asked permission to photograph his cheeks for an article in a medical journal. The musician good-naturedly complied and was flattered when the physician officially dubbed the disorder (characterized by permanently stretched muscle and tissue) "Gillespie pouches."

Bird Falling

As Dizzy Gillespie's star rose, Charlie Parker's fell into terrifying decline. The problem wasn't musical—at least not directly so—but emotional. In 1946, Bird suffered a nervous collapse complicated by heroin addiction and alcoholism. From June through January 1947, he was confined to Camarillo State Hospital in California. After his release, he worked feverishly between 1947 and 1951, performing and recording with the likes of Miles Davis, Max Roach, and others, and touring the States and Europe. During this brief period, he recorded about half of his surviving output.

Dig This

Jazz at Massey Hall, recorded live on May 15, 1953, is some of the best late Bird on record. A veritable bebop summit, it includes Gillespie, Powell, Charles Mingus, and Max Roach with Parker. The CD is available from Original Jazz Classics.

But the monkey was still very much on Parker's back, and in 1951, New York City authorities pulled his cabaret license, banning him from performing on account of criminal drug use. He found work elsewhere when he could, and his license was reinstated in 1953, but Parker was now broken financially, physically, and emotionally. Twice the following year he attempted suicide and finally committed himself to Bellevue Hospital in Manhattan. On March 5, 1955, he made what would be his final public appearance, at Birdland, the New York club named in his honor. Seven days later, he was dead at age 35.

Bop Goes Mainstream

The drug- and alcohol-related deaths of Parker and Powell were hardly unusual among jazz musicians, but the public chalked it up more specifically to the intensity of bebop. The music, they said, burned these guys out. And that just made them seem all the more romantic and appealing. The myth of the "cursed poet" has long been pervasive, and it went into high gear where the bebop generation was concerned. Appalling as were the deaths of Parker, Powell, and others, they lent the music an air of dangerous appeal.

At the same time, Dizzy Gillespie had been commissioned by the U.S. Department of State to tour the world with his music. Dizzy was honored—never mind that the State Department had also sent Louis Armstrong ("a plantation character," Gillespie had once called him) on tour as well. Even Thelonious Monk broke into the mainstream, his face appearing on the cover of *Time* magazine in 1964.

As it entered the mainstream, however, bop began to die. Gillespie, Monk, Art Blakey (father of "hard bop," which we'll explore in Chapter 18), and a few others stayed with the style, but by the late 1950s, the public sought musical "danger" no longer in jazz, but in emerging rock 'n' roll. Jazz took other paths, as we will see in the coming chapters.

Riffs

Parker himself saw no romance in his lifestyle. Talking with a friend, he rolled up his sleeve and pointed out each of the needle tracks on his arm:

This is my home, this is my portfolio, this is my Cadillac.

Beginning in the 1970s, there was much talk about a bop revival, and such musicians as tenor saxophonists Dexter Gordon (*Bouncin' with Dex*, Steeplechase), Johnny Griffin (*Bush Dance,* Galaxy), and altoist Phil Woods (*Bop Stew,* Concord Jazz) did begin playing in the style again. A group of avant gardists, including Anthony Braxton, Archie Shepp, and Pharoah Sanders (all of whom we'll meet in Chapter 19, also revisited bop in the '70s and '80s. More recently, the phenomenal trumpet virtuoso Wynton Marsalis (*Black Codes*, 1985) has recorded in the bop groove.

The conclusion is both true and ironic. Bebop, rebellious, innovative, angry, has now assumed the status of a classic jazz form—right alongside swing and other styles of "traditional" jazz.

The Least You Need to Know

- Bebop grew out of social as well as musical restlessness, a desire to achieve greater social and musical freedom than swing allowed.
- Bebop greatly accelerated the already propulsive beat of swing and further transformed jazz by using underlying harmonic structure, not melody, as the basis for rich, emotionally heated improvisation.
- The two principal bebop pioneers, both independently and together, were Charlie Parker and Dizzy Gillespie.
- For much of its heyday, bebop was an embattled music, under attack from the traditionalists, who the boppers called "moldy figs."
- Bud Powell and Thelonious Monk took bebop piano into two radically different directions.

Chapter 14

When Cool School Was in Session

In This Chapter

- An alternative to bop
- Evolution of the cool style: Lester Young, Kirby Sextet, and others
- Miles Davis: birth of the cool
- The keyboard turns cool, too
- "West Coast" jazz

The beboppers liked to portray themselves as locked in battle against the "moldy figs"—the jazz traditionalists. But if bebop was rebelling against trad jazz, another group of young musicians soon declared war on the revolution itself. In its way, it was a quiet war. And that was precisely the point.

Whereas bop was by definition bumptious and full of fire, the "cool jazz" or "cool school" movement that began in the late '40s was detached and understated. Cool jazz certainly wasn't devoid of emotion, and it presented its own formidable challenges to performance technique (just listen to early Miles Davis or Art Pepper), but it *was* different from bop, and, as this chapter suggests, it still offered unique musical pleasures.

Bopped Out

If you were a young, talented jazz musician in the late 1940s, you were keenly aware that bebop was *the* defining style of this particular moment in the music's history. That many old timers hated the music made it seem even more important. The importance of bop was a fact of musical life.

Not every young musician liked it, however. Bop was fine for a Dizzy Gillespie or a Charlie Parker, who had personalities suited to the hot, headlong music. But what if you didn't have such a personality? Was your choice either to play in a style you didn't really feel or simply put away your horn? Bop was important, and all the youngsters knew it, but what good was it if you just weren't into its steamroller intensity?

A significant minority of young performers, many of them based on the West Coast rather than the East, made the choice to dodge the bop steamroller.

Prelude to a Movement

Talk the Talk

A **nonet** is a nine-person musical ensemble.

Like bop, cool jazz seemed revolutionary when it began making itself heard late in the 1940s. However, the "cool" sound had been a part of jazz for some time before Miles Davis and his *nonet* (a nine-person ensemble) proclaimed the "birth of the cool" in 1950. Remember, jazz and jazz musicians are characteristically skilled at evading two things: the rent collector and easy categorization. As soon as somebody started to define jazz as "hot music," there were musicians who wanted to play it cool.

The New Sound of Lester Young, 1936

Lester Young (1909–59) was born in the Deep South, in Woodville, Mississippi, near New Orleans, but moved with his family to Minneapolis in 1920. There, his father, Willis Handy Young, formed a family band that acquired a legendary local reputation and began touring with carnivals and shows. Lester tried his hand at the violin, trumpet, and drums, before settling on the saxophone at about age 13. Following a dispute with his father in 1927 (when Willis proposed to take the band on a tour of the South, son Lester refused to come along), Young joined Art Bronson's Bostonians and took up the tenor saxophone.

That instrument was becoming popular in jazz, thanks to Coleman Hawkins, and numerous musicians who took up the instrument in the '20s and '30s emulated Hawkins's remarkably lush tone and generally *big* approach to the tenor. The Hawkins style became *the* way to play a tenor saxophone in a jazz ensemble.

But if Lester Young could stand up to his father, he could certainly buck the Hawkins style. Playing with Bennie Moten, King Oliver, Count Basie, and other bands of the late '20s and '30s (including his father's, to which he returned briefly in 1929), Young developed a unique sound—airy, where Hawkins was heavy; thin and clear, where Hawkins was lush; almost without vibrato, where Hawkins reveled in aggressive vibrato. If a Coleman Hawkins phrase is a sip from a brandy snifter, the same phrase from Young's horn is a taste of very dry champagne.

Take Five

There is no more striking one-CD collection of Lester Young than *Ultimate Lester Young—Selected by Wayne Shorter* on Verve. These recordings from the 1930s present "the Prez" at his most fleet. The tenor saxophonist Jerry Jerome provides this picture of the Lester Young sound—a "sound like a French horn. Sort of a deadish, unreedy horn sound. It was magnificent! And the lousiest tenor saxophone you'd ever want to look at. It was a Pan-American, with rubber bands, glue, chewing gum—and he just sat there blowing wonderful stuff." This "deadish, unreedy" sound would become the defining timbre of the cool school.

Young's light, precise, "cool" sound was revolutionary in the '30s, but by the '40s, when he formed his own band, it was as powerfully influential and pervasive as the sound of Hawkins had been a decade earlier. Younger saxophonists, such as Zoot Sims, Gerry Mulligan, Stan Getz, Paul Desmond, and Art Pepper, listened and learned from Young. Sims remarked, "Anyone who *doesn't* play like Lester Young is *wrong*."

Swingin' Cool: The Kirby Sextet

In 1937, during the height of the big band swing era, John Kirby (1908–52) took the helm of a small group at the Onyx Club in Manhattan. It became a sextet the next year, and from 1938 to 1942, it enjoyed a reputation as the nation's leading small ensemble in the swing style.

Kirby had, in fact, taken swing to a new place, leaving behind the fat sound and thick orchestration of the big bands for the equivalent of chamber swing. The arrangements (many of them by the group's trumpeter, Charlie Shavers) were exquisite, complex, but subdued, even quiet. The swing feel was unmistakable, but light and almost machine-like in its precision.

The Kirby Sextet is little remembered today, but like the tenor technique of Lester Young, it served as a model for those young musicians who could find a home neither among the boppers nor the figs.

The Arranger: Gil Evans

Like John Kirby, the name Claude Thornhill (1909–65) rings a bell only among hardcore jazz fans. He led a big band during the swing era, but his style is far removed from that of such contemporaries as Goodman and Basie. His band included instruments from the symphony orchestra, such as a French horn, tuba, and bass clarinet, and the sound he developed shunned the strong vibrato typical of the era, replacing the massed grouping of woodwinds and brass with a fuller, more subtle orchestral pallette—again suggestive of a classical orchestra.

Dig This

John Kirby: 1941–1943 is available on the Classics label and features the sextet at the peak of its popularity. Why isn't this remarkable group more widely remembered?

While Thornhill himself was a skilled and highly original arranger—educated at the Cincinnati Conservatory and the Curtis Institute—he also employed a shy young man from Canada (who had a habit of absent-mindedly munching radishes from a paper sack) named Gil Evans (1912–88). During 1946–47, Evans arranged such bop classics as "Yardbird Suite," "Donna Lee," and "Anthropology" for the Thornhill orchestra, transforming them into cool-toned, richly textured pieces, which created a mild sensation among jazz fans and greatly impressed Thornhill band members Lee Konitz, alto saxophone, and Gerry Mulligan, baritone saxophone—both of whom would soon figure as prominent members of the cool school.

Dig This

It's not hard to be the first on your block to own a Claude Thornhill album. The best collection, on the Affinity label, is called *Tapestries,* featuring a decade of music, from 1937 to 1947.

In Walks Miles

Evans's work for Thornhill impressed another young musician. In 1944, Miles Davis (1926–96) left his family's home in East St. Louis, Illinois, where his father was a prosperous dental surgeon, to come to New York, ostensibly to enroll in the Juilliard School of Music. Davis had made a local name for himself as a trumpeter, and he had no trouble passing his audition for admission to Juilliard. But young Davis was not just dedicated to music, he was committed to bebop.

"I spent my first week in New York looking for Bird and Dizzy," he wrote in his autobiography, and he soon attached himself to Parker, who, although only a half-dozen years older, treated him like a son, encouraging him, and introducing him to fellow boppers. It wasn't long before Davis dropped out of Juilliard and enrolled in Minton's, The Three Deuces, the Spotlite, and the other New York bop clubs.

Miles Davis at Birdland in October 1956.
Photo by "Popsie" Randolph.
Image from the Frank Driggs Collection.

Davis and Parker

Young Miles Davis had an uphill struggle among the geniuses of bop. Frankly, they played rings around him. But Charlie Parker recognized something in the 19-year-old trumpeter and invited him to participate in a November 1945 recording date, and the next month, when Parker left New York for Los Angeles, Davis followed. Parker, however, soon found himself committed to the state hospital at Camarillo, and Davis toured with Billy Eckstine and then returned to New York, to play in Dizzy Gillespie's band.

After Parker returned to New York, he organized a quintet in 1947, which included Davis as well as drummer Max Roach, bassist Tommy Potter, and pianist Duke Jordan. During 1947–48, Miles Davis, under Parker's wing, matured as a bop trumpeter.

Birth of the Cool

In some ways, Davis had grown beyond Parker. By the close of 1948, Davis had tired of trembling in the shadow cast by Bird's erratic, self-destructive behavior. He turned now to Gil Evans, a man as stable as Parker was unbalanced. With such musicians as Gerry Mulligan (baritone saxophone), Lee Konitz (alto), John Lewis (piano), and Max Roach (drums), Davis crowded into Evans's tiny basement apartment on Manhattan's 55th Street to jam.

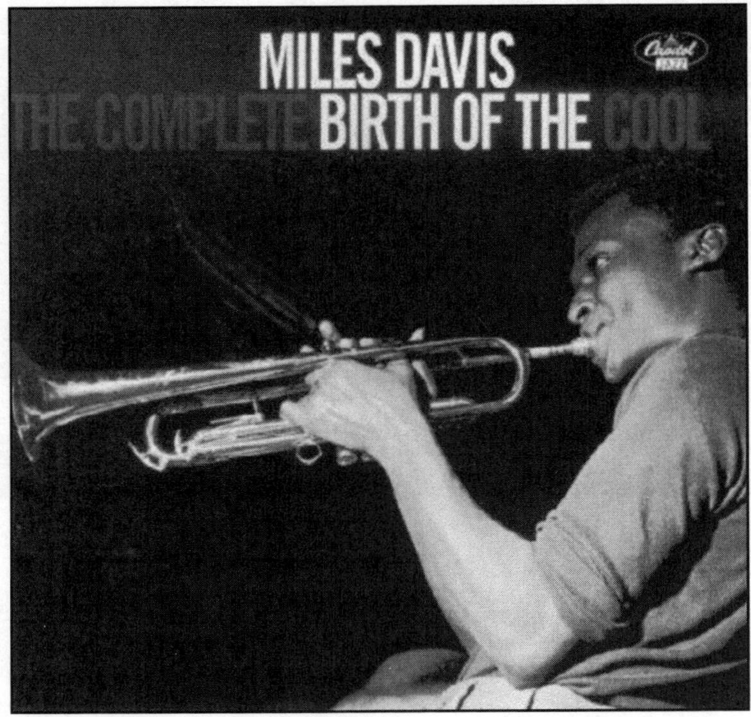

Album art for the CD reissue of Miles Davis's landmark The Complete Birth of the Cool. *Image from Capitol Jazz.*

The result was a cooler alternative to bop. The so-called "cool school" that held its first sessions in Evans's apartment grew from a feeling that bop had run its course and was self-destructing, as evidenced by the downward spiral of Charlie Parker. Davis, the musicians who now gathered about him, and Evans craved a certain discipline and emotional distance. Cool jazz was still technically demanding, but it didn't require the players to walk through the flames the way bop did.

In 1948, Davis formed a nonet—a nine-piece ensemble—that included a French horn and a tuba, but no tenor saxophone. Working with Evans, Davis fashioned the nonet into an instrument capable of great beauty, a sound very different from bop or from swing. "I wanted the instruments to sound like human voices," Davis said. "I looked at the group like it was a choir."

Riffs

The music sounds more like Maurice Ravel than it does like jazz. I, who do not listen to jazz recordings day in and day out, find this music charming and exciting . . .. If Miles Davis were an established "classical" composer, his work would rank high among that of his contemporary colleagues. But it is not really jazz.

—Winthrop Sargent, *classical* reviewer for the *New York Times,* reviewing the nonet.

Davis's work with the nonet was soon dubbed the "Birth of the Cool" and is available on a Capitol CD—called *The Birth of the Cool*—containing recordings from 1949–50. This is a must-have item for all serious jazz fans. Whether you call it jazz or modern classical music hardly matters. The nonet work is simply beautiful, and it is an example of Davis's incredible versatility. He started out in bop, then established the cool sound, and (as we'll see in Chapters 18 and 20) went on to become a hard bop and fusion pioneer.

Cooler and Cooler: Enter the Piano

During the swing era, the piano was generally subordinate to the big band. Masters such as Basie and Ellington used it with grace and power, but more as an ornament than a lead instrument. Bebop pianists like Powell and, in a radically different way, Monk, reclaimed the piano as a central instrument of jazz. In the hands of cool-school pianists, the instrument was used more introspectively and lyrically.

Dig This

The Modern Jazz Quartet, which formed in 1951–52, is often cited with the Davis nonet as an early example of cool jazz; however, it is probably more useful to consider it as a "third stream" phenomenon—that is, a blend of jazz and classical style. For this reason, MJQ is discussed in Chapter 16.

A number of pianists, most notably Nat King Cole, George Shearing, Oscar Peterson, and Erroll Garner, straddled the cool and the mainstream sensibilities. They will be treated in Chapter 15. But three pianists stand out as star students of the cool school: Lennie Tristano, Dave Brubeck, and Bill Evans.

Real Square

Don't make the mistake of thinking that "cool" means unemotional. By the 1950s, Davis's intensity commanded absolute attention. Drummer Jimmy Cobb recalls that a fire broke out at the Sutherland Hotel, where the Miles Davis Quintet was playing. "The club was packed! And the firemen were outside the door putting out the fire, and *nobody left!* Smoke was all in the joint and nobody left. . .. Yeah, Miles was very popular."

Dig This

Until recently, much Tristano had yet to be be reissued on CD. *Wow*, on the Jazz label, is a terrific live recording from 1950, and also now available are *The Complete Atlantic Recordings of Lennie Tristano, Lee Konitz and Wayne Marsh* (six CDs, on Mosaic), and *Lennie Tristano and Wayne Marsh: Intuition* (Capitol Jazz).

Who Is Lennie Tristano?

Lennie Tristano (1919–78) was born in Chicago at the height of the influenza pandemic that engulfed the globe in the wake of World War I. The flu nearly killed him before his first birthday; instead, it left him blind. Fortunately for Tristano, his mother was a pianist and opera singer, and she taught the boy music. He continued his studies at a school for the blind and at the American Conservatory in Chicago. By 1945, he was teaching jazz to the likes of Lee Konitz (who would become a leading alto saxophonist of the cool school) and Bill Russo (a major "third stream" composer, as we will see in Chapter 16). Tenor saxophonist Warne Marsh became a pupil in 1948, and by the early '50s, it is safe to say that Tristano had attracted a kind of cult following among musicians and in-the-know jazz fans.

With Tristano and guitarist Billy Bauer, Konitz and Marsh were the stars of 1949 sextet recordings, which included "Wow" and "Crosscurrent," two cool-school monuments, but also the free-form collective improvisations "Intuition" and "Digression"—which anticipated so-called free jazz (see Chapter 19) by at least a decade.

In his ensemble as well as piano work, Tristano sought to combine a detached spontaneity with a swing-era rhythmic feel. This is cool jazz at its most intensely lyrical, and while it took some years for a broader audience to appreciate Tristano's music, he is now recognized as one of the most significant figures in modern jazz.

Lennie Tristano was a shy man, who became increasingly interested in teaching and decreasingly concerned with performance. While his music is not difficult to listen to—quite the contrary—it is not readily classifiable. For these reasons, it's not surprising that Tristano never had a large following.

The Unlikely Popularity of Dave Brubeck

Something of the same might have been expected from Dave Brubeck (1920–), who studied cello and piano as a boy, worked as a pianist with local West Coast jazz groups from 1933 until he studied music at the College of the Pacific during 1941–42 in Fresno, California. There he formed a 12-piece orchestra and went on to study composition at Mills College in Oakland, where he was a student of the French modern classical composer Darius Milhaud.

Brubeck felt a deep musical connection with the playfully melodic Milhaud, and even named one of his sons Darius. After serving in the army, however, Brubeck resumed his composition studies not with the tuneful Milhaud, but with Arnold Schoenberg, the controversial inventor of the difficult and decidedly unmelodic 12-tone system of composition. This was the limit of Brubeck's modernism; he discovered that he didn't like Schoenberg or his music.

Real Square

If you're looking for the lyrical Tristano, choose recordings from the '40s and early '50s—if you can find them. Beginning in 1955 and into the 1960s (he retired from performance in 1968), Tristano increasingly abandons the lyrical approach for an agitated modern sound. Late Tristano is interesting music, but it's not the "cool school" material that brought him cult status.

Dave Brubeck, 1954. Image from the Library of Congress Prints and Photographs Division, Washington, D.C.

During this postwar period, Brubeck launched a series of innovative small groups, including an octet (1946), a trio (1949), and a long-lived quartet (1951–67). Indeed, the Dave Brubeck Quartet epitomized what came to be called "West Coast jazz"—a branch

Dig This

Brubeck is an influential giant of jazz. *Time Signatures: A Career Retrospective* is a 4-CD set from Columbia spanning 1946 to 1991. If you're looking for a single CD, *Jazz Goes to College*, a Columbia CD reissue of material from 1954, is a classic, as is the later (1959) *Time Out* (Columbia).

of the cool school characterized by clarity of sonic textures, lightness of touch, and a buoyant, lilting quality. The latter was as much a product of the quartet's great saxophonist, Paul Desmond, as it was of Brubeck's talents as composer, arranger, and pianist.

Bouyant and lilting, but also highly cerebral. For many jazz musicians, Brubeck's music seemed all head and no heart—the antithesis of jazz. Yet Brubeck attracted a large and respectful public. Indeed, for many casual jazz listeners of the 1950s and early 1960s, Brubeck was *the* sound of so-called "progressive jazz." It was deemed cool to listen to him, and he was especially popular among college students. For a time, the Dave Brubeck Quartet was probably the best-known combo in the world, and works like "Take Five" were genuine popular hits (still heard a lot today).

Paul Desmond, 1954. Image from the Library of Congress Prints and Photographs Division, Washington, D.C.

Take Five

Brubeck was always an innovator, never content to rest on his laurels. By the 1960s, he had begun exploring unusual meters, such as 5/4 time. Contemporary classical composers had been doing this for years, but jazz, for all its freedom and boldness of rhythmic invention, was still tied to 4/4 time. Brubeck, a white musician, claimed that he was probing jazz's African roots. Four-quarter time was a European invention, Brubeck explained, whereas the rhythms of African music are far more fluid and complex. Ironically, however, most fellow jazz musicians saw these forays into exotic meters as more suited to modern classical music than to jazz.

Sunday at the Village Vanguard with Bill Evans

Often, there seemed to be something slightly...well...*wrong* with this or that musician of the cool school: too intellectual, too European, too quirky, too little resembling jazz. Pianist Bill Evans (1929–80) managed to accomplish what most cool-school musicians ultimately could not do. A pianist of great lyrical intensity who voiced chords with a soft, sweet lushness, Evans had a winning way with a ballad. And that won over even the most casual jazz listener. Yet he also managed to absorb and develop the bop-piano idiom of Bud Powell, taking it to a level of increasing refinement, so that it sounded renewed, fresh. This won over the hardcore jazz fans as well as the musicians. Indeed, Evans became the most influential modern jazz pianist after Bud Powell. Such contemporary piano masters as Chick Corea and Keith Jarrett, whom you'll meet in Chapters 19 and 20, were powerfully influenced by Evans.

After recording with his own group in 1956, Evans recorded with bassist and composer Charles Mingus (see Chapter 19) and then, in 1958, joined Miles Davis. Davis's 1959 album, *Kind of Blue*, became a landmark in cool jazz largely because of Evans's improvisation, which was based not on traditional Western scales but on modes, the scales on which much non-Western ethnic music is based. Thus *modal jazz* became a part of the cool jazz vocabulary, as well as very much a part of Miles Davis's aesthetic.

Talk the Talk

In **modal jazz**, modal scales (such as those that characterize non-Western music) dictate melodic and harmonic content. Modal jazz, popular in the 1950s, provided an alternative to jazz built on conventional scales.

Evans took the cool approach even further in June 1961, with his live recordings from New York's great jazz club, the Village Vanguard. These trio sessions, with bassist Scott LaFaro and drummer Paul Motian, set an early standard for free jazz improvisation—a standard all but impossible for others to attain, since the members of the trio seemed to communicate by mental telepathy. The sessions are nothing less than uncanny.

Dig This

Sunday at the Village Vanguard and *Waltz for Debby* are great Bill Evans albums from 1961, now available on the Original Jazz Classics label.

Intimate, passionate, dreamy, but also capable of really swinging when the need arose, Bill Evans managed to please everyone. Five of his albums won Grammy awards, including the innovative *Conversations with Myself* (1963, still available from Verve), an early experiment in overdubbing, on which Evans plays duets with himself, Tragically, while Evans enjoyed a degree of professional and public success all too rare among jazz musicians, he also shared the all too common affliction of many of his colleagues. Chronic drug addiction ended the life and career of Bill Evans in 1980. He was 51 years old.

Whispering: Gerry Mulligan and Chet Baker

Gerald Joseph Mulligan (1927–96), born on Long Island, New York, grew up in Philadelphia. As a young man, he played various instruments before ultimately settling on the baritone saxophone. It was a choice as impressive as it was challenging. Mulligan developed an understated, delicate approach to the instrument, which perfectly suited cool jazz. After leaving high school in 1944, Mulligan moved to New York to play with a number of bands, and in 1946 became an arranger for Gene Krupa's big band. Soon Mulligan was drawn to the activities of Gil Evans and Miles Davis, joining the Davis nonet in 1948 on the baritone saxophone. In 1951, he went the nonet one better by recording with his own "tentet."

Take Five

Although Mulligan is most closely identified with the West Coast branch of the "cool school," he was extraordinarily versatile and had no problem slipping in and out of any number of styles, including big band, bop, and—astoundingly—Dixieland (a genre in which he played clarinet). But he's best remembered for his cool jazz. The most important albums are *Gerry Mulligan in Paris,* volumes 1 and 2, from Vogue, and two volumes of *California Concerts,* from Pacific Jazz. Interesting, too, is Mulligan's *Re-Birth of the Cool,* a 1992 GRP release that revisits the Miles Davis material from 1950.

Mulligan moved to Los Angeles and, in 1952, met trumpeter Chet Baker, who became part of Mulligan's first quartet—an ensemble that would have been highly unusual because of the inclusion of baritone saxophone, but which created even more of a stir in the jazz world because it lacked the traditional piano. The quartet drew great acclaim, focusing much attention on West Coast jazz and propelling the careers of Mulligan as well as Baker.

Until his death in 1996, Mulligan continually developed and experimented as a musician, forming combos and bands that ranged in size from quartet, to quintet, to another tentet, and up to a 20-piece big band. His 13-piece Concert Jazz Band was one of the few big bands commercially active in the 1960s, and with it, Mulligan toured the world.

In Chet Baker (1929–88), Mulligan in the early 1950s found the perfect trumpeter to complement his own evolving cool style. If Mulligan was a master of musical understatement, Baker had taken an instrument the beboppers used to shout, wail, and scream, and transformed it into a means of whispering. Baker didn't so much play the trumpet as breathe into it, and the effect is one of uncanny intimacy and tenderness.

Chet Baker.
Image from Enja Records.

Nor was a limited *dynamic range* the only constraint Baker imposed on himself. Whereas bop trumpet virtuosos like Dizzy Gillespie delighted in stretching the range of their instrument, typically pushing it into a stratospherically high register, Baker usually limited himself to an octave or less. For this reason, some critics have downplayed his talent as a trumpeter. This is as unfair and misguided as criticizing a black-and-white Picasso drawing for not being a Rembrandt oil painting. Listen to *Mulligan-Baker,* 1951–65 recordings reissued by Prestige, and you will hear how these two quiet masters worked together.

Baker went on to a career independent of Mulligan, gaining recognition not only as the quintessential laid-back West Coast trumpeter, but as a singer of jazz-inflected

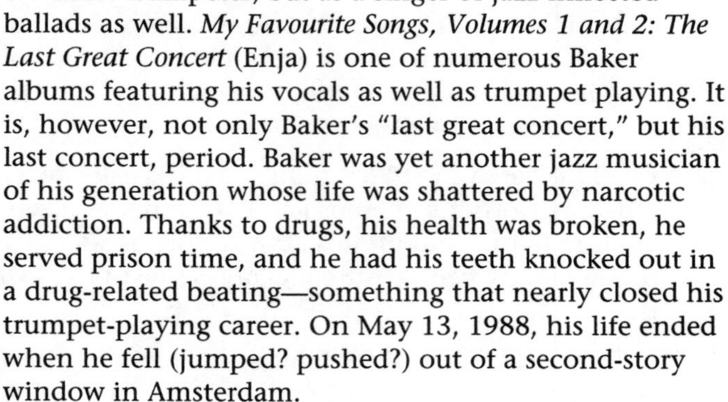

ballads as well. *My Favourite Songs, Volumes 1 and 2: The Last Great Concert* (Enja) is one of numerous Baker albums featuring his vocals as well as trumpet playing. It is, however, not only Baker's "last great concert," but his last concert, period. Baker was yet another jazz musician of his generation whose life was shattered by narcotic addiction. Thanks to drugs, his health was broken, he served prison time, and he had his teeth knocked out in a drug-related beating—something that nearly closed his trumpet-playing career. On May 13, 1988, his life ended when he fell (jumped? pushed?) out of a second-story window in Amsterdam.

Talk the Talk

The **dynamic range** of an instrument or piece of music is the span separating the softest from the loudest passages.

Dig This

Baker fans will want to buy *Chet Baker: The Pacific Jazz Years,* a four-CD set from Pacific Jazz spanning 1952–57.

Straight Time: The Art Pepper Saga

Miles Davis left the bop road of Charlie Parker in part because he believed it led to personal destruction. But Davis—as well as Evans, Baker, and other cool-school musicians—suffered drug-related problems nevertheless. This was also true of a young man named Art Pepper (1925–82), whose 1979 autobiography, *Straight Life: The Story of Art Pepper,* is both harrowing and eloquent, a testament that might apply to any number of jazz musicians.

A West Coast musician who was actually born in L.A., Pepper was introduced to drink and drugs (in the form of marijuana) by his free-spirited mother. He began his career as an alto saxophonist in the bands of Benny Carter and Stan Kenton. In Kenton, Pepper found a strong, protective, and stern father figure, who encouraged him to develop his extraordinary technical prowess and who did his best to keep him off heroin, the drug of choice for jazz musicians. But by the early 1950s, Art Pepper was an addict, and the rest of his career and life were defined and limited by this addiction.

Throughout the 1950s, however, despite the drugs, Pepper was at the height of his form. He fused the technical virtuosity of bop—music played at high velocity—with the light touch and precision of the cool school. The result is hard-swinging jazz that takes wing on seemingly effortless virtuoso flights. *The Artistry of Pepper,* a Pacific Jazz CD featuring recordings from 1956–57, and *Art Pepper Meets the Rhythm Section,* a 1957 date reissued by Original Jazz Classics, preserve these wonderful moments in West Coast jazz history. They are refreshing and astounding albums.

Smack Up, from 1960, is another great Pepper album (reissued on CD by Original Jazz Classics), and its title says more than Pepper probably intended. During the '60s, the altoist's addiction resulted in long prison sentences, which, musically, wiped out for him almost this entire decade.

But the Art Pepper story doesn't end in jail. Beginning in 1969, he embarked on a long struggle toward recovery, and by the mid-1970s besides performing again, he had reinvented himself not as a cool-school horn player, but as hard-driving practitioner of of post-Coltrane hard bop verging on free jazz (Chapter 19). Listen to *Straight Life*, a 1979 album reissued on CD by Original Jazz Classics, to hear where Pepper went.

Despite his recovery, years of abuse had irreversibly damaged Pepper's liver, and he died, prematurely but back on top, at age 57.

Legacy of the Cool

Cool jazz died out as a distinct style by the early 1960s. Many cool-school musicians went into the mainstream or third stream or into free jazz. But the cool style bequeathed to jazz more than a few great recordings. It also revived and revised the improvised *counterpoint* that had been so exciting in early swing.

Improvising counterpoint requires great skill, and cool jazz did indeed demand a new level of control, discipline, and dexterity from musicians. In this way, the cool school really was a *school*, fostering a renewed excellence among jazz performers, which enabled them to embark, with greater confidence and ability, on new musical excursions. But the cool school was also the last dominant jazz style. From the 1960s on, the universe of jazz was composed of a multiplicity of styles, interests, and approaches.

Talk the Talk

Counterpoint is music in which two or more melodic lines are combined in a harmonic relationship that also retains the individuality of each melodic line.

The Least You Need to Know

- The cool school began as an alternative to bop, on the one hand, and traditional jazz, on the other.
- "Cool" does not mean passionless or easy; however, cool jazz is characterized by greater detachment and control than bebop.
- While such musicians as Lester Young laid the groundwork for the cool style, it was Miles Davis who ushered it in with his nonet sessions in 1949–50.
- Many of the cool-school musicians were based on the West Coast rather than on the East Coast, which remained a bastion of bebop.

Part 4
The Elements of Style

Not all jazz musicians embraced bebop or the cool school by the 1950s. Musicians who didn't want to jump into what they considered the "new music," made their way along the so-called mainstream, essentially continuing the swing tradition, but often applying it to new tunes. There was yet another "stream" flowing by the mid-1950s, a "third stream," which combined elements of jazz (especially improvisation) with elements of classical music.

While it is impossible to overstate the importance of African-American musical traditions in jazz, it is all too easy to overlook the Latin influence in the music. While what Jelly Roll Morton called the "Spanish tinge" was present in jazz from it earliest days, Latin jazz came into its own beginning in the 1940s as Cubana Bop. By the early '60s, the samba-like bossa nova beat was the sensual rhythm of a new jazz sound.

Before the end of the '50s, a group of younger musicians were looking for a more assertive and popular jazz sound that would draw on jazz traditions but also embrace "soul," rhythm and blues, and other aspects of black popular music. The result was hard bop—and some of the most intense and exciting jazz yet created.

Chapter 15

Diving into the Mainstream

In This Chapter

- What is mainstream?
- Mainstream piano
- Big band survivors
- The New Orleans tradition lives on
- The vocal scene

Let's have a show of hands of all those who consider themselves average or mainstream.

I'm waiting....

And I'll probably have to wait a long time, since few of us want to be identified as "average" or "mainstream." The connotation of such words is mediocre, unimaginative, safe, dull, and something our parents did, liked, or believed in.

Who wants *that*?

Well, you don't have to be ashamed of enjoying so-called "mainstream" jazz. The best of it—and that's what we'll discuss here—is extraordinarily good music. It's just that the mainstream is nowhere near the cutting edge. If musical adventure is important to you, swim elsewhere. If, however, you just want a good time (and don't care a lot about labels), dive on in. The music's fine.

On the Piano

The piano has been the instrument of choice for some of the most advanced jazz. For example, as we saw in Chapter 10, pianist Art Tatum transformed the stride style, making possible the supercharged sound of bebop great Bud Powell. And it was cool school pianist Bill Evans (Chapter 13) who introduced the concept of modal jazz, a major influence in the '60s. Because the piano is not just a melody instrument, but can play as many notes simultaneously as available fingers and thumbs permit, the piano lends itself to highly advanced, highly individual jazz expressions.

But the piano is also a *familiar* instrument, at home in the nightclub and the living room as well as the concert hall. Because of its expressive possibilities and universal familiarity, the piano has also been a popular vehicle for mainstream jazz.

Nat King Cole

The career of Nat King Cole ended prematurely with his death from lung cancer in 1965 at age 47. Americans—and much of the world—mourned the passing of great popular ballad singer. A much smaller group were saddened by the death of a very exciting jazz pianist, who had been influenced by Earl "Fatha" Hines and who in turn influenced such piano greats as Oscar Peterson.

Take Five

Earl Hines (1905–83) was universally dubbed "Fatha" in tribute to the great influence he exerted on jazz pianists beginning in the 1920s. He developed a uniquely brassy piano style, improvising melodic lines with his right hand phrased like those of a trumpeter (indeed, the trumpet was his first instrument). This style, coupled with wide octave voicings, bold tremolos, and an aggressive attack, has prompted jazz historians to call Hines the first modern jazz pianist.

Hines was also a bandleader during the 1930s and 1940s and, in this sense, a "fatha" to such greats as Charlie Parker, Dizzy Gillespie, Billy Eckstine, and Sarah Vaughan, all of whom got their start in Hines's band.

Hines is well represented on *Piano Man,* recordings from 1939–42, reissued on a Bluebird CD, and on *Tour de Force,* a 1972 solo piano session reissued on CD by Black Lion.

Cole was born in Montgomery, Alabama, in 1919 and grew up in Chicago. His early musical training came with organ and choir work for church, and then he joined brother Eddie's Solid Swingers in 1936. He moved to Hollywood, where he organized a trio with guitarist Oscar Moore and bassist Wesley Prince. Soon, the Nat King Cole Trio became a fixture on the West Coast musical scene. Even in his piano-playing days, Cole did some vocals. His 1940 recording of "Sweet Lorraine" was his first big hit. A long-lived legend has it that Nat's singing career began when a drunk insisted he sing "Sweet Lorraine."

Cole and the trio were essentially swing musicians, but with a light, propulsive touch that no bebopper could criticize as savoring of moldy figs. This is not profound music, but it's very exciting. *Jazz Encounters*, recordings from 1945–50, is a terrific Blue Note CD. If you want more, the four-CD *Complete Early Transcriptions* (1938–41) is available from Jazz Classics. Laserlight's five-CD *The Trio Recordings*, spanning 1940–56, is usually budget priced.

Riffs

This particular customer kept insisting on a certain song, and I told him I didn't know that one but I would sing..."Sweet Lorraine."

—Nat King Cole

The trio was tipped 15 cents—a nickel apiece—and the customer requested a second tune. Again, Nat didn't know it, but asked, "Is there something else you would like?"

"Yes," the customer said, "I would like my 15 cents back."

—Maria Cole

Nat King Cole singing at the Paramount Theater, New York, January 20, 1949.
Photo by "Popsie" Randolph.
Image from the Frank Driggs Collection.

Oscar Peterson

Canadian-born Oscar Peterson (1925–) is a prodigious talent who has probably recorded more music than any other pianist in jazz history. This has its downside as well as its up; for a lot of those recordings start to sound the same. However, when you've got a style inspired by Nat King Cole and a technique that comes close to Art Tatum's, that's not all bad.

The Oscar Peterson Trio, 1960. Ed Thigpen is on drums, Ray Brown on bass.
Image from the Frank Driggs Collection.

Dig This

Peterson suffered a massive stroke in 1993 but dedicated himself to two years of intensive physical therapy and returned to performance. *The More I See You*, released in 1995 by Telarc, is a brilliant session that includes an 87-year-old Clark Terry on flugelhorn, a 90-year-old Doc Cheatham on trumpet, and a youthful 68-year-old Ray Brown on bass. If the jazz lifestyle claimed its share of young men, it can also, apparently, confer near-eternal youth.

Through much of the 1950s and 1960s, the piano of Oscar Peterson was the way many casual fans believed jazz *should* sound. Combining elements of swing as well as bop, but declaring allegiance to neither style, Peterson's piano is a case study in the mainstream sound. And anyone who is this popular for so long—Peterson's still going strong—is bound to draw criticism. Some have called him superficial and flashy. Others complain that he lacks soul. And still others point out that he visits and revisits the standard tunes more than a few times too often.

The fact is, while some of this criticism is probably justified at least some of the time, it comes from critics and not musicians. Peterson has played with musicians of every stripe: from Billie Holiday to Lester Young to Roy Eldridge to Dizzy Gillespie to Count Basie to Louis Armstrong. No complaints from them.

You will probably enjoy Peterson most in a trio setting. *At the Stratford Shakespearian Festival*, recorded live on August 8, 1956, is a masterpiece reissued by Verve on

CD. From the 1960s, you shouldn't miss *Oscar Peterson Trio + One*, another Verve CD reissue. (Trumpeter Clark Terry is the "one.")

Take Five

Oscar Peterson's sidemen frequently played practical jokes on the pianist. Before a 1953 performance in Japan, bassist Ray Brown went to a Pachinko parlor and copped a handful of the little steel balls that are used in this popular Japanese game. He put the balls in Peterson's piano. At the first chords, the piano twanged and sizzled. While still playing with one hand, Peterson reached in with his other, pulled the balls out one by one, and, one by one, threw them at Brown's bass. All kept playing.

George Shearing

Shearing was born blind in London in 1919 and received only three years of formal musical training at the Linden Lodge School For the Blind, which he attended between the ages of 12 and 16. Most of his musical education came from listening to the recordings of Earl Hines, Fats Waller, Teddy Wilson, and Art Tatum. But it was as if the music simply flowed into him, because when he immigrated to the United States in 1947, he was a thoroughly accomplished jazz pianist.

Shearing was strongly attracted to the bop idiom, but soon developed his own unique "Shearing sound." This can be heard on a Savoy LP (watch for its reissue on CD) titled *So Rare*. The characteristic Shearing sound is built on a block-chord style sometimes called "locked hands." It was in part inspired by the distinctive sound of the saxophone section of the Glenn Miller band.

Dig This

The Swingin's Mutual, a Capitol CD reissue of music from 1960–61, is Shearing (with the George Shearing Quintet) at his best.

Erroll Garner

Erroll Garner (1921–77) is the most important of all the mainstream pianists because he managed so thoroughly to combine idiosyncratic creativity (a sound all his own)

Dig This

Garner was a composer as well as pianist. His biggest hit was the haunting "Misty," the tune that Clint Eastwood used as the centerpiece of his 1971 film *Play Misty For Me,* a thriller about a jazz DJ and a psychotic female admirer that anticipates *Fatal Attraction* by two decades. If you're a jazz fan (or a Clint Eastwood fan), go to the video store and rent the movie.

with tremendous popular appeal. In contrast to the other pianists we've just discussed, Garner was entirely self-taught and, indeed, never learned how to read music. He perfected a virtuoso style and technique that rhythmically played the left hand against the right. Garner would introduce the beat with his left hand, only to play chords just behind the beat with his right. Add to this Garner's lyrical sense of ornamentation plus his delightful free-form introductions (musical essays in themselves), and the result is a sound unlike that of any other jazz pianist. Yet it never strikes one as quirky or odd. It's pretty. There's just no other word for it.

The must-have Erroll Garner recording is *Concert by the Sea,* from 1955 and reissued on CD by Columbia, featuring Garner and his trio (Eddie Calhoun on bass and Denzil Best on drums). Play this for so-called jazz experts who try to warn you away from mainstream music.

Dinosaurs

"Mainstream" seems like a pretty generic label, but, actually, it has an inventor. The term was coined by jazz critic Stanley Dance specifically to describe the work of trumpeter Buck Clayton in the 1950s. Clayton (1911–91) was best known as a major soloist in the Count Basie band during the 1930s and 1940s (before joining Basie, he had led a band based in China!), but went on the 1950s to organize a series of recordings for Columbia Records collectively titled Jam Sessions. These have been reissued as a three-CD set by Mosaic, and if your knee-jerk response to the word "mainstream" is a yawn, these recordings will rewire your reflexes. Yes, it's swing music in an era dominated by bop and the cool school. No, it's hardly cutting edge. But the music of these "dinosaurs" is alive—and kicking!

The Ellington Band

Artistically, Duke Ellington, vintage 1950s, was as exciting as ever. His orchestra still boasted an extraordinary line-up of soloists, including trumpeters Clark Terry, Ray Nance, Cat Anderson, and Willie Cook; trombonists Buster Cooper and Britt Woodman; and the reed section that had played with him for more than a decade, among them Johnny Hodges (after an absence in the early '50s) on alto saxophone and Paul Gonsalves on tenor. Commercially, however, the 1950s were something of a slump period for Ellington, who nevertheless survived when so many other big bands folded. *The Complete Capitol Recordings of Duke Ellington,* a 5-CD Mosaic set, covers the period from 1953 to 1955 and contains much that even Ellington's fans are not familiar with.

Duke Ellington and his orchestra were big enough to survive the general postwar demise of the big bands. He is pictured here in the 1950s, in a publicity shot for one of his Carnegie Hall concerts. Image from Lawrence Cohn.

The 1960s saw Ellington composing several works of sacred and symphonic music—hardly "mainstream" jazz. More definitely mainstream, however, are the only recordings Duke made with Louis Armstrong, reissued on a great two-CD set from Roulette misleadingly titled *The Duke Ellington-Louis Armstrong Years*. (This recording date spanned a mere two days in 1961.)

Dig This

The 1960s saw Ellington record with free-jazz icon John Coltrane (see chapters 18 and 19) to produce *Duke Ellington and John Coltrane* (MCA). *The Far East Suite*, available on a Bluebird CD, one of 25 jazz suites Ellington wrote, is in many ways the most attractive—although less well known than *Black, Brown and Beige*, a masterpiece from 1943, a highlight of the two-CD *Carnegie Hall Concerts (January 1943)* on Prestige.

Gentle Ben

One of the Ellington band's greatest alumni was tenor saxophonist Ben Webster (1909–73)—with Coleman Hawkins (his mentor) and Lester Young, one of the "big three" jazz tenormen. Webster could growl out musical stomps like nobody else, but it was his gentle, lyrical warmth for which he is best remembered. Listen to *Meet You at the Fair*, an Impulse! CD reissue of 1964 sides, and the earlier (1957) *Soulville* (Verve), in which Webster is showcased with the wonderful Oscar Peterson Trio.

Basie Drives On

If the '50s were a bleak period for big bands, you'd never know it from Count Basie. In 1952, while other swing organizations were folding left and right, Basie formed what he nicknamed his "New Testament" band (the swing-era group was the "Old Testament") and enjoyed great popularity and continued artistic excellence. Among Basie's

Dig This

The Discovery label issued two LPs featuring the Third Herd (*Third Herd*, volumes 1 and 2), which are widely available in secondhand record stores. For those who lack a turntable, music from late in the Second Herd period is available on a superb Capitol CD: *Keeper of the Flame: Complete Capitol Recordings* (1948–49).

biggest hits during the '50s was *Count Basie Swings, Joe Williams Sings*, available on CD from Verve. Also from Verve, the instrumental *April in Paris*, which includes the title cut that Basie fans of the mid-1950s couldn't get enough of. Basie offers stylish, ultra-cool music in a decade that, often, was neither stylish nor cool.

Herman's Third Herd

Woody Herman was another swing-era survivor, who kept reinventing his bands to suit the times. His First Herd, active in the early '40s, was influenced by Duke Ellington; his Second Herd, from the late '40s, verged on the cool school; and his Third Herd formed in the '50s, retreated a bit into more conservative, danceable music with a boppish accent.

Traps, the Drum Wonder

Bernard—Buddy—Rich made his stage debut in his parent's vaudeville act in 1919, two years after he had been born in New York. He was tap dancing and playing drums on Broadway by four (as "Traps, the Drum Wonder"), was touring nationally and internationally by six, and, at the ripe old age of 11, was leading his own band.

During the swing years, Rich was a highly sought-after drummer, whose sheer velocity and phenomenal dexterity prompted audiences and critics to acclaim Rich as the world's greatest drummer. No one agreed with this appraisal more than Rich himself, who not only brimmed with self-confidence, but mercilessly pushed himself as well as those with whom he worked. He was notorious for hiring sidemen, chewing them up, then spitting them out—often in front of an audience.

During the 1930s and early 1940s, Rich played with the swing bands of Joe Marsala. Bunny Berigan, Harry James, Artie Shaw, Benny Carter, and Tommy Dorsey before joining the Marine Corps during part of World War II. Returning to the Dorsey organization after the war, he played with Dorsey and James, as well as others through the 1950s and early 1960s.

Rich had a powerful personality and an acid sense of humor, which appealed to a much wider public than those who regularly listened to jazz. He packed enough star power to buck the prevailing trend and start a highly successful big band in 1966 in an era when most bands had long since folded. He led this organization until his death in 1987.

You can hear Rich at his hard-driving best on albums he made with his big band during the late 1960s and early 1970s: *Mercy, Mercy* (World Pacific, 1968), *Rich in London* (RCA, 1971), and *Time Being* (Bluebird, 1972).

New Orleans and Dixieland Revivals

While bandleaders like Ellington and Basie, as well as Harry James, Benny Goodman, and Buddy Rich, continued to perform swing-oriented music profitably (if sometimes repetitively) through the 1950s, '60s, and even '70s, the New Orleans and Dixieland music that predated swing never died.

The Crash of '29

Black Tuesday: October 29, 1929. The stock market tumbled, and most of the world descended into an economic depression that, among many other things, made much of the headlong, carefree jazz of the preceding decade seem suddenly irrelevant. Classic jazz, founded on the New Orleans and Dixieland sound, rapidly gave way to the more sophisticated rhythms and arrangements of the swing era.

Feetwarmers

But not everyone turned their backs on the New Orleans tradition. In 1932, the great New Orleans soprano saxophonist and clarinetist Sidney Bechet formed the New Orleans Feetwarmers, a sextet that kept the New Orleans tradition very much alive. The rich Bechet sound, while it smacks of traditional jazz, is also timeless. It never really sounds old fashioned. *The Chronological Sidney Bechet, 1923–36*, a Classics CD, features the Feetwarmers as well as other work.

Dig This

Bechet continued to record well into the 1950s, and it is always a pleasure to hear him play. Bechet was greatly admired in France. Vogue, a French import label, has reissued *Le Legende de Sidney Bechet* (recordings from 1949–58) and *Parisian Encounter* (from 1958), both outstanding sessions.

Manone, Prima, Waller

Bechet preserved and perpetuated a style of New Orleans jazz that is both lyrical and earthy. Wingy Manone and Louis Prima, white musicians, kept the Dixieland tradition (New Orleans jazz as interpreted by white musicians) alive in the '30s.

Joseph Matthews Manone (1900–82) acquired his nickname, Wingy, when, as a 10-year-old in New Orleans, he was "winged" by a streetcar, losing his right arm. Despite this handicap, Manone became an exciting Dixieland trumpet player who punctuated his instrumentals with humorous, jive-style vocals.

Dig This

Manone is best represented on *Wingy Manone Collection*, vol. 4, which covers 1935–36, and is available on the Collector's Classics label.

Like Manone, Louis Prima (1911–78) was a white musician born in New Orleans and, also like

Real Square

Jazz provokes passionate opinions, and some self-styled jazz mavens may put you down for listening to Dixieland, which has long been considered uncool in some circles. Just remember that jazz is about inclusion; it's about the blending of many cultures and traditions. Don't be too quick to cut yourself off from anything the music offers.

Talk the Talk

The great swing tenorman Lester Young, notorious for inventing obscure equivalents for common words, always referred to the cops as "Bob Crosbys." Why? No one knows.

Manone, played in the Dixieland vein throughout the '30s and '40s. In contrast to Manone, however, he went on to success in swing (composing the swing standard "Sing, Sing, Sing") and ultimately in early rhythm and blues and rock 'n' roll. It is Prima in his pop R&B incarnation that is best represented on record, most notably the *Capitol Collectors Series,* which features sessions from 1956–62.

As practitioners of Dixieland, the white musicians Manone and Prima shared with the black pianist-bandleader-composer Fats Waller a sense of comedy that was always a part of the New Orleans musical tradition. While Waller was the most uproarious of the three—a great, moon-faced, pop-eyed balloon of a man—he also more fully transcended the buffoonery. Manone and Prima were ultimately superficial musicians—what you heard was all there was—whereas Waller was capable of making extraordinary, enduring music. Stash has issued a two-volume *Definitive Fats Waller. His Piano His Rhythm* is volume one, and *Hallelujah* is volume two. These recordings cover Waller's later years, 1935–1939, but at any time in his career, Fats Waller was a musical giant.

Bob Crosby and His Bobcats

It probably wasn't easy being Bing Crosby's younger brother, but Bob Crosby (1913–93) managed better than might be expected, fashioning his Bobcats into the hottest Dixieland band of the 1930s and early forties. The recording to get is *South Rampart Street Parade,* a GRP CD featuring sessions from 1936 to 1942.

Muggsy Spanier's Ragtime Band

Chicagoan Muggsy Spanier (1906–67) was not an innovative cornetist, but he had the moxie to play very spirited Dixieland, always verging on the cornball, but never quite crossing the line. *The Ragtime Band Sessions,* a Bluebird CD, reissues classic feel-good tunes from 1939. This is the ultimate retro party music.

Yerba Buena Breakthrough

The bands of Bob Crosby and Muggsy Spanier played Dixieland, to be sure, but it took Lu (short for Lucious) Watters (1911–), a California trumpet player, to bring back New Orleans-style jazz in the small-band tradition of King Oliver. When he organized the

Yerba Buena Jazz Band in 1939, most of the jazz world not only considered the likes of King Oliver and Jelly Roll Morton passé, they hardly lamented the loss. But Watters loved the music, and the group he assembled triggered a steady Dixieland revival that endures to this day. The Good Time Jazz label has issued *The Complete Good Time Jazz Recordings* on four CDs, and a live recording of a 1963 session, *Together Again*, is available on CD from Merry Makers.

Preservation Hall

While the Yerba Buena Jazz Band did more to promote the Dixieland revival, no traditional New Orleans group is better known than the Preservation Hall Jazz Band. The group was not organized by a musician, but by Larry Borenstein, a New Orleans art dealer who wanted traditional jazz played in his gallery on St. Peter Street. In 1961, Borenstein bought the building adjacent to his gallery and christened it Preservation Hall. A very popular attraction in New Orleans, the band also tours worldwide. *The Best of Preservation Hall Jazz Band* is a 1989 Columbia CD that presents a fine selection of traditional New Orleans jazz from this unique ensemble.

Giving Voice

If one were to identify a mainstream within the mainstream, especially during the 1950s, it would be vocal music. The important jazz singers of this era were also pop singers, and for many casual listeners, pop vocal was as close as they would ever come to hearing jazz.

Nat King Cole: Part Two

We've already met Nat King Cole as a fine swing pianist. At first, vocals were sideline for this quintessentially suave performer, but with the release of "Mona Lisa" in 1950, Cole became primarily a singer of pop ballads. *Big Band Cole*, a Blue Note CD offering releases from 1950 to 1961, features Cole's vocals set against accompaniments from Stan Kenton and Count Basie and should satisfy retro pop as well as jazz fans.

Talk the Talk

Tormé's distinctive suede-toned voice earned him the nickname "The Velvet Fog." It is a voice that remained consistent in quality and timbre from his early years through the end of his life, and it imparted to his vocals a timeless quality.

Mel Tormé

Born in 1925, Chicagoan Mel Tormé first sang in public at age three and, the next year, made his radio debut. By nine, he was acting in films. By fifteen, he had published his first composition. He sang with big bands, including one of Artie Shaw's ensembles, then made his way as a popular—but always jazz-oriented—solo singer from the 1940s on.

Mel Tormé, the "Velvet Fog."
Image from the Frank Driggs Collection.

Tormé was one of those rare musicians who enjoyed great success both in the jazz and pop worlds, and was also one of those even rarer musicians who managed to achieve popular success while never losing the respect of other jazz musicians. Tormé recorded extensively for the Concord Jazz label. One of his best releases is *Fujitsu-Concord Festival (1990)*.

Peggy Lee

The mainstream '50s were a good time for female jazz-oriented vocalists. Peggy Lee (1920–) got her start with Benny Goodman (1942–43), but really came into her own in the 1950s. She didn't possess a large voice, and she wasn't one of the great jazz improvisers, but her musical sense was highly atmospheric, and for that reason, she has appealed to jazz as well as popular audiences. *Black Coffee*, from MCA/Decca, is a bargain-priced two-CD set featuring jazz as well as pop.

Rosemary Clooney

Like Lee, Rosemary Clooney (1928–) is more a jazz-influenced pop singer than strictly a jazz vocalist; nevertheless, her work is greatly energized in a jazz setting, as is apparent on *Everything's Coming Up Rosie*, a 1977 release from Concord Jazz.

Catch-All

If "mainstream jazz" seems like a catch-all category, well, it is. Jazz has consistently invited critical commentary and, with it, efforts to group and classify the various styles. The music has just as stoutly resisted such pigeonholing. A good thing, too.

The Least You Need to Know

- "Mainstream" is a catch-all term covering jazz artists (principally of the 1950s) who chose not to rush to the music's cutting edge.
- While mainstream jazz was widespread, the piano and the voice were the mainstream instruments of choice.
- Only a handful of big bands survived into the 1950s (Ellington's and Basie's among them), but the decade also saw the birth of a lively movement to preserve New Orleans jazz traditions.
- Some "mainstream" musicians survived and prospered by developing powerful public presences. Ellington and Basie did this, as did Buddy Rich.
- A number of extraordinary jazz-oriented vocalists found happy homes in the 1950s mainstream, including Mel Tormé, Peggy Lee, and Rosemary Clooney.

Chapter 16

A Swim in the Third Stream: Jazz with a Classical Accent

In This Chapter

- Gershwin: first great bridge between classical and jazz realms
- Stravinsky and other key modern classical composers were inspired by jazz
- Classical composers who contributed to jazz
- "Primitive" roots of jazz and modern classical music
- Symphonic jazz and progressive jazz
- The Modern Jazz Quartet: jazz "chamber music"

In a 1957 lecture at Brandeis University, the American composer Gunther Schuller (1925–) coined the term "third stream" to describe a style of music that combines elements of modern Western "classical" or "art" music with ethnic or vernacular music. As it is used currently, "third stream" refers specifically to music that combines elements of contemporary classical music (one stream) with elements of jazz (another stream) to produce a *third* stream.

While the term may have been coined in the late 1950s, combinations of jazz and classical music have been around since the 1920s. At its best, this hybrid music is highly interesting, enriching both jazz as well as classical music traditions. But the course of third-stream music has never been tranquil and has provoked controversy among classical enthusiasts and jazz fans alike. This chapter explores some of the interaction between musical traditions.

Gershwin Gives a Lesson

The ambition of George Gershwin was restless and boundless. He wanted it all: success as a popular composer as well as the artistic accolades normally reserved for creators of so-called "serious" music. To a remarkable degree, he achieved his ambition, as we saw in Chapter 9, with such works as *Rhapsody in Blue* and *Porgy and Bess.*

But this did not satisfy Gershwin. He studied classical composition and orchestration, and as we also saw in Chapter 9, he even sought lessons from the modern French classicist Maurice Ravel—who ended up taking lessons from Gershwin.

Dig This

If you are interested in the "classical" Gerswhin, you'll find many CDs available. Three of the best are *Gershwin: 100th Birthday Celebration* (RCA), *Gershwin Centennial Edition: Complete Orchestral Collection* (Telarc), and *Gershwin: Piano Works* (Dag Achatz, pianist; on the BIS label).

Ravel, Milhaud, Stravinsky

There is no denying that many classical afficionados, even today, have looked down their noses at jazz. Many 20th-century composers (in contrast to afficionados), however, have welcomed jazz, finding in it a way to invigorate the classical idiom. It's no secret that 20th-century classical composers often find it difficult to engage an audience for dissonant and demanding works. Jazz offered the rhythmic and tonal complexities many modern classical musicians desired, without striking listeners as alien, remote, overly intellectual, or emotionally distant.

Maurice Ravel, whose Piano Concerto in G *was influenced by the jazzlike music of George Gershwin. Image from arttoday.com.*

A Frenchman Cool

In jazz, Maurice Ravel found the perfect foil to his own cool musical temperament—a temperament so remote and precise that Igor Stravinsky once compared him to "the most perfect of Swiss watchmakers." To be sure, one does not hear full-out improvisational swing in Ravel, but the echoes of Gershwin (who used elements of jazz, though he was not a jazz composer) in the beautiful *Piano Concerto in G Major* (1931) are unmistakable.

Dig This

The catalogue of one major music chain lists no fewer than 40 available recordings of Ravel's *Piano Concerto in G Major.* My favorite is the 1993 recording by Alicia de Larrocha on RCA, which also includes the composer's *Concerto for the Left Hand* (written for a pianist who had lost his right arm in World War I) and other piano works.

A Frenchman Playful

Ravel's younger countryman, Darius Milhaud (1892–1972) was warmer in temperament and more playful and daring musically. His delightful ballets *Le Boeuf sur le toit* (1919; sometimes translated as *The Nothing-Doing Bar*) and *La Création du monde* (1923; *The Creation of the World*) smack of 1920s jazz—not as sanitized by Gershwin, but as played in the nightclubs of Paris.

Milhaud was not content merely to borrow a few jazz passages and effects, however. He began exploring *polytonality,* the simultaneous use of more than one key. Polytonality is a characteristic of some non-Western ethnic music and also of early jazz. Just listen to some of the traditional New Orleans bands. When Dave Brubeck (see Chapter 14) wanted to push the envelope of jazz experimentation, he became Milhaud's student, in effect trying to connect with some of the ethnic roots of jazz by working with a modern European composer. Truly, music is a universal language that ultimately knows no boundaries of time or place.

Dig This

Milhaud is widely recorded. *La Création du Monde* and *Le Boeuf sur le Toit,* both conducted by Leonard Bernstein, are available on an EMI/Angel CD. The Qualiton label has issued a recording of Milhaud's rarely heard *Concerto for Marimba and Vibraphone,* another delightful jazz-inspired work.

Russian Fire

Trained in the conservative romantic tradition of great Russian orchestral music (one of his teachers was Nikolai Rimsky-Korsakov, the composer of the popular *Scheherezade*), Igor Stravinsky (1882–1971) developed into a musical revolutionary. The ballet choreographer Sergey Diaghilev commissioned *The Firebird* ballet in 1910, which was followed by *Petrushka* the next year and then *The Rite of Spring* (*Le Sacre du printemps*). Premiered at the Théatre des Champs Élysées in Paris on May 29, 1913, *Rite*

Talk the Talk

Polytonality is the simultaneous use of more than one key. While frequently encountered in various non-Western ethnic musical traditions, polytonality is rare in Western music.

Dig This

Recordings of the epoch-making *Rite of Spring* are legion. You can't go wrong with Pierre Boulez's 1995 interpretation on the Sony Classical label. *L'Histoire du soldat* is available in several recorded versions. The one conducted by John Carewe on Everest (released in 1997) is very good—and has the added advantage of including Stravinsky's *Ebony Concerto* (with Woody Herman both conducting and playing the clarinet) and Milhaud's *La Création du monde.*

touched off a full-scale riot, as factions of the audience responded to its wild rhythms and unresolved dissonances with unbridled enthusiasm or unchecked outrage.

Superficially, *The Rite of Spring* has little to do with jazz, but, on a deeper level, its appeal is similar. Stravinsky wrote a piece of music that was radically modern precisely because it evoked a world of *primitive* rhythms and harmonies. Jazz developed similarly as music that was at once modern and yet rooted in ancient African musical traditions.

For his part, as the 20th century progressed, Stravinsky heard the similarities between his music and jazz, and he took great pleasure in jazz. Works such as *The Soldier's Tale* (*L'Histoire du soldat*), from 1918, used ragtime and early jazz meters. In turn, by the 1940s, a host of jazz composers and performers paid homage to Stravinsky. Charlie Parker rated him highly, remarking of his *Song of the Nightingale*, "that's music at its best." Bandleader Boyd Raeburn, for example, wrote a piece called *Boyd Meets Stravinsky*, and composer George Russell wrote *Bird in Igor's Yard* in 1949.

Commissions and Collaborations

While some audiences and critics tried to keep jazz and "art music" separated, many musicians in both camps were eager to build bridges. We saw in Chapter 9 that Benny Goodman played Carnegie Hall, that bastion of classical music, with great success. He also performed such classical clarinet works as the Mozart *Clarinet Quintet* and *Clarinet Concerto*. Coleman Hawkins likewise performed at the Metropolitan Opera House in New York.

With Stravinsky

Even more significant than the fact that jazz musicians could successfully play in concert halls was that modern classical composers of the caliber of Stravinsky and the Hungarian master Bela Bartok eagerly wrote for jazz instrumentalists and bandleaders.

Igor Stravinsky as depicted by another 20th-century giant, Pablo Picasso, 1924. Image from arttoday.com.

In 1946, Igor Stravinsky, greatly impressed by Woody Herman's First Herd, wrote the *Ebony Concerto* for clarinet and asked Herman and his band to premiere the work. Since its premiere, the concerto has been recorded numerous times and is one of Stravinsky's more popular works. Yet jazz critics never warmed to the piece, complaining that it not only failed to swing, but lacked even the non-jazz rhythmic vitality characteristic of Stravinsky's most appealing compositions. Despite its possible shortcomings, the *Ebony Concerto* is an important—and highly enjoyable—experiment in combining the modern classical and jazz sensibilities.

Dig This

The classic recording of Benny Goodman playing Mozart is from the 1950s, *Mozart at Tanglewood* (RCA), with Goodman and the Boston Symphony Orchestra conducted by Charles Munch playing the *Clarinet Concerto* and a smaller ensemble playing the *Clarinet Quintet*. You can also hear Goodman play the Mozart *Quintet* and Bartok's *Contrasts for Violin, Clarinet, and Piano* on a Magic Talent reissue. This includes a performance of *Rhapsody in Blue* conducted by the great Arturo Toscanini, with Goodman taking the clarinet solos.

With Bartok, Copland, Hindemith, and Gould

Benny Goodman commissioned more works from classical composers than any other jazz musician. From Bela Bartok, he received *Contrasts*, an extraordinary duet for clarinet and violin, with piano accompaniment. From Aaron Copland, often called the "Dean of American Composers," he commissioned *Concerto for Clarinet*. While not an overtly

Riffs

Eager to impress the maestro, Herman recalls that his band rushed to the rehearsal hall dressing rooms to…

…put on a dark blue shirt and tie—things that are not normal with musicians—because it was such a great honor that this man had come. So Stravinsky arrived, wearing a sweatshirt and a pair of slacks and a towel around his neck, ready to go to work.

Dig This

The Carewe *L'Historie du soldat* on Everest (mentioned above) includes an excellent recording of *Ebony Concerto* with Woody Herman as soloist and conductor.

jazzy work (except for the syncopated rhythms of the second movement), it is one of Copland's most beautiful and, indeed, one of the loveliest works for clarinet and orchestra ever written.

Rather more challenging to the listener is *Concerto for Clarinet and Orchestra*, by the German master Paul Hindemith—again, less a work of jazz than of modern classical music. More solidly in the jazz idiom is Morton Gould's *Derivations for Clarinet and Band.*

An Octopus and a Summer Sequence

The '30s, '40s, and '50s saw the sporadic creation of a number of classically inspired jazz works (or jazz-inspired classical works), including Red Norvo's 1933 *Dance of the Octopus*. Norvo (1908–) played jazz vibes as well as xylophone, and his highly atmospheric *Dance of the Octopus* created a sensation. (It also presents a rare opportunity to hear Benny Goodman playing *bass* clarinet!) Classic Norvo sides, including *Octopus* and Norvo's version of the Bix Beiderbecke composition *In a Mist* (a piece often compared to the work of the French Impressionist composer Claude Debussy), are available on the Hep label (as *Dance of the Octopus*), a Scottish import available in larger record stores.

At the same Carnegie Hall concert in which the Woody Herman band premiered *Ebony Concerto*, the ensemble played the romantic and lyrical *Summer Sequence* (1946), by Ralph Burns (1922–). Burns also wrote other classically tinged pieces for the Herman organization, including *Apple Honey* and *Bijou*. These are all lovely works, which deserve to be heard more often today.

Symphonic Jazz

Many jazz critics and historians use the term "third stream" to refer to all classical-jazz hybrids. This, however, is not in keeping with the spirit of the word as coined by Gunther Schuller. As Schuller saw it, third stream was a combination of Western art music and ethnic or vernacular music brought together, in part, through the jazz device of improvisation. A lot of classically influenced jazz lacks the improvisational element and is, therefore, more appropriately referred to as *symphonic jazz*.

Whiteman's Aspirations

We've already seen (in Chapter 9) that orchestra leader Paul "Pops" Whiteman, determined to "make a lady out of jazz," commissioned *Rhapsody in Blue* from George Gershwin. The 1924 performance was so successful that Whiteman went on to commission symphonic jazz works from such American composers as George Antheil (*Jazz Symphony*, 1925), Ferde Grofé (*Metropolis*, 1928), Duke Ellington (*The Blue Belles of Harlem,* 1942), and Igor Stravinsky (*Scherzo à la Russe*, 1944), among others.

Dig This

Contrasts is available on the Magic Talent release mentioned above and also on *Benny Goodman Collector's Edition*, a CBS Masterworks CD that also includes the Copland and Hindemith clarinet concertos and the Gould *Derivations*. This is *the* recording to buy for Goodman and the modern classics.

Charlie Parker Takes on Strings

Listen closely to any number of Charlie Parker solos, and you will here snatches of Stravinsky and Bartok, composers Bird greatly admired (along with Sergei Prokofiev, Paul Hindemith, Claude Debussy, Maurice Ravel, and avant-garde visionary Edgard Varèse).

Parker, the quintessential bebop performer, was greatly attracted by the idea of performing against a background of strings—an orchestral palette that seems light-years distant from bop. Had Parker secured great orchestral arrangements, his work with strings might have been landmarks of the stature of so much else that he did. But the results are conventional and disappointing.

Dig This

You can hear *Apple Honey, Bijou,* and other Burns compositions on *Thundering Herds, 1945–1947,* a Columbia CD. Unfortunately, the earlier, more comprehensive three-record LP set, *Thundering Herds,* from which this CD was taken, is no longer in print. If you have a turntable and can find the album in a used-record store, buy it. It has a full-length performance of *Summer Sequence,* along with other Herman hits.

The Enigmatic Claude Thornhill

If Parker's interest in classical music never quite resulted in music as interesting as his best efforts, Claude Thornhill (1909–65) created a big band sound that was—at its best—symphonic without sacrificing a sense of swing and jazz identity. Thornhill's music is a bit like Greek olives: an acquired taste that, once acquired, stays with you for life. Thornhill enjoyed a reasonable level of popularity and was influential on Miles Davis, among others. Yet he never caught on big, and the last 15 years of his career were spent largely in obscurity.

Talk the Talk

Symphonic jazz combines elements of classical orchestral music with jazz but is fully written out, leaving no room for improvisation.

Dig This

If you're interested in hearing Gershwin as played by Whiteman, both *Rhapsody in Blue* and *An American in Paris* are on *Paul Whiteman: The Complete Capitol Recordings*, a CD reissue of material from 1942–51.

Dig This

As of this writing, *Bird with Strings*, live recordings long available on a Columbia LP, had yet to be released on CD. But you can hear studio sides on *Charlie Parker with Strings: The Master Takes* on a 1995 Verve CD.

Fortunately, Thornhill is waiting to be rediscovered. His brand of symphonic jazz, with tunes and arrangements that often remind one of Debussy, yet which always swing, is well worth sampling. *Best of the Big Bands: Claude Thornhill* is available from Legacy, and *Claude Thornhill and his Orchestra* is a Jazz Hour CD.

Kenton: Classical Dissonance

Claude Thornhill's music failed to capture a broad public. To many, it just seemed odd—the work of a bandleader who insisted on going his own way. In this, Thornhill resembled Stan Kenton (1911–79), another bandleader who followed his own path. But Stan Kenton was able to put a name to that path—he called it *progressive jazz*—and others were willing to follow him.

Stan Kenton (1912–79) began writing music as a teenager in Wichita, Kansas, then found work as a pianist and arranger for a number of 1930s dance bands. He formed his own band in 1940 but really came into his own during the early '50s, when he became identified with progressive jazz.

Not that he ever wholly abandoned swing. He always had a battery of outstanding jazz improvisers, such as saxophonists Lee Konitz and Art Pepper, trumpeter Conte Candoli, trombonist Frank Rosolino, and many others. Nevertheless, Kenton put the emphasis not on solo work, but on elaborate ensemble arrangements, which typically included such "exotic" (that is, non-jazz) instruments as bass saxophone, tuba, French horn, strings, and the mellophonium—an instrument Kenton himself commissioned, a kind of trumpet crossed with a French horn. Into the idiosyncratic mix, Kenton also threw a few Latin-American harmonies and rhythms.

Kenton organized large ensembles—culminating in the 43-piece Innovations in Modern Music Orchestra—that played loudly and with great precision. In an era marked by bop's general retreat from large groups, the Kenton orchestras, bucking the trend, couldn't fail to garner public attention.

Many jazz critics found the concept of progressive jazz hollow and pretentious, but at its best, it was a genuinely adventurous musical movement. Composer-arranger Bob Graettinger (1923–57) created *City of Glass* for the Kenton orchestra in 1948, a genuine jazz symphony of fascinating complexity. This is challenging music to listen to, but it is unlike anything else you have ever heard and rewards close attention.

Talk the Talk

Progressive jazz is a term coined by Stan Kenton to describe his idiosyncratic, elaborately arranged, and classically inflected music. While progressive jazz (perhaps surprisingly) appealed to mainstream audiences, some critics classify it with "cool jazz."

Modern Jazz Quartet: Modern Classic

So far in this chapter, we have looked at performers who sought, in varying ways, to combine musical elements of jazz and classical composition. Pianist John Lewis, vibraphonist Milt Jackson, bassist Ray Brown, and drummer Kenny Clarke, who had met one another as the rhythm section of the 1946 Dizzy Gillespie Orchestra, sought to combine jazz and classical streams not on the level of composition, but as an approach to performance.

Dig This

City of Glass is available on a Capitol CD, together with another fascinating Graettinger composition, *Thermopylae*, and shorter works. Almost a half-century old, this music still sounds like something from the future. For a broader picture of Kenton's output, including his more swing-oriented work, try the four-CD *Retrospective* set from Capitol, which spans 1943 to 1968.

Most connoisseurs of classical music will tell you that the most eloquent expression of their favorite composers comes not in the symphony or the opera—the truly *big* forms—but in the string quartet and other the chamber ensembles, the most intimate musical forms. Lewis, Jackson, Brown (soon replaced on bass by Percy Heath), and Clarke (soon replaced by Connie Kay) came together first as the Milt Jackson Quartet (1951) and then as the Modern Jazz Quartet (1952) to create in jazz what classical musicians created in chamber music: an enduring, elegant, intimate musical experience.

MJQ has played with a symphony orchestra (conducted by Gunther Schuller) and with the Beaux Art String Quartet, an important classical chamber ensemble, but the group's third-stream identity comes less from these literal associations with classical music than from a kind of timeless commitment to excellence. MJQ has endured. In 1974, Milt Jackson withdrew for a time, and the quartet broke up, only to reconvene in 1981, but with changes in personnel, the quartet has continued to perform and record into the 1990s.

What is truly marvelous about the Modern Jazz Quartet is that they combine the spirit of classical music with the unmistakable feeling and content of jazz. The four-CD *MJQ: 40 Years,* from Atlantic, is a worthy investment, covering 1952 through 1988, but you can also enjoy vintage MJQ on *Django,* recordings from 1953–55, reissued on Original Jazz Classics, or the 1993 *Celebration,* an Atlantic CD. In every sense, MJQ provides a classic listening experience and is one of the most successful realizations of the third stream idea.

Real Square

While critics and self-styled connoisseurs split hairs, most *musicians* agree: good music is good music, period. Follow the musicians' example and avoid the mistake of partitioning the musical world into strictly divided "classical" and "jazz" realms.

Jazz in the Conservatory

By the 1950s, the cultural gap between jazz and classical music was narrowing in another important way. The music was being taught and developed in academic settings. Whereas four decades earlier, the home of jazz had been the bordello and then the speakeasy, now it was also the classroom.

Professor Gunther Schuller

Gunther Schuller (1925–) was born in New York City to a family of classical musicians, his grandfather having been a conductor in Germany, and his father a longtime violinist with the New York Philharmonic. Schuller became a French-horn virtuoso, playing with the Cincinnati Symphony Orchestra and the Metropolitan Opera, but he also found himself magnetically drawn to the music of Duke Ellington. He created symphonic adaptations of a number of Ellington's works and, in 1955, wrote *Symphonic Tribute to Duke Ellington.*

Schuller never became a jazz musician in the conventional sense of a soloist and improviser, but he did appear with such ensembles as the Modern Jazz Quartet, and he wrote and lectured widely about jazz and aspects of other popular music. He taught at the new School of Jazz, in Lenox, Massachusetts in 1959, then was appointed music director of the First International Jazz Festival in Washington in 1962. From 1964 to 1967, he taught at the Yale School of Music.

As a composer, Schuller was all over the musical map, exploring the most remote regions of modern 12-tone classical composition as well as jazz and many styles and traditions in between. In the 1970s, he developed an interest in ragtime and played a key role in reviving popular interest in the music of Scott Joplin. While pianist Max Morath had earlier kept the flame of ragtime alive on piano, Schuller (president of the New England Conservatory of Music, 1967–77) organized the New England Conservatory Ragtime Ensemble, which re-created orchestral ragtime—a sound that had not been widely heard since early in the 20th century.

Take Five

Schuller is a fascinating and thoroughly remarkable musician, whose contributions to American music encompass performance, composition, and education, as well as cultural preservation—especially in the case of ragtime. His most important recording of original jazz compositions is on *Jumpin' into the Future,* available on CD from GM Records, which was justly acclaimed when it was released in 1989. This is an eye-opening modern big-band recording.

If you are interested in hearing Schuller as a non-jazz contemporary composer, a good place to start is *Impromptus and Cadenzas, Octet,* an Arabesque CD.

Schuller is probably best known to the public for his ragtime recordings. His *Scott Joplin: The Red Back Book,* a marvelous re-creation of the ragtime band sound, climbed onto the pop charts and received a Grammy when it was released in 1973 and is still available on CD from EMI Angel. In 1990, Schuller and his New England Ragtime Ensemble recorded *The Art of the Rag*, featuring works by Joplin and others, on the GM label.

Schuller's authoritative and highly readable *Early Jazz* and *The Swing Era* are essential books in any serious jazz library.

The Excursions of John Lewis

John Lewis (1920–), longtime leader of the Modern Jazz Quartet, is a bop pianist and an educator (having served at the Lenox School of Jazz, at the City College of New York, and at Harvard University), and a composer. Perhaps his single best-known work is *Django*, which may be heard on the MJQ recording mentioned earlier. His most characteristic compositions are truly third stream works, combining jazz with a very conservative classical tradition, embodying the kinds of harmonic and melodic approaches a Mozart or a Haydn would have been comfortable with. Lewis writes delicate, elegantly simple, and often very beautiful music. It

Dig This

John Lewis: Private Concert is a recent (1991) Emarcy release that gives a good glimpse of Lewis's work outside of MJQ. Remarkable, too, are Lewis's recordings of the *Bach Preludes and Fugues,* issued in two CD volumes on the Philips label.

is work of great integrity, demonstrating that, despite controversy, third stream music can be enduring and thoroughly delightful.

Experiment in Jazz: Bill Russo

Born in Chicago in 1928, Bill Russo studied as a teenager with Lennie Tristano (Chapter 14) and played trombone in several bands. From 1947 to 1950, he led an orchestra called Experiment in Jazz, but his real musical laboratory was the Stan Kenton Orchestra, for which he was arranger and composer (as well as trombonist) from 1950 to 1954.

Russo was the force behind much of what Kenton termed progressive jazz in the early 1950s, creating compositions and arrangements that fed Kenton's obsession with a big brass sound. *Halls of Brass*, a work from Russo's Kenton period, demands a virtuosity from the horns that perfectly suited Kenton's skilled, disciplined, and powerful brass section.

Dig This

The Innovations Orchestra, reissued on CD by Capitol Jazz/Blue Note, includes *Halls of Brass* and other Russo compositions for Kenton.

After he left Kenton in 1954, Russo began composing more fully in the third stream, especially for his own large ensemble, the Russo Orchestra. A distinguished educator, Russo has taught at the Lenox School of Jazz, the Manhattan School of Music, and has directed the Center for New Music at Chicago's Columbia College. He has also written standard texts on jazz composition and arranging.

Ran Blake: The Ethnic Influence

Born in Massachusetts in 1935, Ran Blake has been closely identified with third stream music since the 1960s and has worked closely with John Lewis and Gunther Schuller. In 1973, Schuller appointed Blake chairman of the third stream department of the New England Conservatory of Music.

Blake brings to third stream music a strong improvisational element as well as elements from non-Western ethnic traditions. His piano solo work is highly dramatic, and audiences thrill to the explosions of sound that erupt from his keyboard. In contrast to more traditional jazz improvisers, Blake often emphasizes melodic structure, carrying the melody while allowing chord structure to lapse. The result is fresh and even startling.

Make no mistake, Ran Blake could be in the avant-garde chapter (Chapter 19) just as well as here. His music is idiosyncratic and challenging, but it is also exciting. A wonderful introduction to the work of Ran Blake may be had in *Duke Dreams*, a tribute and transformation of music by Duke Ellington and Billy Strayhorn, released in 1981 and available on a Soul Note CD. If you enjoy this album, try *Epistrophy* next, a 1991

Soul Note release that reinterprets 12 songs by Thelonious Monk—in ways even Monk wouldn't have thought of. Characteristically, Blake weaves rhythmic and melodic wreathes around the Monk tunes rather than improvising on the chord changes, as a more conventional jazz musician would.

"America's Classical Music"?

When jazz composer, bandleader, pianist, and educator Billy Taylor called jazz "America's classical music," he provoked some controversy among those who thought that he was unnecessarily trying to "elevate" jazz to a higher cultural status. But this wasn't Taylor's intention. As the third stream experience demonstrates, jazz is "classical" in that, like the music of Mozart or Beethoven, it has a certain timelessness. Compounded of ethnic as well as popular traditions, it also transcends these, with an identity all its own.

Many jazz fans and jazz critics see third stream music as a curiosity, quirky and interesting, perhaps, but ultimately an out-of-the-way aspect of jazz. Yet, in a sense, all jazz is "third stream" music, innovatively combining aspects of a variety of musical voices and cultures.

The Least You Need to Know

- Beginning with George Gershwin and Maurice Ravel, jazz and classical music have mutually benefitted from a lively interchange.
- Both jazz and much modern classical music share an impulse to connect with "primitive" cultural and musical roots.
- Third stream music combines elements of classical and jazz traditions, with emphasis on jazz improvisation; symphonic jazz also combines classical and jazz elements but does not include improvisation. Progressive jazz is a term coined by Stan Kenton in the 1950s to describe large-scale orchestral jazz, incorporating elements of symphonic-style orchestral composition.
- John Lewis and the Modern Jazz Quartet created the jazz equivalent of classical chamber music.

Chapter 17

Dash of Salsa and Bit of Bossa Nova: Jazz Goes Latin

In This Chapter

- Latin music and the heritage of jazz
- Latin dance comes to America
- From Latin dance to Afro-Cuban jazz
- The Cubana Bop phenomenon
- Everybody does the bossa nova
- Latin goes avant garde

It comes as no news that the roots of jazz run deep into West Africa. However, African traditions are not the music's only ethnic element. Jelly Roll Morton believed that authentic jazz always has a "Spanish tinge." "Latin jazz," "salsa," and "bossa nova" are distinct styles of jazz, but many jazz masters do more than simply add Latin touches to the music, they write or perform in ways that acknowledge a "Spanish tinge" running deep in the music. The rhythms and harmonies identified with Spanish—and especially Afro-Cuban—ethnic music seem naturally suited to the jazz idiom, and in this chapter, we'll explore some of the exciting Latin dimensions of jazz.

Talk the Talk

Habanera is a Spanish word meaning dance of Havana and is a slow, Cuban folk dance that has provided composers with one of the most familiar of Spanish rhythms.

Dig This

Bauzá died in 1993. His extraordinary contribution to Latin jazz might have been all but forgotten had he not formed a 23-piece big band during the last two years before his death. Bauzá's *The Tanga Suite*, a beautiful, large-scale example of Afro-Cuban jazz, is available on a 1992 CD of that name, released on the Messidor label.

Talk the Talk

Cubop, short for Cubana Bop, is the name applied to a Latin-inspired form of bop introduced by the Afro-Cuban musicians Machito and Mario Bauzá and additionally developed by Dizzy Gillespie.

Jelly Roll's "Spanish Tinge"

Jelly Roll Morton's pronouncement that the "Spanish tinge" added just the "right seasoning" to jazz was no idle observation. A number of Morton's compositions, including *New Orleans Joys* (also called *New Orleans Blues*), *The Crave,* and *Mamanita,* make use of the most familiar Spanish rhythm, that of the *habanera.*

A slow Cuban folk dance (the name means dance of Havana), the habanera provides an *ostinato*—a repeated rhythmic figure—that instantly signals a Latin feeling about the music. The habanera pattern is both simple and flexible, capable of great variation without losing its Latin identity. It is, therefore, a highly effective foundation on which to build a tune.

In fact, the habanera rhythm is found even earlier than the music of Jelly Roll Morton. Ragtime, one of the precursors of jazz, offers many examples of the "Spanish tinge," from *Cubanola (Cuban Danza)* by Neil Moret as early as 1902, to Scott Joplin's *Solace: A Mexican Serenade,* to the second section of W. C. Handy's celebrated *St. Louis Blues,* composed in 1914.

Caravan

If the "Spanish tinge" was part of jazz from the beginning—from the days of ragtime, even before there was anything actually called jazz—it did not fully enter the Anglo musical mainstream until the 1930s. During that decade, a host of Latin dances became widely popular, especially the tango and the rhumba. Popular bandleaders, such as Don Azipiazú and Xavier Cugat, promoted the Latin ballroom beat.

Duke Ellington's great Puerto Rican trombonist, Juan Tizol, wrote two memorable Latin jazz classics, *Caravan* (1937) and *Conga Brava* (1940). Both can be heard on just about any Ellington disk from the late '30s or early '40s, such as *The Carnegie Hall Concerts (December 1947)* from Prestige.

The Afro-Cubans

But Azipiazú and Cugat were hardly jazz musicians. Mario Bauzá was. Born in Havana in 1911, he played bass clarinet in the Havana Symphony Orchestra before he moved to New York City in 1930 and found work as a trumpeter with Noble Sissle, the vaudeville and Broadway composer-bandleader most famous for his partnership with ragtime composer-pianist Eubie Blake. From 1933 to 1938, he appeared with the Chick Webb Orchestra as trumpeter and music director. He played with Don Redman in 1938–39 and with Cab Calloway from 1939 to 1941. During this period, he brought Dizzy Gillespie into the Calloway band. For his part, as we are about to see, Gillespie became intensely interested in Afro-Cuban music through Bauzá.

Dig This

The Pablo label has released on CD *Mucho Macho Machito*, a compilation of terrific Cubana Bop from 1948. Here is Afro-Cuban jazz at its best and most authentic.

In 1941, Bauzá joined a band called the Afro-Cubans, led by his brother-in-law, one Frank Raul Grillo (1912–84), a Cuban vocalist better known by the single name of Machito. For the Afro-Cubans, Bauzá created arrangements that blended excellent jazz feeling with highly charged, even frenetic Cuban rhythms. The result was Cubana Bop, sometimes called *Cubop*.

Cubana Bop

Cubana Bop—Cubop—instantly attracted one of bebop's founding fathers, Dizzy Gillespie. Inspired by his contact with Bauzá during the time they had spent together in the Cab Calloway band, Gillespie hired Chano Pozo, a phenomenal Cuban conga (an ethnic Afro-Cuban drum) player in 1947. Pozo and bongo player Chiquitico joined Gillespie in a Carnegie Hall concert on September 29, 1947 and created a sensation. Gillespie and collaborator George Russell wrote "Cubana Be, Cubana Bop" to make full use of Pozo's prodigious rhythmical powers. In so doing, they laid the foundation for much Latin-flavored jazz and popular music that followed.

Dig This

The 1947 Carnegie Hall concert with Chano Pozo was released on an Artistry LP, *Live at Carnegie Hall* (search used record stores). It is not available on CD; however, *Gillespiana* (Verve CD, from 1960) features Latin material, and *Dizzy Gillespie y Machito*, live in 1975, is on Original Jazz Classics. *Dizzy Gillespie: The Complete RCA Recordings, 1937–1949* is a magnificent two-CD set, including Gillespie's forays into Cubop and much more.

Tragically, it remained a foundation only. Little more than a year after he began working with Gillespie, Chano Pozo—who apparently had connections to the underworld—was gunned down in a New York bar.

An identified Cuban street musician playing a conga in Havana. Image from arttoday.com

Mainstream Latin

Thanks to Bauzá, Machito, and Gillespie, the Latin influence soon entered the jazz mainstream and was regularly heard in recordings by any number of big bands.

Stan Kenton Takes on Bongos

As usual, Stan Kenton took on the latest trend in an especially big way. Jack Costanzo appeared with the Kenton band during the late 1940s as a *bongo* soloist and was featured in such ambitious works as *Chorale for Brass, Piano, and Bongo*, written in 1947 for Kenton by Pete Rugolo, and *Fugue for Rhythm Section*, another 1947 Rugolo work. Some critics have called these pieces pretentious, but the spotlight cast on bongos in the Kenton organization did much to popularize Latin rhythms. One of Kenton's best known Latin recordings is *23° N—82° W* (the location of Cuba), composed by Bill Russo.

Talk the Talk

Bongo drums are a pair of small Afro-Cuban drums played with bare hands and capable of producing a range of tones, timbres, and musical effects.

Arguably Kenton's most successful foray into Afro-Cuban music was *Cuban Fire*, a six-part suite composed and arranged by Johnny Richards and recorded in 1956. Conceived on a scale comparable to Duke Ellington's numerous suites, *Cuban Fire* uses a 27-piece orchestra, including six percussionists, two French horns, and six trumpets. But there is more to this music than massive forces. Top-notch soloists and an impressive arrangement make this an important recording. It is available on CD from Capitol.

Cal Tjader

Born in St. Louis in 1925, Cal Tjader was not only *not* Cuban, he had no Latin ethnic heritage at all. After study at San Francisco State, he began his jazz career playing drums with Dave Brubeck's trio in the late 1940s and early 1950s, then worked with bandleader and steel guitarist Alvino Rey before going on to front his own band until 1953, when he joined George Shearing's band. At this time, he began to play vibes as well as percussion and worked with such Latin jazz artists as Willie Bobo, Mongo Santamaria, and Armanda Perez. But it was bassist Al McKibbon who really encouraged Tjader's developing love for Afro-Latin jazz.

Tjader left Shearing and started a number of his own groups, specializing in Afro-Cuban and Latin jazz, with percussionists Bobo and Santamaria later joining him. Listen to *Black Orchid* on Fantasy, a CD that reissues two LP albums, *Cal Tjader Goes Latin* (1956) and *Cal Tjader Quintet* (1959), and you'll understand why Tjader is considered the most important non-Latin practitioner of Latin jazz. The expressive range of his work in the Latin vein is highly impressive.

Tito Puente

While Tjader emerged as the leading non-ethnic exponent of Latin jazz, Mario Bauzá remained the field's most important musician of Latin heritage. With Bauzá's death in 1993, that honor went to Tito Puente (1923–). A native of New York City, Puente had an ambition to be a dancer but suffered an early accident that permanently injured his Achilles tendon. After service in the U.S. Navy during World War II, Puente enrolled in Juilliard, then worked in the bands of Noro Morales, Machito, and Pupi Campo before forming his own group in the late 1940s. By the early 1950s, Puente was spearheading a craze for the mambo, which swept the nation. From this point on, Puente's success was mainly a crossover phenomenon, straddling the worlds of Latin jazz and Latin pop.

Tito Puente, veteran practitioner of Latin jazz. Image from Online Talent Agency.

If you want to hear Puente at his jazziest, go back to the 1950s and *Dance Mania,* a BMG CD reissue of material from 1958. Puente claims to have been the originator of big-band mambo, and this album backs him up. More recent Puente has demonstrated the musician's return to a jazz idiom. *Royal T,* on the Concord Picante label, features Latin bop-oriented jazz recorded in 1993.

Black Orpheus

To think of 1950s America is to unleash a flood of mainstream Rock Hudson-Doris Day images stamped all over with "Made in America." Yet, by the late 1950s, international influences were making themselves felt even in mainstream America, and, in 1959, sophisticated moviegoers were buzzing about a new French-Portuguese movie set in Buenos Aires. An updated retelling of the classical myth of Orpheus and Eurydice, it was called *Black Orpheus* and was the story of a street-car conductor and a country girl who fall in love during Rio's carnival. (The Oscar-winning *Black Orpheus* is rightly considered a film classic and is widely available for rental at larger video stores.)

Dig This

San Francisco-born pianist-composer Vince Guaraldi (1928–76) wrote and recorded *Jazz Impressions of Black Orpheus* in 1962 (available on an Original Jazz Classics CD), which combines brilliant improvisation with a solid bossa beat.

Not the least of the film's attractions was a score by Brazilian composer Luis Bonfa and Brazilian composer-guitar virtuoso Antonio Carlos Jobim. The score introduced American audiences to Brazilian popular music in general and to Jobim in particular, setting the stage for a bossa nova craze in the next decade, but more immediately launching Jobim's international career.

Born in 1927, Jobim would build his popularity on the bossa nova, but the depth of his musicianship went beyond skillfully exploiting this musical style. He combined the bossa beat with a cool jazz sensibility and a feeling for melody inspired (he repeatedly said) by the songs of Cole Porter. In *Elis and Tom* (Verve, 1974), for example, Jobim joins poetic lyrics to simple melodies wedded to cool jazz chord progressions. It is a delicate and irresistible combination.

Talk the Talk

The **samba**, which became a popular ballroom dance in the United States by the late 1930s, originated as a lively, complexly syncopated, duple-meter folk dance of Afro-Brazilian origin.

Jazz Samba

The Brazilian influence had quietly figured in American popular music as early as the 1930s, when the *samba*, a lively, complexly syncopated, duple-meter (two beats to a measure) traditional dance of Afro-Brazilian origin, was introduced into this country by popular song composer Vincent Youmans ("Carioca," 1933). The dance didn't really catch on big until 1939, when it was featured at the New York World's Fair and then widely popularized by the bubbly Brazilian-born film star Carmen Miranda.

The very popularity of the samba may have discouraged "serious" jazz musicians from exploring its many rhythmic possibilities for at least a decade until Charlie Parker ("Tico, Tico") and Stan Kenton ("Baia") embraced the samba in the early 1950s.

In the meantime, by the late 1950s, musicians in Brazil, including Jobim, were developing the samba in a more sedate, sophisticated, yet breezy style known as the *bossa nova*, meaning "new wrinkle" or "new wave."

Dig This

Laurindo Almeida (1917–95) is generally credited with having introduced Brazilian guitar to jazz. He is less generally recognized for having brought an early version of bossa nova to the United States with recordings made as early as 1954. *Brazilliance* (volume 1), a CD reissue from World Pacific, is worth purchasing just to hear Almeida transform the samba into a bossa beat.

Stan Getz and Charlie Byrd

As transformed into the bossa nova, the samba suddenly seemed a perfect fit with the new cool jazz (see Chapter 14) sensibility that was especially popular among West Coast jazz musicians. It was rhythmically complex—hitting 16 beats every two bars, with the accent on beats 1, 4, 7, 11, and 14, so that the rhythm was actually spaced out as 3-3-4-3-3—yet very relaxed and laid back, evoking a blend of equatorial breezes and urbane sophistication.

Tenor saxophonist Stan Getz joined guitarist Charlie Byrd on *Jazz Samba*, one of the most popular, delightful, and remarkable of all jazz albums. Released in 1962 by Verve, it is still available as a CD on the DCC Compact Classics label. More than any single album, *Jazz Samba* ushered into the United States the bossa nova craze, and made "Desafinado" and "One-Note Samba" pop hits.

Talk the Talk

The **bossa nova** (Brazilian Portuguese for "new wrinkle" or "new wave") is a musical style of Brazilian origin that blends elements of the samba with elements of cool jazz.

Herbie Mann

Herbert Jay Solomon—better known as Herbie Mann—was born in New York in 1930 and started playing jazz flute (as well as tenor saxophone and bass clarinet) professionally in the early 1950s. By the mid- to late 1950s, Mann was playing in a laid-back

Real Square

Don't confuse the jazz treatment of the samba with the cornball "Latin" ballroom dances of the 1950s, such as the cha-cha. Like the Argentine tango, the Brazilian samba is as much a state of mind as it is a dance. It embodies deeply rooted national and cultural identities, and it is a musical form capable of great sophistication.

Dig This

Also sample Mann's non-Latin work. One of his finest albums is *Flute Souffle*, from 1957 and reissued on an Original Jazz Classics CD.

bop style that verged on cool, but he was and continues to be a musician of very wide-ranging tastes (something some jazz "purists" object to!), and in 1962, he was in the vanguard of American jazz musicians recording Brazilian-inspired music.

The most important of Mann's bossa nova albums, *Do the Bossa Nova with Herbie Mann*, released by Atlantic in 1962, has not been reissued on CD; however, Mann returned to the Brazilian idiom frequently, and *America/ Brasil*, a 1997 album, is available on the Lightyear label, as is *Caminho de Casa*, a 1990 release from Chesky.

Bossa Nova Breezes In

The 1962 albums by Getz and Byrd and by Herbie Mann crossed over from jazz into the pop realm, and for a time in the early 1960s, it seemed that everyone, everywhere was playing to a bossa nova beat.

The Girl from Ipanema Goes Walking

In 1963, Astrud Gilberto, a rather primly appealing vocalist born in Bahia, Brazil in 1940, recorded with Stan Getz one of Jobim's songs. Called "The Girl from Ipanema," it shot to the top of U.S. pop charts and for a time was heard wherever one tuned the radio dial. "The Girl from Ipanema" planted the bossa beat firmly in the popular ear.

The Bossa Beat Comes to Carnegie Hall

In 1962, Gilberto, Getz, and Charlie Byrd appeared in concert at Carnegie Hall with Dizzy Gillespie. Gilberto's "Girl from Ipanema" recording came out the next year, and another Carnegie Hall concert followed in 1964. During this brief span—1962–64—a number of jazz artists tried their hand at bossa nova, including the venerable but always adventurous Coleman Hawkins with a recording of Jobim's "Desafinado" (*Desafinado: Bossa Nova and Jazz Samba*, 1962, reissued on CD by MCA), but it was Getz, Byrd, and Gilberto who most thoroughly explored the jazz possibilities of this popular form. *The Bossa Nova Years (Girl from Ipanema)* is a multiple-CD set that may be too much of a good thing for some tastes, but it is a remarkable collection in any case. Spanning 1962–64, it is available on the DCC label and includes the original hit recording of "Girl from Ipanema" as well as the 1964 Carnegie concert.

Joao and Astrud Gilberto

Astrud Gilberto was not a professional singer when she was asked to sing the English lyrics to "Girl from Iapanema" in the 1963 recording with Getz, Jobim, and her husband, Joao Gilberto. Yet her demure, somewhat distant delivery of the song suited it perfectly and struck a chord with the public, launching a quietly successful career for her. *Look at the Rainbow,* a Verve CD reissue of recordings made in 1965–66, is a pleasant set of bossa vocals and features classy arrangements by Gil Evans.

Of more interest musically is the work of Gilberto's husband (they later divorced), Joao Gilberto, generally regarded as the most important of modern Brazilian popular singers and guitarists. With Jobim, Joao Gilberto was the artist most responsible for developing the samba into the bossa nova. *Amoroso/Brasil,* a Warner Bros. CD combining two LPs from 1976 and 1980, presents Joao Gilberto at his romantic best, not only as a vocalist but on guitar as well. This is popular music with a touch of the exotic and a jazzy, swinging feel.

Salsa to Go: Some Innovations

The 1970s and 1980s took Latin jazz in some exciting new directions. The Argentine tenor saxophonist Gato Barbieri (1934–) had been bringing tropical, jungle-like sounds into free jazz and avant-garde jazz since the 1960s, even using ethnic South American Indian instruments for added effect. Barbieri's approach to his own instrument is often unconventional, as he sometimes hums and blows at the same time, producing very intriguing, highly expressive, other-worldly distortions. At the same time, Barbieri is capable of a sensual and romantic vibrato that keeps the music from drifting very far off into avant-garde realms.

Dig This

Lake's work with Jump Up was more successful in live performance than on record. *Jump Up,* a 1981 Gramavision release, is now hard to find.

Barbieri made a major popular hit with his soundtrack to the sexually steamy Marlon Brando film *Last Tango in Paris* in 1972. The soundtrack, recently reissued on a United Artists CD, is wonderfully atmospheric, brooding, and exotic music that still remains very much on the cutting edge.

Talk the Talk

Reggae is popular music of Jamaican origin, combining strains of calypso, soul, and rock 'n' roll. Rhythmically, the offbeats are strongly accented, and, politically, the reggae lyrics often pack a protest punch.

The Art Ensemble of Chicago, whom we will meet in Chapter 19, a boldly avant-garde group, ventured into another aspect of Latin music, the Carribean popular form known as *reggae,* on their *Nice Guys* album of 1978 (available on CD from

ECM). In 1981, another avant-gardist, flutist and saxophone player Oliver Lake, engaged reggae jubilantly and with good-natured humor through his band Jump Up.

Nana Vasconcelos (1944–), a Brazilian percussionist, took Brazilian-inspired jazz in exciting directions, playing with the Pat Metheny fusion groups (see Chapter 20) and also on his own, as in *Saudades*, a 1979 ECM release, featuring Vasconcelos on a wide array of ethnic percussion instruments.

More recently, Afro-Cuban jazz has been reinvigorated by the Havana-born clarinetist and alto saxophonist Paquito D'Rivera. *Who's Smoking?!* returns Latin jazz to the red heat of Cubop. It was released in 1991 on the Candid label.

Give a listen to these and other recordings by Latin jazz musicians from the 1980s and 1990s. You will be amazed at the vitality and variety of this often-neglected ethnically inspired branch of jazz.

The Least You Need to Know

- The Latin influence has figured importantly in jazz since the music's earliest years.
- The Latin element came to the jazz forefront during the late 1930s and into 1940s, after the popularity of Latin ballroom dances accustomed the popular ear to Latin rhythms.
- The most important early (1940s) Latin jazz was Cubana Bop or Cubop, pioneered by Mario Bauzá and Machito and further developed by Dizzy Gillespie.
- By the early 1960s, Brazilian music, in the form of the bossa nova, had become an important element in cool jazz.

Chapter 18

Bopping Harder: Hard Bop Takes a Stand

In This Chapter

- What is hard bop?
- Hard bop vs. bop and the cool school
- The founders of hard bop
- The hard bop careers of Miles Davis and John Coltrane
- The twilight of hard bop

We have seen that bebop was in part a reaction against swing and that the jazz of the cool school was a departure from the emotional hyperintensity of bop. Some jazz historians interpret hard bop as a rebellion against the cool school. These commentators see tenor saxophonist Sonny Rollins, pianist Horace Silver, drummer Art Blakey, and alto saxophonist Cannonball Adderley (four of the principal figures of hard bop) as objecting to the softer, more emotionally remote aspects of the cool school.

Well, this is one way to think about it, but the development of hard bop probably had less to do with one musical style reacting to another than it was a function of geography. By the middle 1950s and early 1960s, the cool school had caught on really big in California. Hard bop was an East Coast intensification of East Coast bop and for the most part simply ignored what was happening out West.

Anyway, if you like your jazz hot and hard-driving, rather than cool and laid-back, you'll want to hang around New York rather than take flight to L.A. This chapter will keep you company.

Uncool

Maybe bebop was doomed to fall victim to its own importance. Up-and-coming artists in the late 1940s and early 1950s couldn't help but hear what was going on. The *happening* jazz, the important jazz, the innovative jazz was all in the bebop vein. As we saw in Chapter 14, this was fine for those young musicians whose personal and artistic temperament—not to mention *chops*—suited bop. But what could you do if bop just wasn't your thing?

Talk the Talk

Chops is synonymous with technique and musical skill—the ability to play fast, loud, and nimbly.

For some artists, the detachment and discipline of cool jazz offered a viable alternative to bop. For others, however, the answer was not to step back and cool off, but to blow even harder and hotter and heavier.

This is a bit misleading. Hard bop was and is sometimes called "*soul jazz*," and it's not just that the hard boppers played louder and heavier than their bop colleagues, they added *soul*—that is, additional elements of traditional and popular African-American music. This included dark, heavy, earthy timbres and blues-like melodies and inflections of pitch. Harmonies often reminded listeners of the music played in some African-American church services. But all of this—heavy, earthy, soulful—was played with a hard-driving intensity. Like the boppers, the hard boppers were typically fast and nimble instrumentalists.

Talk the Talk

Soul jazz is another word for hard bop, a style combining elements of bebop with elements of the blues, rhythm and blues, and African-American gospel music, all at intense, hard-driving tempos.

Young Sonny Rollins

He was born Theodore Walter Rollins in New York in 1930, but was always called Sonny. As a little boy, he played piano before discovering the alto saxophone at age 11. A few years later, he took up the tenor saxophone. By the time he was in high school, Rollins was leading a group that featured alto saxophonist Jackie McLean, pianist Kenny Drew, and drummer Art Taylor—all of whom would go on to prominent jazz careers. At 18, Rollins was rehearsing with Thelonious Monk, and from 1949 to 1954 he was recording with all of the bop greats, including Charlie Parker, Bud Powell, and Max Roach.

Dig This

Although you can find early Sonny Rollins on period recordings by Davis, Monk, and others, there's also an extraordinary seven-CD set from prestige, *Sonny Rollins: The Complete Prestige Recordings*, spanning 1949–56. A major jazz musician, Rollins deserves such a comprehensive set.

Rollins's early recordings with trombonist J.J. Johnson, Powell (both 1949), and Miles Davis (1951) set the jazz world on fire. Three of his 1954 compositions, *Airegin, Doxy,* and *Oleo* became instant jazz standards. Here was a major *bop* musician.

But like so many others, Rollins was plagued by drug addiction. In 1955, while working to overcome his drug problems, Rollins joined the Max Roach-Clifford Brown Quintet, which, as we will see in a moment, was one of the major new hard bop groups.

Innovation was the keynote of Sonny Rollins's mid-1950s career. He composed *Valse Hot* in 3/4 time—then virtually unheard of in jazz, though now fairly commonplace. He introduced calypso rhythms into his music (*St. Thomas*), and he explored new approaches to improvisation in such works as *Blue 7.* With the kind of wit typical of Thelonious Monk, Rollins even transformed such non-jazz chestnuts as the corny cowboy songs "I'm an Old Cowhand" and "Wagon Wheels" into hard bop jazz!

Dig This

The 1957 *Way Out West,* one of Rollins's finest albums, features "I'm an Old Cowhand" and "Wagon Wheels" cooked up Rollins style. The album is available from Original Jazz Classics. Check out OJC's catalog for other Rollins recordings from the mid-1950s.

As the 1950s drew to a close, there seemed to be no stopping Sonny Rollins. Then, in 1959, he suddenly dropped out of sight.

Well, not quite. While he did not play club dates or cut any records between August 1959 and November 1961, he became a local legend as a solitary figure given to blowing his tenor on the Williamsburg Bridge.

By the time he returned to full-time performance in 1962, the cutting edge of jazz had passed him by, and hard bop had begun to fade. Rollins, as we will see in Chapter 19, turned to free jazz as well as to R&B and pop sounds.

Stan Getz Makes a Discovery

In 1950, the tenor saxophonist Stan Getz, at the height of his popularity, made a guest appearance in Hartford, Connecticut, with a local trio led by pianist Horace Silver. Getz liked what he heard and hired the trio to tour with him for the next year. This gave Silver valuable exposure and the kick he needed to leave Connecticut for New York in 1951. There he worked with the likes of Coleman Hawkins, Lester Young, Oscar Pettiford, and Art Blakey, becoming a Blue Note recording artist in 1952 and remaining with this seminal jazz label for almost three decades.

Talk the Talk

Funk may be taken as a synonym for *soul jazz,* but it is also a style of African-American soul music, characterized by complex syncopation in duple meter.

Silver had been born in Norwalk, Connecticut, the son of a man who had been raised in Cape Verde, at the time a Portuguese island province off the coast of Senegal, Africa.

As a boy, Horace delighted in his father's performances of Cape Verdean folk music and thus acquired a connection to West African "root music" more immediate than other jazz musicians. But Silver was also influenced early on by boogie-woogie piano, the blues, and, more than anything else, the bop of Bud Powell and Thelonious Monk. Fresh out of high school, he was leading his own piano trio.

A Blue Note record label from 1948. Image from the author's collection.

Take Five

Blue Note is one of the most important of the great jazz record labels. Founded in New York by Alfred Lion in 1939, the company began recording the likes of Sidney Bechet, Earl Hines, and other major figures. During the 1940s, Blue Note recorded many traditional artists, including James P. Johnson and more Bechet, as well as Ike Quebec, a tenor saxophonist who also became the label's A & R (artists and repertory) director. It was Quebec who turned Blue Note into a bop label, and by the 1950s, Blue Note was recognized as a specialist in contemporary jazz.

With the 1971 death of Francis Wolff, one of the label's guiding executives, Blue Note began recording fusion and commercially oriented material, but by the mid-1970s, the company also began reissuing recordings from its large and important back catalogue. Today, the label is recognized both for its ongoing reissue program and for recording important younger jazz artists.

In New York, Silver matured rapidly and pushed to the forefront of the hard bop movement, in part through his charter membership in the pioneering hard-bop Jazz Messengers ensemble. He brought to the new style all the elements of his musical background, including R&B and gospel, as well as strong echoes of the Cape Verdean traditions (in *Cape Verdean Blues* and the important 1960 composition *Song for My Father*). Indeed, by mid-1960s, Silver had moved out of hard bop and was composing and playing in a variety of styles, ranging from *funk* to ethnic to pop.

But it is as a prime mover of hard bop that Silver may well be best remembered (though he is still a long way from the end of his career!). Not only did he combine the basic elements of the style, he also organized ensembles that gave many young jazz musicians their start, and he composed original works important in hard bop, such as *The Preacher, Doodlin'*, and *Opus de Funk*.

Dig This

Horace Silver and the Jazz Messengers is vintage hard bop from 1954 to 55 and is available as a Blue Note CD. Don't be put off by the title of a CD reissue of 1959 recordings by the best quintet Silver assembled, *Finger Poppin' with the Horace Silver Quintet.* Reissued by Blue Note, this CD is a prime example of late hard bop as it became more "soul"-oriented and funky. *Juicy Lucy* is a funk classic.

Album art from Horace Silver and the Jazz Messengers, *a Blue Note release.*
Image from Blue Note.

Enter Miles

And then came Miles. "Giants of jazz" is a phrase much heard and much abused, but if it can be justly applied to anyone, surely Miles Davis merits the title. An important young figure in bop, he was, as we saw in Chapter 14, a principal architect of the cool school. Protean in sensibility, he also figured prominently in hard bop, forming in 1958 perhaps his greatest band, a sextet that included tenor saxophonist John Coltrane (who would soon eclipse Sonny Rollins as the most important hard bop exponent of the instrument), pianist Red Garland, altoist Cannonball Adderley, bassist Paul Chambers, and drummer Philly Joe Jones. If this was Davis's greatest band, it was also resolutely a hard bop band. Coltrane and Adderley joined Bill Evans and Wynton Kelly on Davis's single most famous album, *Kind of Blue*, released in 1959 by Columbia and available today on CD. The miracle of this album is that the soloists, Davis, Coltrane, and Adderley, are profoundly different from one another, yet work perfectly together without sacrificing any of those differences. And few jazz albums offer an all-star line-up like this!

Dig This

Miles Ahead (1957), *Porgy and Bess* (1958), and *Sketches of Spain* (1960) were all albums of this period that had nothing to do with hard bop, but it would be criminal not to mention them. All three are classic collaborations with the great arranger Gil Evans, and all are available in CD form from Columbia. These are wonderful recordings that belong in every serious jazz collection.

Of Brass and Reeds

The heyday of hard bop was not long, perhaps five or a half-dozen years, during which a handful of names became most thoroughly identified with the style: Rollins, Silver, Blakey, and Adderley. But hard bop also offered opportunity to a host of other musicians, especially brass and reed players, capable of pushing a hard-driving, funky sound.

Blowing Harder

In addition to Davis, the leading hard bop trumpeters were Art Farmer, Freddie Hubbard, Donald Byrd, Clifford Brown, and Cannonball Adderley's brother Nat Adderley. Representative albums include *Meet the Jazztet* (1960, an MCA/Chess CD), for Farmer—and noteworthy, too, as the recording debut of pianist McCoy Tyner; *Goin' Up* (1960, a Blue Note CD), for Hubbard; and *At the Half Note Café, Volumes 1 and 2* (1960, a Blue Note CD), for Byrd. Strictly speaking, Nat Adderley played cornet rather than trumpet, developing a sound that exploited the lowest registers of the instrument and that perfectly complemented his brother's saxophone in Cannonball's popular quintet. *That's Nat*, a recording from 1955, is great early hard bop and has been reissued by Savoy on CD. *Work Songs*, from 1960, features hard bop guitarist Wes Montgomery and is a minor classic. It is available on CD from Original Jazz Classics.

Album art for Freddie Hubbard's early album, Goin' Up.
Image from Blue Note.

Clifford Brown, whose career was cut short in a car accident at age 25, is one of the greatest of the hard bop trumpet players. We will discuss him, in connection with Max Roach, in a moment.

Hard bop brought back to the jazz forefront the trombone, an instrument that both bop and the cool school had somewhat neglected. J.J. Johnson and Kai Winding were the leading exponents of the instrument in the hard bop style, and Johnson is considered by many to be the finest jazz trombonist of all time, period. He did play in the bop style, but it was as a pioneer of hard bop that he is best known. *The Eminent Jay Jay Johnson*, featuring recordings from 1953 to 55, has been reissued on CD in two volumes by Blue Note.

In 1954, Johnson formed a two-trombone quintet with the Danish-born Kai Winding. *The Great Kai and J.J.*, recorded in 1960, available on an MCA/Impulse! CD, presents him to advantage in a hard bop setting.

The New Reedmen

In addition to Cannonball Adderley, whom we shall discuss shortly, Oliver Nelson and Jackie McLean emerged as hard bop alto saxophonists to reckon with. Nelson we will discuss toward the end of the chapter, in connection with the great hard bop summation album, *Blues and the Abstract Truth*. McLean is a widely recorded musician who is still somehow underrated. *Bluesnik*, recorded in 1961 and featuring a young Freddie Hubbard, is available on a Blue Note CD.

If bop tended to favor the alto saxophone, hard bop, with its demand for a heavier, gutsier sound, offered gainful employment to a small legion of tenormen. While

Rollins was the best known of these, Johnny Griffin, Clifford Jordan, Hank Mobley, and Stanley Turrentine also deserve to be singled out for an extended hearing.

Dig This

A Blowing Session, a 1957 recording available on CD from Blue Note, unites Griffin with two other—very different—tenor soloists, Hank Mobley and the legendary John Coltrane. It is a classic hard bop encounter.

Griffin earned the distinction of being dubbed "the world's fastest saxophonist," a facility he honed playing with the stars of bebop in the late 1940s and early 1950s. You can hear him to hard bop advantage on *The Congregation*, a Blue Note CD reissue of a 1957 recording.

Clifford Jordan's hard bop work is well represented by *Blowing in from Chicago* (1957, reissued by Blue Note) and on *Spellbound*, a 1960 recording reissued by Original Jazz Classics. Mobley's most notable hard bop recording is *Soul Station*, from 1960 and reissued on a Blue Note CD, featuring bassist Paul Chambers and drummer Art Blakey, both hard bop mainstays. For Stanley Turrentine, listen to *Up at Minton's*, from 1961, a Blue Note CD reissue.

Brown and Roach

Clifford Brown, affectionately known as Brownie, was born in Wilmington, Delaware, in 1930, began taking trumpet lessons at age 13, and was effectively coached by his high school band director. He studied math and music at college and, while still a student, began appearing professionally in Philadelphia, where he was encouraged by no less than Charlie Parker and trumpeter Fats Navarro, who particularly befriended and encouraged him.

Dig This

Columbia's *The Beginning and the End* offers some of the earliest Clifford Brown and a live recording made the night before his death. At this writing unavailable on CD, this is a moving tribute that is worth hunting for on vinyl.

In contrast to many young jazz musicians, Brown neither drank nor used drugs. In 1950, he narrowly cheated death in an automobile accident that laid him up for almost a year. On June 26, 1956, he wasn't so lucky. He was killed in a car wreck.

By 1950, Brown had established a reputation as a trumpeter fit for comparison with Miles Davis and Dizzy Gillespie. In 1954, he formed the Brown-Roach Quintet with Max Roach, already a giant among bop drummers and now ready to take on the hard bop idiom. GNP offers *The Best of Max Roach and Clifford Brown in Concert*, recordings of the quintet from 1954.

Cannonball

Julian "Cannonball" Adderley (1928–75) earned both praise and, perhaps, a degree of criticism for his upbeat, affirmative approach to the alto saxophone. The other great reedmen of his generation tended toward brooding introspection or high-speed frenzy. Adderley was exuberant and joyous. This made for remarkable chemistry when he was part of the Miles Davis Sextet, which included John Coltrane, a man of very different musical temperament.

Adderley can be heard on Davis's *Kind of Blue*, mentioned earlier, *Milestones* (Columbia, 1958), as well as on *Somethin' Else*, a Blue Note reissue from 1958. On *Something Else*, Miles Davis paid Adderley the ultimate compliment by appearing as a sideman.

Jazz Messengers

Born in Pittsburgh in 1919, drummer Art Blakey was hard bop's elder statesman, rabbi, and guru. He was a brilliant and brilliantly inventive drummer, who played so loud and long that he ultimately lost most of his hearing. This didn't end his career, anymore than it had ended Beethoven's. Like that master, he continued to hear the music in his head, and he kept playing until his death in 1992.

But Blakey was more than a drummer. He was a finder and developer of jazz talent, and in 1955, he and Horace Silver formed a cooperative jazz ensemble they called the Jazz Messengers. The name was borrowed from an octet Blakey had formed back in 1947, after Billy Eckstine disbanded the band Blakey had joined in 1944.

Silver left the Messengers in 1956, and Blakey was now leader of a group that endured into the early 1990s. For almost 40 years, Blakey nurtured the talents of a veritable jazz who's who, including Donald Byrd, Hank Mobley, Jackie McLean, Johnny Griffin, Freddie Hubbard, and such recent figures as Wynton and Branford Marsalis (see Chapter 21), Keith Jarrett, and Chuck Mangione.

Take Five

Blakey was so thoroughly devoted to jazz that he became the subject of this legend quoted in Bill Crow's *Jazz Anecdotes* (Oxford University Press, 1990):

Art was driving to an out-of-town job and passed through a village where traffic was completely tied up because of a funeral procession. Since he couldn't get past the cemetery until the service was over, he got out and listened to the eulogy. The minister spoke at length about the virtues of the deceased, and then asked if anyone had anything else to add. After a silence...Art said, "If nobody has anything to say about the departed, I'd like to say a few words about jazz!"

The Jazz Messengers was perhaps the single most important hard bop ensemble. A six-CD set, *The Complete Blue Note Recordings of Art Blakey's 1960 Jazz Messengers,* is available from Blue Note, but if you are not quite so ambitious (or so well supplied with cash), *Moanin': Art Blakey and the Jazz Messengers* (from 1958) is a great single-CD Blue Note Reissue, as is *The Big Beat* (from 1960).

Dig This

Besides *Kind of Blue,* the classic Davis sextet recording, hard bop Coltrane is epitomized on *Giant Steps,* a 1959 album that counts on most critics' lists as among the most important jazz recordings ever made. *Heavyweight Champion: The Complete Atlantic Recordings* is a boxed set that covers 1959 to 1961, the period in which Coltrane made the transition from hard bop to the avant garde. It is packed with very exciting music. We will return to Coltrane in Chapter 19.

Here Comes 'Trane

If hard bopper Art Blakey had a profound influence on jazz by virtue of having mentored and nurtured so much talent, John Coltrane exerted great influence simply by his example. Countless players sought to imitate his sound on tenor saxophone and even took to doubling on soprano because Coltrane had doubled on soprano. Countless more musicians have pored over his improvisations.

Yet few dedicated Coltrane enthusiasts think of him as a hard bop musician. Most concentrate on his later avant-garde and free jazz work. The fact is that Coltrane's style evolved gradually. He began as a rather tentative bop player, who joined the Miles Davis Quintet in 1955, before his chops were equal to his musical ideas.

Davis not only helped develop Coltrane's talent, he almost certainly saved his life—by firing him, in 1957, because of his heroin addiction. Coltrane kicked the habit—permanently—and played with the Thelonious Monk Quartet before rejoining Davis in 1958.

At this point, Davis was leader of his famed hard bop sextet, which gave 'Trane the room he needed to create what jazz critic Ira Gitler called "sheets of sound," cascading chordal improvisation that came faster and more furiously than anyone had ever heard before.

Dig This

Roach's hard bop direction culminated in the *Freedom Now Suite,* an album from 1960 (reissued on CD by Columbia) presenting a seven-part suite dealing with African-American history. This is an unusual didactic direction for hard bop, but the album is a classic of protest and is very moving music.

Roach Post-Brown

The two years drummer Max Roach co-led a quintet with Clifford Brown (1954–55) produced great hard bop. But Roach had a musical life before teaming with Brown, and he has had a long career afterward.

He came to hard bop by way of bop, playing with Parker, Gillespie, and others and considered by many the most inventive bop drummer of all, eschewing the "bombs" and other heavy-handed bop percussion clichés in favor of a more subtle approach involving skilled modulation of pitch and volume and virtuoso use of the brushes.

After working with Miles Davis on the *Birth of the Cool* sessions (see Chapter 14), Roach collaborated with Clifford Brown on a hard bop quintet. Following Brown's death, Roach organized a new quintet, Max Roach Plus 4. *Max Roach Plus Four*, recorded in 1956, has been reissued on CD by Em Arcy and is an exciting introduction to Roach as a leader and as a soloist.

The Blues and the Abstract Truth

In 1961, Oliver Nelson, alto and tenor saxophonist, recorded original compositions with young trumpeter Freddie Hubbard, altoist and flutist Eric Dolphy, baritone saxophonist George Barrow, pianist Bill Evans, bassist Paul Chambers, and drummer Roy Haynes. The result was the classic *Blues and the Abstract Truth*, reissued on CD by Impulse!

Hard Bop Meets Hard Facts

Blues and the Abstract Truth was one of several albums of the early 1960s that presented high-quality hard bop even as it signaled the demise of the form. The principal sidemen on this album—Hubbard, Dolphy, Evans, and Chambers—would very soon abandon the hard bop idiom altogether.

Hard bop had pushed the jazz envelope into the realms of avant garde and free jazz (the genre in which the likes of John Coltrane, Eric Dolphy, and some other hard boppers would make their major reputations), but more importantly, hard bop had also pushed jazz into R&B and pop genres.

Wes Montgomery. Image from author's collection.

Hard bop tore down some of the barriers that had separated jazz from many more commercial forms of popular music. This was liberating and invigorating for jazz, but by the early to mid-1960s, those hard boppers who did not move on to new forms of jazz found themselves lured squarely into pop. Wes Montgomery, for example, a hard bop guitarist whose *Incredible Jazz Guitar of Wes Montgomery* (1960, on CD from Original Jazz Classics) is one of the more significant hard bop documents, suddenly crossed over in 1965 with *Goin' Out of My Head* (Verve), a big pop hit that changed his musical orientation forever. Much the same was true for Cannonball Adderley (with his 1966 *Mercy, Mercy, Mercy*) and, to lesser degrees, for Freddie Hubbard and Horace Silver. Before the decade of the 1960s was out, hard bop had indeed come to a hard end.

The Least You Need to Know

- Hard bop took elements of bebop and added more African-American "soul," including liberal doses of blues, rhythm and blues, and black gospel tradition.
- The major founders of hard bop were Sonny Rollins, Horace Silver, Art Blakey, and Cannonball Adderley.
- Both Miles Davis and John Coltrane passed through a hard bop phase, contributing mightily to the style.
- Incorporating as it did elements of African-American popular music, hard bop soon crossed over into such pop realms as rhythm and blues and funk, as well as into fusion (see Chapter 20).

Part 5

Wild Side or Mild Side?

For some musicians, jazz is about musical tradition. For others, it's all about freedom. Beginning in the 1950s and exploding into the 1960s and beyond, certain jazz musicians abandoned traditional ideas of improvisation based on melody or chord structures and embraced new, freer ideas often based on sheer instinct. Avant-garde and free jazz pushed the limits of what musicians could play and, often, of what audiences could accept.

If jazz inspiration didn't flag, rock 'n' roll did, becoming increasingly bland and commercial during the 1970s. Well before the end of the decade, it seemed that fusion had precious little left to fuse, and some jazz musicians, unwilling to give up the larger audience rock-driven electric jazz had won for them, now looked to pop music for inspiration. Crossover or "contemporary jazz" was born.

We can talk about roots, tradition, and styles, but jazz is finally intensely personal music—both for the musicians and for their audience. One of the most creative activities a jazz fan engages in is building a personal record collection, reflecting his knowledge of the music as well as his own feelings about it. Read on for a guide to starting your own jazz record library.

Chapter 19

Welcome to the Edge: Avant-Garde and Free Jazz

In This Chapter

- Lennie Tristano introduces two free jazz pieces
- A music for its time
- What's "free" about free jazz?
- The early avant-garde masters: Monk, Coltrane, Coleman, and Mingus
- Pushing the envelope all the way

The United States Food and Drug Administration has strict rules about these things. Any strong medicine must bear a warning label. In the realm of jazz, no medicine is stronger than what practitioners of the avant-garde and free jazz offer. The warning label? How about: MAY CAUSE YOU TO UNPLUG CD PLAYER. But this one's a possibility, too: MAY EXPAND HORIZONS AND INDUCE AN OPEN MIND.

From its very roots in the music of West African slaves, jazz has been about freedom, and freedom is precisely the issue that underlies avant-garde and free jazz: freedom to explore new musical territory, freedom to improvise in new ways, freedom from the musical past, freedom from melody (in some cases), and (in some instances) even freedom from basic scales, chord structures, and rhythmic structures.

Does this mean that the ultimate expression of freedom is noise? This chapter will help you decide.

"Intuition" and "Digression": Freeing Up Jazz

As you may recall from Chapter 16, Igor Stravinsky's ballet *The Rite of Spring* brought into the world such radical sounds that it touched off a street riot when it was premiered in Paris on May 29, 1913. While nothing so dramatic happened in 1949 when pianist-composer Lennie Tristano (first encountered in Chapter 14) recorded "Intuition" and "Digression" with his sextet, the pieces were, for jazz, as innovative as Stravinsky's ballet was for classical music.

Dig This

The 1949 session featuring "Intuition" and "Digression" is available on an excellent Capitol/EMI CD titled *Intuition.*

Talk the Talk

The terms **free jazz** and **avant-garde jazz** are often used interchangeably to describe the free-form jazz of Ornette Coleman and later musicians. Some critics differentiate, however, reserving "free jazz" for music that is wholly improvisational and follows no pattern, and "avant-garde" simply to describe experimental music that may or may not adhere to rules or pattern. Some commentators in the early 1960s referred to avant-garde jazz simply as *the New Thing.*

They are highly improvisational works—nothing new there, of course. But it is the range and degree of improvisation that makes these pieces radical. Early jazz—from New Orleans jazz through much of the music of the swing period—involved improvisation principally based on melodic lines. Some advanced swing and all bebop made the underlying chord patterns, not the melodic line, the basis for improvisation. Depending how the musician interpreted these patterns, the resulting improvisations could stray very far from recognizable tunes. Many listeners found this exciting, others merely bewildering.

And for still others, like Lennie Tristano in 1949, even chord-based improvisation didn't allow sufficient freedom for invention. Tristano began improvising both instinctively and collectively. Both "Intuition" and "Digression" begin with brief thematic statements, then the sextet wanders off freely, governed only by individual imagination and a kind of collective imagination, a feel or instinct for where the group should take the music next.

In one sense, Tristano was reaching well ahead of his time. Many musicians and hard core Tristano fans were excited by "Intuition" and "Digression". Many others, however, dismissed (or downright condemned) these pieces as nonmusic. People who neither liked nor understood jazz had brushed off bebop as make-it-up-as-you-go-along music. Well, here was music that *really was* made up as it went along! Yet free jazz would become increasingly important by the end of the 1950s, into the 1960s, and beyond.

In another sense, however, Tristano was very much *of* his time. Think about the world in 1949. It was just four years out of the second global war of the century and, for all anyone knew, was years, months, days, or moments from a third global war that, given the availability of weapons of mass destruction, would probably spell the end of the world. The wars of the century were the most extreme symptoms of a world in which traditional structures, ideas, tastes, and values were either crumbling or fluid.

In the arts, traditional literary forms such as the novel and the poem had been transformed. Old-fashioned storytelling was still around but so were "stream-of-consciousness" and "automatic writing," in which authors went along for the ride as they relinquished control of their words to the unconscious mind. Rhymed metrical poems were still being written but so was "free verse," poetry structured not according to abstract rules, but as the spirit moved the poet. In the visual arts, too, traditionalists were still creating painting and sculpture that "imitated" surface reality, but the most important painters and sculptors had broken free of the need to imitate and reproduce. And in modern classical music, we know that things were never the same after Stravinsky.

Riffs

Modern classical or "art music" was often even more adventurous than jazz. Avant-gardist John Cage (1912–92) wrote such works as "Imaginary Landscape No. 4" (1951), for 12 randomly tuned radios, 24 performers, and conductor; and "4'33"" (Four Minutes and Thirty-three Seconds, 1952), in which the musicians remain silent onstage for four minutes, thirty-three seconds. Even Igor Stravinsky was unamused. "I look forward to a work of major length from this composer," he remarked of it acidly.

Free jazz was radical, but it was a radical response to politically, socially, humanly, and artistically radical times. If the 18th century, the "Age of Reason," called for the orderly music of a Haydn or Mozart, the years after World War II (a period the British poet W.H. Auden dubbed the Age of Anxiety) seemed to call for either disorderly music or music that searched for new, inner orders. For global war and the possibility of instantaneous universal annihilation, among many other things, had robbed the old external orders of their foundations.

Thelonious Assault

As we saw in Chapter 18, Thelonious Sphere Monk came of age among the beboppers, but was spurned by some of them, who thought he was merely crazy. Monk was certainly capable of improvising, writing, and playing in the bop style—and doing so with great lyricism. With the exception of Monk—"'Round Midnight," for example—bebop is not known for gorgeous melodies. But Monk also wrote, improvised, and played music characterized by idiosyncratic rhythms with bizarre offbeats, silences, and accents, and he wrote tunes that seem to consist of all wrong notes (listen to "Gallop's Gallop," for example). In "Brilliant Corners," perhaps Monk's single most unorthodox work, conventional scales are left by the wayside, rhythm is stretched and compressed, and chords often consist of quirky "crushed" clusters of notes.

Take Five

To paraphrase the antiwar anthem of the 1960s, Give Monk a Chance. Once you're hooked on his music, you'll want it all, and next time your favorite stock splits, why not plow some of the profits into *The Complete Riverside Recordings*? This is a 15-CD set of great Monk spanning 1955–1961 and is as essential to any serious collector of jazz as, say, the Budapest Quartet's complete Beethoven string quartets are to the committed classical collector.

If you don't want to make a 15-CD commitment just yet, the original 1956 *Brilliant Corners* album has been released on CD by Original Jazz Classics. *The Thelonious Monk Orchestra at Town Hall* (1959) is on Original Jazz Classics, and *Monk's Dream* (1962) is available from Columbia.

Yet "Brilliant Corners" never sounds chaotic. Monk's genius was such that he traveled in musical realms into which no one followed, yet what he produced has an inner coherence, power, and beauty.

Thelonious Sphere Monk. Image from the Frank Driggs Collection.

Even the most open-minded critics occasionally level this charge against free jazz: It may be interesting, but it fails to *move* the listener. This is never the case with Thelonious Monk. Strange sounds? To be sure. But there is always something compelling, fascinating, and intensely felt about the music of this early avant-garde master.

The Coltrane Legend and Legacy

Intensity of feeling is a strong point of another early avant-gardist. We met John Coltrane briefly in Chapter 18, but by the mid-1960s, Coltrane had moved well beyond hard bop and was far into the realm of the avant-garde. In contrast to many experimental musicians, however, Coltrane's adventure was not a lonely one. His intensity was truly compelling, attracting other committed musicians to his side, and also drawing an audience far larger than any avant-garde artist could hope for. By 1965, when he was entering into his most advanced musical period, John Coltrane was a very well-paid musician.

With Monk

Coltrane played with Miles Davis from 1955 until Davis fired him in 1957 when his heroin addiction made him unreliable (Chapter 18). The experience sobered Coltrane—literally. He permanently kicked his drug habit and briefly joined the Thelonious Monk Quartet. If you can afford to invest in the monster 15-CD *Complete Riverside Recordings* mentioned earlier, you will own Monk's work with Coltrane (and much else, of course). *Thelonious Monk and John Coltrane* is a Milestone vinyl two-LP set yet to be released on CD; however, *Thelonious with John Coltrane*, from Original Jazz Classics, is available on CD and features wonderful music from 1958.

Committed Monk and 'Trane fans speak reverently of the 1958 sessions the two collaborated on at New York's famed Five Spot. Only recently did a tape, made by Coltrane's first wife, Juanita, turn up. Blue Note has released this mesmerizing material on *Discovery! at the Five Spot.*

Riffs

The intense Coltrane worked to exhaustion, as critic Scott Yanow observes:

Although the cause of [Coltrane's] death on July 17, 1967 [at age 41] was listed as liver cancer, in reality it was probably overwork. Coltrane used to practice ten to twelve hours a day and when he had a job (which featured marathon solos), he would often spend his breaks practicing in his dressing room! It was only through such singlemindedness that he could reach such a phenomenal technical level, but the net result was his premature death.

The "Classic Quartet"

Working together was a growth experience for Monk as well as for Coltrane, who went on in 1960 to form what fans have come to call the "classic quartet," consisting of pianist McCoy Tyner, drummer Elvin Jones, and (after several others) bassist Jimmy Garrison.

My Favorite Things, recorded by the quartet in 1960 (and reissued on an Atlantic CD) electrified the jazz world when it was released. The title cut, featuring 'Trane on soprano saxophone, pared down the chords and revved up the intensity, setting an example of modal improvisation that proved highly influential. This is an essential document of modern jazz.

John Coltrane, as photographed by "Popsie" Randloph. Image from the Frank Driggs Collection.

A Love Supreme

Between 1960 and 1965, Coltrane blazed deeper and deeper trails into the avant-garde. In live performance, he became legendary for monumental solos that could stretch to as much as three-quarters of an hour. Audiences were riveted to every second. Signed in 1961 as the first artist on the brand new Impulse! label, Coltrane was recorded at Birdland in 1963 on an album released as *Live at Birdland*. Now available on an Impulse! CD, this may be Coltrane's single best album. It moves into uncharted territory, yet is always guided by some uncanny compass toward an intense beauty.

Coltrane's journey led him through experimental territory and into spiritual realms. *A Love Supreme* (recorded by Impulse! in December 1964 and reissued on CD) meant a great deal to Coltrane personally as a kind of hymn to God. It is very moving music that signaled a final change in direction. During the last two years of his life, Coltrane embraced even freer experimentation, taking unpredictable turns. *Expression* (originally recorded by Impulse! in 1967 and reissued on CD by GRP) is music from Coltrane's final sessions and features 'Trane not only on tenor saxophone, but also on flute. This is music best enjoyed and appreciated if one comes to it having heard some of Coltrane's work from earlier in the decade.

Take Five

Established in 1960 as a subsidiary of ABC-Paramount, Impulse! immediately signed such advanced jazz artists as John Coltrane, Kai Winding, J.J. Johnson, Cecil Taylor, and hard bop/avant-garde tenorman Archie Shepp, advertising that "The New Wave of Jazz Is on Impulse!"

While Impulse! also offered recordings by numerous mainstream artists, it was the label of choice for fans of the cutting edge. During his later career, Coltrane recorded exclusively for the company, which never fully recovered from his death in 1967. The importance of Impulse! as an avant-garde label diminished, but beginning in the 1980s, the label has reissued much of its now classic material.

Ornette Coleman's "Free Jazz"

Alto saxophonist Ornette Coleman's very first recording, *The Music of Ornette Coleman: Something Else!!!,* made in 1958 for the Contemporary label, is available on CD as from Original Jazz Classics. It is a revelation. At 28, Ornette Coleman burst upon the jazz scene with a style that seemed fully developed. Moreover, it was the radical, free-jazz sound that, over the succeeding decades, would win him a small legion of dedicated fans and a host of vociferous detractors.

Real Square

Free jazz and avant-garde jazz are not for everyone. If you don't like the music, don't be intimidated, and *don't* give up on it at first hearing. Give it a chance. Most new or complex music is an acquired taste that rewards repeated hearing. Also, don't make the mistake of lumping all of this music together. The practitioners of avant-garde and free jazz are, if anything, individuals. They write a wide range of *different* music.

Ornette Coleman's music may sound frenetic and random on first hearing. To be sure, it is intense and wailing, but, while avant-garde, it is also grounded in African and African-American folk music as well as in the blues. It is at once abstract and angular, with bursts of rapid-fire notes and unpredictable turns and tempo changes, but it is also earthy, raw, and primal.

While these qualities are evident in Coleman's music from his first recording, he actually developed them over a period of years, beginning when he first took up the saxophone at 14 in his hometown of

Fort Worth, Texas. He was influenced early on by Charlie Parker, then played in carnival bands touring Texas and the Southwest before moving to New Orleans in 1948, where he worked menial non-musical jobs. By 1950, he was in Los Angeles playing rhythm and blues, from time to time attempting to inject his original voice into the music, only to be discouraged by unresponsive audiences and colleagues.

Dig This

For the truly adventurous, *Beauty Is a Rare Thing: The Complete Atlantic Recordings* offers six CDs of Coleman's highly challenging work. An excellent one-CD sampling is from Blue Note, *At the "Golden Circle" in Stockholm*, volume 1.

Coleman found work as an elevator operator and used his spare time to study harmony and musical theory. He performed catch-as-catch-can in underground L.A. jazz clubs and was finally discovered by bassists Red Mitchell and Percy Heath (of the Modern Jazz Quartet). After the Contemporary recording date, Coleman, encouraged and sponsored by John Lewis, attended the Lenox School of Jazz and moved to New York, where he either amazed or outraged audiences and fellow musicians alike with improvisational works that avoided chord structures.

Coleman's music is both intensely exciting and exhausting to listen to. While he has garnered as many detractors as advocates, not even his harshest critics ever question his integrity, and he has continued to perform and to develop his music.

Pithecanthropus Erectus

The jazz avant-garde has never been a unified movement to the degree that swing, bop, cool jazz, or hard bop were. Avant-gardists have taken music in many directions. Charles Mingus (1922–79), virtuoso bass player and composer, embraced—even as he surged beyond—all the jazz traditions Ornette Coleman seemed simply to reject. Indeed, Mingus, notoriously opinionated and irascible, loudly denounced Coleman and his music.

Charles Mingus was honored on a 1997 U.S. postage stamp. Image from the author's collection.

Take Five

Mingus had a legendary temper and was fired by the customarily easygoing Duke Ellington because of a fight with trombonist Juan Tizol. Mingus presented his side of the story in his autobiography, explaining that Tizol had called him a "nigger" who couldn't read music, then lunged at him with "a bolo knife"—onstage during a performance at Harlem's Apollo Theater. After the show, Ellington called Mingus into his dressing room:

"'Now, Charles,' he says, looking amused, putting Cartier links into the cuffs of his beautiful handmade shirt, 'you could have forewarned me—you left me out of the act entirely!

"'... I must say I never saw a large man so agile—I never saw *anybody* make such tremendous leaps! The gambado over the piano carrying your bass was colossal. When you exited after that, I thought, "That man's really afraid of Juan's knife, and at the speed he's going, he's probably home in bed now." But no, back you came through the same door with your bass still intact. For a moment, I was hopeful you decided to sit down and play but instead you slashed Juan's chair in two with a fire axe!

"'Really, Charles, that's destructive. Everybody knows Juan has a knife, but nobody ever took it seriously—he likes to pull it out and show it to people, you understand.

"'So I'm afraid, Charles—I've never fired anybody—you'll have to quit my band. I don't need any new problems. Juan's an old problem, I can cope with that, but you seem to have a whole bag of new tricks. I must ask you to be kind enough to give me your notice, Charles.'

"The charming way he says it, like he's paying you a compliment. Feeling honored, you shake hands and resign."

Mingus started out in swing—even doing a stint with Ellington—then moved to bop and, in 1955, founded an experimental Jazz Workshop, which included such major innovative and avant-garde figures as flutist, bass clarinetist, and alto saxophonist Eric Dolphy, altoist Jackie McLean, and multiple reed player Rahsaan Roland Kirk.

During the workshop years, Mingus turned out extraordinary compositions, including *My Jelly Roll Soul, Orange Was the Color of Her Dress, Goodbye Pork Pie Hat,* and the slyly brilliant protest against the segregation policies of Arkansas Governor Orval Faubus, *Fables of Faubus*. This period of Mingus's career is well represented on *New Tijuana Moods* (a Bluebird CD), *Blues and Roots* (Atlantic), and *Mingus Ah Um* (Columbia).

With Eric Dolphy

Born in Los Angeles in 1928, Eric Dolphy was a master of the flute, bass clarinet, and alto saxophone. He became a member of the Charles Mingus Quartet and inspired Mingus to bolder levels of experimentation. Dolphy's improvisational style was marked by Grand Canyon-like leaps from low to high notes, punctuated by nonmusical murmurs and other speech-like sounds. He played with a variety of innovative artists, including Ornette Coleman and John Coltrane, but he always returned to work in Mingus ensembles, including his quintet and sextet. *Mingus at Antibes*, recorded in 1960 by Atlantic and available on an Atlantic CD, features Dolphy in the pianoless quartet setting.

Dig This

Dolphy fans treasure the 1964 *Out to Lunch* album cut for Blue Note in February 1964, just four months before his death. It's now available as a Blue Note CD.

The career of Eric Dolphy, one of the most inventive yet approachable exponents of free jazz, was tragically cut short in 1964 when, at age 36, he succumbed to a diabetic coma.

Mingus Dynasty

Despite financial disaster following his attempt to start avant-garde promotional and recording companies, Charles Mingus continued to perform and compose, venturing into the composition of larger-scale works and music for large ensembles, including the truly marvelous *Cumbia and Jazz Fusion* (1976–77), available on an Atlantic CD and featuring a large and colorful complement of percussion and winds.

Dig This

More Mingus? *The Black Saint and the Sinner Lady* (Impulse!, 1963) and *Mingus Mingus Mingus Mingus Mingus* (Impulse!, 1963) are two strikingly different aspects of this modern master at the height of his powers. *Black Saint* is a full-length suite, while *Mingus...* features seven great compositions, including the incomparable "Mood Indigo."

By the later 1970s, Mingus was diagnosed as suffering from ALS—better known as Lou Gherig's Disease, an ultimately fatal degeneration of the central nervous system. Shortly before his death, in 1978, he was honored by President Jimmy Carter in a White House ceremony.

He was also honored by his wife, Susan Graham Ungaro Mingus, who formed the Mingus Dynasty, a group consisting primarily of Mingus sidemen, dedicated to performing his works. *Mingus Dynasty Live at the Village Vanguard* is an excellent 1984 session on a Storyville CD. More recently, the Mingus Big Band has been playing and recording Mingus works. Listen to *Mingus Big Band—Live* (Dreyfus Records, 1996).

Piano Four Hands

Mingus may have been personally difficult, but his music, advanced though it is, can be enjoyed by just about anyone. It is rich in melodic content and in texture, and it is by turns moody and witty. The work of pianist-composer Cecil Taylor is not nearly as accessible, and, like that of Ornette Coleman, it draws as many vigorous detractors as passionate enthusiasts.

What's so challenging about Taylor?

He is a no-holds-barred *atonal* improviser, who treats the piano as if it were a set of drums. Instead of chords, even dissonant chords, Taylor often plays bursts of *tone clusters*, blocks of sound from adjacent keys. The music is typically intense, which can be exciting, demanding, or just plain irritating.

While Cecil Taylor's music is definitely not for everyone, it should be heard. A good way to ease into Taylor is through a 1961 recording, now available on CD from Candid, called *New York R&B*. If you like bebop, chances are you'll enjoy this album. From here, proceed to *Unit Structures*, originally recorded in 1966 and reissued on CD by Blue Note.

Here's another pair of hands—and a different, but still avant-garde approach to the piano. Keith Jarrett was born in Allentown, Pennsylvania, in 1945 and was a piano prodigy, starting to play at three and giving his first recital at five. Moving to New York in 1965, he spent some time with Art Blakey and the Jazz Messengers, and after work with others, played fusion with Miles Davis during 1969–71.

His stint with Davis was the last time he would perform on electric keyboards. He returned to the acoustic piano and launched a series of solo concerts. These are extraordinary concert-length improvisations that, while acoustic, are electrifying. Stylistically, the solo concerts blend jazz, classical, and non-Western (mostly Far Eastern) musical traditions with a power and imagination that are both dramatic and meditative. Start with *The Köln Concert* (1971, ECM).

Talk the Talk

Tone clusters are dissonant chords consisting of adjacent notes. Clusters are often heard in **atonal** music—that is, music that is not written in a particular key. To ears accustomed to music centered on a particular key or scale, atonal work sounds dissonant.

The Wildest Ones

The discordant intensity of Cecil Taylor possesses an internal logic that emerges on repeated hearing. But free jazz offers even wilder territory to explore, in which logic, internal or otherwise, is pretty hard to find.

Dig This

Sun Ra often made it difficult to take his music seriously, since he and his Arkestra arrayed themselves in bizarre (and rather cheesy) costumes intended to evoke connections with other worlds as well as with ancient Egypt. Sun Ra also employed non-musical entertainment in many of his live concerts, including, at one point, fire-eaters and plate spinners.

Sun Ra

He was either Herman "Sonny" Blount (1914–93) from Birmingham, Alabama, or Sun Ra, from another planet. The latter was his claim, but it was as Sonny Blount that he led his own band in the '30s and worked as a pianist and arranger for Fletcher Henderson in the '40s. In 1953 (as Sun Ra), he formed a big band he called the Arkestra and started playing highly advanced bebop. Almost before anyone else, he also got into electric keyboards and other amplified instruments, and he soon began playing free jazz.

How free? *Other Planes of There,* recorded in 1964 and available on CD from Evidence, is a mixture of mystical and avant-garde elements, rich in *polyrhythmic* passages, full of odd orchestration, chants, and other sounds. If this sounds strange, it most definitely is, but it's also highly compelling, hypnotically fascinating orchestral music. *Jazz in Silhouette,* also available on Evidence, is a slightly more recognizable example of Sun Ra's avant/big-band style.

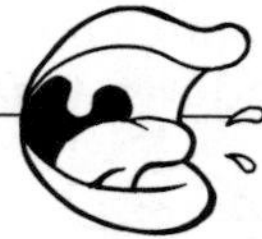

Talk the Talk

Multiphonics is the sounding of simultaneous notes, like a chord, on an instrument conventionally capable of playing only one note at a time.

Pharoah Sanders

Farrell—Pharoah sounds much better—Sanders was born in Little Rock, Arkansas, in 1940, and started playing tenor saxophone as an "unofficial" fifth member of the John Coltrane Quartet in 1962. Sanders wowed audiences and fellow musicians alike with his wild improvisations in the screech range of his horn and his use of *multiphonics,* the sounding of simultaneous notes, like a chord, on an instrument conventionally capable of playing one note at a time.

Real Square

Spelling bee finalists will insist that Pharoah is spelled Pharaoh. True enough for the rulers of ancient Egypt, but not for this tenorman.

Sanders is so exciting a player that he made free jazz really fun to listen to, and his 1969 *Karma* (available on CD from Impulse!) was deservedly a hit record. In contrast to most other avant-gardists, Sanders has retreated over the course of his later career and is now more of a bop-style musician than an exponent of experimental jazz.

Rahsaan Roland Kirk

Rahsaan Roland Kirk (1936–77) is especially difficult to categorize, having played swing, bop, hard bop, R&B, avant-garde music, and New Orleans jazz! Blind since age two, he began playing tenor saxophone professionally while still a teenager and also discovered at this time the saxello (a variant of the B-flat soprano saxophone) and the straight (as opposed to conventionally curved) E-flat alto saxophone. He made modifications to both instruments, calling his version of the modified saxello a manzello and the modified straight alto a stritch. The modifications he made—with tape and rubber bands—allowed him to play his conventional tenor saxophone (also modified), the manzello, and the stritch simultaneously, all three mouthpieces in his mouth at the same time! Thus he was a saxophonist capable of playing chords.

Needless to day, the sight of Kirk blowing was nothing short of extraordinary. Was it a gimmick? Well, it certainly served Kirk effectively as one, but he also used it to unique musical purposes, as can be heard on the fine sampler album, *Does Your House Have Lions: The Rahsaan Roland Kirk Anthology*, a two-CD compilation from Rhino.

Braxton

While Sanders made his peace with bop, Anthony Braxton, "multireedist" (alto saxophone, clarinet, contrabass clarinet, and so on) and composer, has resolutely pursued his own path, producing a prodigious quantity of music in a variety of avant-garde styles. Born in Chicago, Braxton studied jazz as well as modern classical music, supplemented by university work in philosophy. Active in the Chicago-based avant-garde collective Association for the Advancement of Creative Musicians, he frequently confounds the jazz world by demonstrating his facility with "straight" jazz, only to take what he does to extremes that seem very remote from all jazz traditions. Indeed, many of his pieces involve elements of theater and visual art, and none of his compositions are titled in the conventional sense, but are instead labeled with animal or geometric icons.

Anthony Braxton. Image from the Tricentric Foundation (via the Internet).

Braxton often improvises or performs highly abstract solos, but he is also capable of writing humorous pieces for such ensembles as marching band. In any given performance, he may play clarinet, saxophone, contrabass clarinet, or even flute and piano. This might be called truly *free* jazz—unrestricted in style or instrumentation—were it not for the unique logic of Braxton's idiosyncratic system of composition.

Braxton's output is considerable, but a good initial approach to this composer is through his *Dortmund (Quartet—1967)* album, available on CD from Hat Art. *Dortmund* combines forays into highly abstract free jazz with elements of swinging bebop, brilliantly colorful percussion, and even circus-like music.

The Art Ensemble of Chicago

Since 1971, Chicago has also been home to the Art Ensemble of Chicago, a free jazz quintet consisting of Roscoe Mitchell and (until recently) Joseph Jarman (on reeds, vibes, marimba, and an assortment of very strange winds, ranging from toy whistles to conch shells), Lester Bowie (on brass, harmonica, celeste, and other instruments), Malachi Favors (bass, zither, banjo, and so on), and Don Moye (who plays a collection of ethnic and homemade percussion instruments he dubs "sun percussion"). The Art Ensemble developed out of the Association for the Advancement of Creative Musicians in 1965 and was officially founded in Paris in 1969.

The Art Ensemble is one of the most important avant-garde jazz groups and certainly among the most delightfully inventive. Live performances are as much a treat for the eyes as for the ears, with displays of miscellaneous instruments ranging from beautiful African percussion pieces to bicycle horns, gongs, sirens, and various toys. Jazz purists may protest the group's theatricality, but let them stay home.

Dig This

Live is a 1972 Delmark recording available on CD and featuring the Art Ensemble in all its aspects: funny, furious, and fascinating.

Groups like the Art Ensemble are not for purists or for anyone who wants their music *either* this way *or* that. "Free jazz" is not merely free of tonal and rhythmic restrictions, it is about freedom to choose whatever direction offers itself as the most creative at the moment. If you have trouble with that concept, you will never like free jazz, but if, like Ralph Waldo Emerson, you would inscribe the word WHIM above your doorway, the musical explorers in this chapter are for you.

The Least You Need to Know

- At the root of all jazz is the issue of freedom, and avant-garde or free jazz is a natural outgrowth of this issue.
- The extremes of avant-garde and free jazz are very much a part of the postwar era, a time in which traditional concepts of art, order, and reality itself were called into question.
- Lennie Tristano, Thelonious Monk, John Coltrane, Ornette Coleman, and Charles Mingus were the great pioneers of avant-garde jazz.
- Much recent free jazz reaches back into the ethnic roots of the music, becoming modern by returning to the "primitive."

Chapter 20

Fusion Power: Jazz Rocks

In This Chapter

- Jazz musicians react to rock
- Miles Davis brings rock into jazz
- Rockers react to jazz
- The 1970s: Jazz electrifies
- Fusion embraces jazz and rock with a dash of folk
- The key fusion groups

On January 10, 1956, Memphis singer Elvis Aron Presley walked into RCA's Nashville studio and recorded "Heartbreak Hotel." Over the next 27 months, until he was inducted into the army in March 1958, Presley recorded "Hound Dog," "Jailhouse Rock," "Love Me Tender," "Don't Be Cruel," "All Shook Up," and much more.

The rest, as they say, is history.

Rock 'n' roll burst upon the scene, slumped a bit in the early 1960s, was revived when the Beatles crossed the Atlantic and Dylan went electric, and it has been going strong ever since, the longest-lived popular music phenomenon in history and a central fixture of the popular culture of America and most of the world.

Not everybody has liked it. Many jazz and pop musicians of the 1950s, for example, saw the new music as luring away an already dwindling audience (although any number of 1950s jazz musicians made extra bread as studio players backing up early rock 'n' roll recording acts). At first, in some jazz quarters, resentment ran high. By the

1960s, most jazz musicians simply turned a deaf ear, hoping rock would just go away. But other jazz artists not only listened to the music, but actively engaged it. By the mid-1970s, a hybrid style combining rock and jazz was being called fusion. Let's hear some of it.

If You Can't Beat 'Em...

By the 1960s, jazz musicians had plenty to worry about. The jazz life had never been easy, but now it was getting even harder to make a living. A number of musicians moved to Europe or at least toured there, where jazz was better received than in the States. In the '20s, the "Jazz Age," the whole world moved to the tempo of jazz. During the swing era, the mid-1930s to the mid-1940s, popular music and swing jazz were virtually synonymous.

Then came the fragmentation of jazz styles: bop from swing, and hard bop and the cool school from bop. Mainstream jazz kept plugging along during this period, but its audience was aging. The cool school soon eased into pleasant pop, in part via the bossa nova fad of the early 1960s, and many hard boppers went the way of pop or R&B or soul, while others pursued the less lucrative paths of free jazz and the avant garde.

By the 1960s, jazz was as exciting as ever—given its increased variety, maybe *more* exciting—but its audience was dwindling even as the pop-music industry was becoming larger and more powerful: a juggernaut, a steam roller.

Miles Again

I think it was Lyndon Johnson who once observed that, given a choice, he'd rather be on top of a steam roller than under one. Miles Davis, who had already embraced bop and hard bop, saw the steam roller coming and, by the later 1960s, was looking for a way to get on top. Since 1963, a young pianist named Herbie Hancock had been part of one incarnation of the Davis Quintet. In 1967, Davis began using Hancock on electric piano. For his part, Hancock infused his keyboard work with rock rhythms and feeling as well as jazz.

Herbie Hancock

Hancock was first heard on electric keyboards with Davis in 1967, but the 1968 *In a Silent Way* is the first breakthrough album, which clearly shows the roots of fusion. It is available on CD from Columbia.

Born in Chicago in 1940, Hancock studied classical piano (performing Mozart with the Chicago Symphony Orchestra at age 11) and went on to compose and play in a late bop or "post-bop" idiom before joining the Miles Davis Quintet in 1963 and moving increasingly toward a rock-inflected sound by the late 1960s. The early Hancock sound is beautifully represented on *Maiden Voyage*, recorded in 1965 and reissued by Blue Note on CD.

Keyboardist-composer Chick Corea. Image from Ron Moss Management.

In 1968, Chick Corea replaced Hancock on electric piano in the Davis group, and Hancock went on to lead his own ensembles. During the '70s, he formed The Herbie Hancock Sextet, a jazz-rock group that also drew on African and Indian musical sources. The Sextet may be heard on *Mwandishi: The Complete Warner Bros. Recordings*, a two-CD reissue of material from 1972.

Hancock formed the Headhunters in 1973 and crossed over into pop, most successfully with his 1983 MTV hit, "Rockit," but he has also continued to record in the jazz vein.

A Jazz Guitar Starts a Rockin'

While Davis was edging toward a fusion of jazz and rock, a young Texas guitarist, Larry Coryell, teamed up with a quartet led by Gary Burton, a vibes player, who had been mixing elements of rock, jazz, and country. With Coryell, the group began performing jazz-rock, producing *Duster*, a 1967 album that combined jazz, rock, and country and that came as a revelation to jazz musicians willing to open their ears to it. Many consider this the first fusion album. Originally released by RCA, it is available on CD from Koch Jazz.

Blood, Sweat, Tears, and Chicago

Many jazz musicians may have seen themselves as the underdogs going up against rock, but there were also rock musicians who not only respected jazz, but wanted to learn from it and incorporate it into their sound. The most important of these groups in the late sixties were Blood, Sweat and Tears and Chicago (originally called Chicago Transit Authority).

BS&T, which attracted fairly sophisticated rock fans, used horn arrangements reminiscent of Stan Kenton in their 1968 *Child Is the Father to the Man*, while Chicago employed somewhat more homogenized, but still jazzy, horns in its 1969 *Chicago Transit Authority*.

Yet both BS&T and Chicago lacked significant improvisational elements, and the next advance in the fusion of the two styles would come not from the rock side, but from jazz.

Bitches Brew

In August 1969, Miles Davis recorded *Bitches Brew*, a landmark fusion document (available as a double CD from Columbia). The personnel who collaborated on this extremely important recording—essential to any comprehensive jazz collection—are a young who's who of fusion musicians: Wayne Shorter on soprano saxophone; John McLaughlin on guitar; Chick Corea on keyboards (with Larry Young and Joe Zawinul on some cuts as well); and a percussion section that includes Jack DeJohnette.

Bitches Brew is a set of long, complex works, and it has never and will never please jazz purists, who react to it much the way that Bob Dylan's folkier fans responded to his introduction of electric instruments in 1965. They just don't like it. Nevertheless, *Bitches Brew* turned on many rock fans (and musicians) to jazz, even as it did manage to win over numerous jazz aficionados and musicians to the possibilities of rock. Certainly, the album made the fusion style, which figured prominently in the 1970s and 1980s, possible. Davis brought improvisational genius to the thick sonic textures of rock, and the musician who had gotten his start in resolutely undanceable bebop, now propelled his vision of jazz through hard-rocking flashes of a dance beat.

Electrification Program

In the wake of Davis's *Bitches Brew*, a number of young jazz musicians began to see the future in a synthesis of jazz and rock. In many cases, the transition to a fusion style was signaled by a migration from acoustic to electric instruments.

Chick Corea

Born in Chelsea, Massachusetts, in 1941, Armando Anthony "Chick" Corea emerged as a piano prodigy at age four and, as a youngster, was attracted to the music of Horace Silver and Bud Powell. During the early '60s, young Corea played with the Latin jazz bands of Mongo Santamaria and Willie Bobo, and with Blue Mitchell, Herbie Mann, and Stan Getz. His debut album as a leader, *Tones for Joan's Bones*, came in 1966 and verges on the avant-garde. The hard bop *Now He Sings, Now He Sobs* came in 1968 (and is available on a Blue Note CD).

In 1968, Corea joined Miles Davis, gradually replacing Herbie Hancock and easing into electric piano. During this period, he worked with Davis on *Bitches Brew* and other jazz-rock projects, but when he left Davis in 1970, he returned to the avant-garde mode, playing acoustic works in Circle, a quartet that included Anthony Braxton (Chapter 19) among its members. The following year, Corea left Circle to form his own band, Return to Forever, originally a Brazilian-style group (which counted among its members the Brazilian vocalist Flora Purim, whose 1973 *Butterfly Dreams* is a thing of great beauty still available on an Original Jazz Classics CD). By 1972, Corea transformed Return to Forever into a high-octane fusion band, featuring Al DiMeola on guitar.

Dig This

You can hear Return to Forever in its original Brazilian incarnation on *Light as a Feather*, a 1972 Polydor release now available on CD. A lot of jazz fans love this first incarnation and hate the second, *Hymn of the Seventh Galaxy*, another Polydor release, from 1973. It showcases the group in its full-speed-ahead fusion version.

The music of Return to Forever, one of the most important of all fusion groups, was heavily rock-oriented, but it was also highly improvisational in the spirit of jazz.

Return to Forever dissolved in the late 1970s, and it wasn't until 1985 that Corea formed a new fusion group, the Elektric Band, which featured electric bassist John Patitucci. *Light Years* (on the GRP label) is perhaps the most all-around satisfying recording of the Elektric Band.

Al DiMeola

A native of Jersey City, New Jersey, Al DiMeola was not yet 20 years old when he replaced Bill Connors as guitarist in Chick Corea's Return to Forever in 1974. This catapulted him to fame as he helped propel the group into high-energy fusion—though he also drew criticism for favoring technical proficiency over feeling. In addition to his work with Corea, DiMeola recorded such impressive albums as *Land of the Midnight Sun* (1976, Columbia), which features extended and complex fusion works.

DiMeola ventured beyond fusion into such albums as *Heart of the Immigrants*, a 1993 exploration on the Mesa label of the rich depths of the Argentine tango.

The Bass Plugs In

Electronic amplification profoundly changed the texture of popular music. Perhaps the role it most revolutionized was that of the bass. The acoustic double bass played a vital part in small-ensemble jazz, to be sure, but amplification made the bass guitar possible, which meant that bass parts could really be heard, and they could be played rapidly, nimbly, and melodically. No longer would the bass be relegated to the rhythm section.

Perhaps the greatest of the jazz-oriented electric bassists was Jaco Pastorius. Born in 1951 in Norristown, Pennsylvania, Pastorius was both blessed and cursed with an

Dig This

Stanley Clarke (1951–) is master of both the acoustic and electric bass. His early album *Stanley Clarke,* a 1974 Epic release, is available on CD. Together with *Children of Forever* (released in 1972 by Polydor and now available from One Way Records), it is fresh early fusion. Like Clarke, John Patitucci (1959–) plays acoustic as well as electric bass and may be heard to advantage on the 1991 *Hear of the Bass* (from Stretch) with Chick Corea.

aggressive ego that enabled him to muscle the electric bass into the front ranks of lead instruments. He played with the Pat Metheny Group, which was (as we shall see in a moment) one of the key fusion organizations, and with another important group, Weather Report. He also toured on his own and with his own ensemble, Word of Mouth.

If you like electric bass, you must hear Pastorius, and a good place to start is *Jaco Pastorius*, a 1976 Epic release now available on CD.

Pastorius's career was that of a shooting star. The 1980s were, for him, muffled by drug abuse, and he died of injuries sustained in a barroom brawl at the Midnight Club in Fort Lauderdale, Florida, on September 21, 1987.

Ditto the Fiddle

The violin never became a prime jazz instrument in the way that the trumpet and saxophone have, yet it had at least two great early virtuosos, Stephane Grappelli and Joe Venuti (Chapter 9). These musicians specialized in swing (Grappelli) and in swing, classic jazz, and Dixieland (Venuti). But after them, the violin essentially disappeared from jazz until—surprisingly—the advent of fusion. For if the violin leaps to mind as a jazz instrument, it seems light-years away from rock.

Dig This

Upon the Wings of Music (1975, Atlantic) is perhaps Ponty's most interesting fusion recording and is certainly regarded by musicians as his most influential.

French-born (1942–) Jean-Luc Ponty has transformed the violin into an extraordinary fusion instrument. The son of a violin teacher, Ponty started playing at five and, at 13, left school to embark on a classical concert career. After studying at the prestigious Paris Conservatory, he was awarded that institution's Premier Prix and went on to play with the classical Concerts Lamoureux Orchestra. By the late '50s, he had been introduced to jazz and, by the early 1960s, had turned to it exclusively.

Ponty recorded an album with the avant-garde rock musician Frank Zappa in 1969 (*King Kong: Ponty Plays Zappa*, on Pacific Jazz), started a free-jazz band in the early 1970s, then toured with Zappa's Mothers of Invention in 1973, before touring with the Mahavishnu Orchestra during 1974–75. After this, Ponty fronted his own bands.

Ponty's versatility is phenomenal—he can play swing, bop, free jazz, and fusion with seemingly equal facility. His rhythmically driving fusion not only exploits the qualities of the violin, it draws on the full range of rock instrumental effects as well, including fuzz tone and distortion. Ponty created a rock violin technique and also pioneered various electronic modifications to the instrument, beginning by simply amplifying a conventional violin, then moving to a special five-string electronic violin, and to the violectra, an instrument tuned an octave lower than a conventional violin.

A New Group Causes Con-Fusion

You are deep into a book that claims to provide a map of jazz but has repeatedly warned that jazz musicians typically resist pigeonholing. Often, they just don't cooperate by meekly falling into this musical category or that. Pat Metheny, a Missouri-born (1954) guitarist, played with the great fusion bassist Jaco Pastorius and with pioneer jazz-country-rock musician Gary Burton before starting the Pat Metheny Group in 1978. Its debut album, *Pat Metheny Group* (ECM, 1978), coming after two excellent albums by Metheny with Pastorius and others (*Bright Size Life*, ECM, 1975, and *Watercolours*, 1977), has been classified as fusion by many, as folk-rock by some, and as swinging rock-jazz with a folk influence by others. Essentially, the music, while electric, is more swinging than rocking, and the melodies do savor of folk.

Dig This

When Metheny teamed up with avant-gardist Ornette Coleman, fans of both musicians had reason to be skeptical. But *Song X* (Geffen, 1985) turns out to be highly provocative music-making, which once again demonstrates the protean identity of jazz and the protean personalities of two important jazz musicians.

The multiple streams of *Pat Metheny Group* foreshadowed things to come. Throughout the balance of the '70s, '80s, and '90s, Metheny has ventured in and around fusion, free jazz, the avant garde, and pop crossover. One of the Group's most successful recent albums, *We Live Here* (Geffen, 1994), combines pop rhythms with a fusion sound reminiscent of hard bop guitarist Wes Montgomery (an early influence on Metheny). If, back in the 1970s, fusion required jazz fans to open their minds and ears to rock, Metheny's recent work requires fusion enthusiasts to accept the broader world of pop.

Weather Report and Mahavishnu

In Chapter 10, we saw that early soloists like Louis Armstrong transformed jazz from a medium for collective improvisation to one that focused on the soloist. This evolutionary step was reversed by Weather Report, one of the earliest (founded December 1970) and most important fusion groups. Weather Report stressed ensemble playing and engaged in collective improvisation rather than solo work.

The charter members of Weather Report were Joe Zawinul, an electronic keyboardist, Wayne Shorter, on soprano and tenor saxophone, Miroslav Vitous, double bass,

Alphonse Mouzon, drums, and Airto Moreira, on an assortment of additional percussion. The group performed and recorded, with numerous personnel changes, through the middle of the 1980s.

Both Shorter and Zawinul were Miles Davis alumni (though Zawinul was never a regular member of any Davis band), who had learned from that master how to play rock without losing the feel of jazz. At its best, it is this true fusion of the two musical styles that makes Weather Report an exciting group. *I Sing the Body Electric*, the group's second recording, made in 1972 and available on CD, may be its very best, though Zawinul fans might favor 1974's *Mysterious Traveller* (available on a Columbia CD), which really showcases keyboards (and also includes vocals).

Weather Report was frequently compared to a fusion group guitarist John McLaughlin formed in 1971 and named after the spiritual name McLaughlin's guru (it was an era during which Eastern mysticism was popular in the West) had bestowed on him. In addition to McLaughlin, the Mahavishnu Orchestra debuted with violinist Jerry Goodman (later replaced by Jean-Luc Ponty), Jan Hammer on keyboards, Rick Laird on electric bass guitar, and Billy Cobham on drums.

Dig This

Inner Mounting Flame (1971) and *Birds of Fire* (1972) are the two standout albums of the Mahavishnu Orchestra. Enthusiasts agree: this is what fusion is all about. The albums are available as Columbia CDs.

Mahavishnu combines three distinct strains: hard, high-volume, danceable rock, mantra-like ostinato patterns drawn from Eastern religious music, and high-energy, high-velocity improvisation very much in the jazz tradition. In 1974, new personnel were added, including brass, bringing the ensemble to eleven. But this incarnation was not as successful as the first, and an attempt to revive the ensemble in the 1980s simply didn't succeed.

The Durable Spyro Gyra

Although fusion continues as a viable style, it's been subject to the same stylistic and, dare we say, economic forces that pulled upon the practitioners of hard bop. Once the barriers separating jazz from rock had fallen, those between fusion and a broader, more commercial pop sound could not long endure.

Talk the Talk

A **studio group** is an ensemble that does not tour or perform live, but records exclusively. It is often an ad hoc group.

In 1975, alto and soprano saxophone player Jay Beckenstein and pianist Jeremy Wall founded Spyro Gyra as a *studio group*, brought together for the sole purpose of recording. By 1979, the band had graduated to a full-time recording, performing, and touring ensemble, going through a number of personnel changes, but always producing essentially the same lightweight pop fusion.

Critics have consistently lambasted Spyro Gyra for its easy-listening melange of jazz, pop, and R&B, but audiences have loved it for years. Indeed, Spyro Gyra is all about building rapport one audience at a time, because the band's success has been the result of live tours for more than two decades. A non-vocal ensemble, Spyro Gyra ran up against pop-radio stations that were not interested in playing instrumentals. Only through dint of a rigorous touring schedule—and (even the critics admit) a high level of professional skill—did the band win its audience.

Lightweight? Yes. So what? Spyro Gyra is an upbeat and enjoyable example of what happens when musical styles become fluid, mix, and blend.

Dig This

You can dig into Spyro Gyra at almost any point in its history and hear music in a consistent pop-fusion style. One of the best albums is *Dreams Beyond Control*, from 1993 on GRP.

Spyro Gyra and the more industrial-weight groups and individuals who preceded it in the fusion enterprise broke through some very thick walls separating not only divergent musical traditions, but cultural identities as well. Some jazz fans found this unnerving. Many, as we will see in the next chapter, have been even less happy about the jazz musicians who went pop.

The Least You Need to Know

- Many jazz musicians saw rock as a threat to their livelihood, but a few embraced it as a means to reach a wider audience.
- Miles Davis's *Bitches Brew* was the landmark album that launched fusion.
- Fusion introduced electric instruments into the jazz arsenal, with electronic keyboards and bass guitars the most important.
- By the mid-1970s, groups such as Weather Report, the Mahavishnu Orchestra, and Spyro Gyra became important forces in fusion. Individual improvisation, a hallmark of jazz since the early days of Louis Armstrong, gave way to collective improvisation.
- As with hard bop, fusion embraced so many elements of pop that many fusion musicians crossed over into the pop realm.

Chapter 21

Pop Go the Jazzmen: Some Crossover Artists

In This Chapter

- The gap between jazz and pop narrows
- Louis Armstrong—as a crossover artist
- Eckstine: from bop to pop
- The case of Nat King Cole
- New Orleans pop
- Crossover trumpets and reeds
- Guitar and keyboard offerings

For jazz aficionados, this is the chapter in which many hitherto open minds will finally close. David Sanborn, Grover Washington, Jr., Chuck Mangione, Kenny G., George Benson, Joe Sample—much that the radio and record-store bins have called jazz since the 1980s, the music's mavens would label (and dismiss as) instrumental pop.

Perhaps this is justified. It's true that the artists in this chapter have "crossed over," moved from various styles more universally accepted as jazz (often hard bop and fusion) to milder "feel good" music or "mood music" or some other pop variation. But let's look at the history of jazz before we banish the crossover artists from this book. Historically, jazz has embraced many forms of music, from ethnic folk, to ballroom dance, to marching band music, to classical, to avant-garde and free forms, to blues, soul, R&B, to rock 'n' roll. Historically, jazz has torn down barriers, not put them up. The crossover artists here are all rooted in jazz, even if they have departed from it, and many crossover both ways, playing pop one day and straight-ahead jazz the next. So let's continue to be adventurous and explore the borderlands between jazz and pop.

Dig This

Armstrong as a crossover artist? One of his biggest hits was the title song from the Broadway musical *Hello, Dolly!* It and other pop favorites are featured on a CD of that title from MCA Jazz. "What a Wonderful World"—pretty sappy unless you hear Louis sing it—became an Armstrong hit well after his death. It is featured, with other pop selections, on *What a Wonderful World,* a 1968 Decca Jazz recording. If you have children or an abiding affection for Walt Disney, there's even *Disney Songs the Satchmo Way* on the Disney label.

The Big Bands in Eclipse

By the late 1940s and early 1950s, the hot news in professional jazz was not the demise of this or that big band—they were folding daily, it seemed—but that the Ellington band managed to endure, Basie to prosper, Herman to survive, and Kenton to do quite well. The point is this: The survival, let alone the success, of a big band had become big news.

Even before Elvis Presley and rock 'n' roll burst upon the scene (Chapter 20), jazz—a truly popular music—was in trouble. Bop, cool jazz, and hard bop all certainly had artistic validity and attracted committed followers, but it was nothing like the legions of fans swing had commanded. Just as, beginning with the bop era, the big band had shrunk to the combo, so the jazz audience now became more concentrated. Lovers of bop were probably more enthusiastic and certainly more knowledgeable than the bulk of the swing audience had been, but their numbers were far fewer—and, consequently, their influence in the popular musical marketplace much less.

Why Satchmo Loved Lombardo

Louis "Satchmo" Armstrong. Most jazz historians agree that "modern" jazz—that is, jazz focused on the improvisations of a soloist—began with him. For some, this is the equivalent of saying that jazz itself, for all practical purposes, began with Armstrong.

Guy Lombardo. Dubbed by jazz enthusiasts the "king of corn," he billed himself and his big band, the Royal Canadians, as purveyors of "the sweetest music this side of heaven." For almost 50 years, beginning with his first national broadcast from Chicago in 1929, Lombardo enjoyed tremendous popularity, introducing more than 300 songs and selling in excess of 250,000,000 recordings. Starting in 1954, Lombardo broadcast annual New Year's Eve concerts. Even people who *never* listened to Lombardo 364 days out of the year listened that night. Doubtless many people thought that he wrote "Auld Lang Syne."

Louis Armstrong and Guy Lombardo. Musically worlds apart, yes?

Yes—and no. Armstrong freely praised Lombardo and his band. He admired its professionalism and polish. Most of all, he admired its success. He didn't care that Lombardo was the "king of corn." What Lombardo did was skillful, and it worked. Armstrong, for some the inventor of modern jazz, embraced Lombardo as he did Bing Crosby, Frank Sinatra, Dean Martin, Barbra Streisand, Leonard Bernstein—as well as Ella Fitzgerald, Duke Ellington, and Oscar Peterson. Armstrong even took on Broadway, scoring a smash hit with the glitziest of show tunes, "Hello, Dolly."

When Armstrong died in 1971, newspapers called him the most widely known American of his day. Was it jazz who got him to this point? Yes—but, then, Armstrong also played anything that worked.

Riffs

Louis Armstrong was not alone in his regard for the likes of Guy Lombardo. Free-lance musician and writer Bill Crow (*Jazz Anecdotes*, Oxford University Press, 1990) comments on the astounding range of Charlie Parker's musical interests:

One of the delightful features of Parker's improvised choruses was his ability to extract quotes from various musical sources and weave them into his own lines.... He was interested in every kind of music. The quotes he used during an evening's performance might be extracted from Stravinsky, Mantovani, Bo Diddley, Guy Lombardo, television commercials, or any other music he might have been listening to.

Eckstine and Cole: Bop to Big Bucks

Born William Clarence Eckstein (1914) in Pittsburgh, Eckstine changed the spelling of his name after he won an amateur singing contest in 1933. He left Howard University, where he had been enrolled and, by 1937, was singing professionally in Chicago. He became the lead vocalist in Earl Hines's big band in 1939, staying with Hines until 1943. More than a singer, Eckstine had an ear for the new music and persuaded Hines to hire young Dizzy Gillespie and Charlie Parker. Moved by emerging bop, Eckstine formed his own band in 1944 and hired Gillespie, Parker, Miles Davis, trumpeter Fats Navarro, mellow tenor saxophonist Gene "Jug" Ammons, tenorman Dexter Gordon, pianist-composer-arranger Tadd Dameron, drummer Art Blakey, and other movers and shakers of bop.

Musicians and critics loved the Eckstine band. The public, however, was indifferent, and in 1947, the leader became one of the first important jazz musicians to cross over into pop. Eckstine launched a highly successful career as a popular singer with hits that included "Caravan," "Prisoner of Love," "You Go to My Head," and "That Old Black Magic."

Many critics have compared the rich, warm baritone of Billy Eckstine to that of Frank Sinatra, claiming that Eckstine's popularity might have

Dig This

A key retrospective album of Eckstine's bebop band is *Mister B and the Band*, from Savoy and encompassing 1945–47. Early Eckstine vocals—*before* and during the period in which he fronted his big band—are found on *I Want to Talk About You* (1940–45), from Xanadu.

Dig This

Hear a great popular voice on Billy Eckstine's *No Cover, No Minimum,* a live nightclub session from 1960 reissued on CD by Roulette. This isn't bop—it isn't even jazz—but the wonderful songs and delivery to match are irresistible.

Dig This

A good cross-section of Cole's pop vocalizing is heard on *Nat King Cole Story,* recordings from 1961 reissued on a two-CD Capitol set.

Real Square

Truly sophisticated jazz enthusiasts appreciate Fountain's verve and skill, even if they don't much like his music. Be warned, however, that, in some musical quarters you risk being labeled a yahoo if you admit liking the music. Also be aware that Fountain's albums are quite uneven in quality. Listen before you buy.

approached or even eclipsed that of "The Voice"—if only he had been white.

Maybe.

But racism couldn't stop the rise of another jazz artist turned pop star. We've already met Nat King Cole in Chapter 15, primarily in the context of his early work as a formidable swing pianist and leader of a successful trio. We saw how vocals were a sideline of the trio's repertoire until "Sweet Lorraine," "The Christmas Song" (you know, "Chestnuts roasting by an open fire," composed by Mel Tormé), "Nature Boy," and, most of all, "Mona Lisa" became bigger hits than anyone playing swing piano could ever hope to have.

Cole sold millions of vocal records, was heard all over the radio dial, and had an active live career. He even became the first African American to star in a network TV variety series, *The Nat King Cole Show,* during 1956–57. Jazz musicians may have mourned his full-time entry into pop, but he featured many of them on his TV show, including Count Basie, Ella Fitzgerald, Stan Kenton, Mel Tormé—and Billy Eckstine.

Fountain of Hits

The crossover music of an Eckstine or a Cole had a contemporary sound. Most pop music is by definition contemporary, but two New Orleans musicians reached back into the Dixieland past for pop hits. They did not seek to re-create the early 20th-century New Orleans sound in the way that Lu Watters or Preservation Hall did (Chapter 15), but imparted to Dixieland a contemporary crossover appeal.

Pete Fountain was born in New Orleans in 1930, started clarinet by age 12, and was a member of the Junior Dixieland Band at 18. At 20, he was recording, and by the mid-1950s—in no small measure through appearances on hyper-bland bandleader Lawrence Welk's popular television program—he was by far the most famous of all New Orleans clarinetists, past or present.

Fountain is not a great jazz clarinetist, but he is a very accomplished musician who plays the most hackneyed Dixieland warhorses (*Basin Street Blues, When the Saints Go Marching In, Way Down Yonder in New Orleans,* and so on) with such genuine enthusiasm that you'd almost believe the tunes were brand new or, at least, just discovered. He is best enjoyed in live recordings, as on *Live at the Ryman*, a Sacramento CD from 1992.

The trumpet equivalent of Pete Fountain is his somewhat older (born 1922) New Orleans contemporary, Al Hirt. Indeed, during the mid-1950s he led a group that included Fountain as a member.

Riffs

Fans of Wynton Marsalis may give precious little thought to Al Hirt, but both are New Orleans natives, and it was Hirt who gave Wynton his first trumpet. Ellis Marsalis, Wynton's father, played piano in Hirt's band at his club in the city.

Based in Dixieland, Hirt also ventured into more contemporary pop and even country music in the 1960s, only to return to Dixieland. He is a superb technician, having been trained at the Cincinnati Conservatory and having played with both the Tommy and Jimmy Dorsey bands. Savvy jazz musicians and aficionados generally praise his skill while lamenting the fact that he didn't stretch more and make greater musical use of his formidable chops. Listen to Hirt play the favorites on *That's a Plenty*, a Pro Arte CD recorded in 1988.

Trumpets Go Pop (and It Feels So Good)

The trumpet and cornet have long been among the most popular jazz instruments in part because they are among the most assertive. Trumpet players are often featured soloists in jazz ensembles, and it is little wonder that, beginning with Harry James in the late '40s and early '50s, a number of them readily crossed over into pop.

Born in 1940, trumpeter and flugelhorn player Chuck Mangione acquired impeccable jazz credentials, playing informally in his native Rochester, New York, with such visiting luminaries as Dizzy Gillespie and Kai Winding, then studying at the Eastman School of Music, earning a B.A. in 1963. After moving to New York in the mid-1960s, he led a hard-bop group, the Jazz Brothers, with his brother, pianist Gap Mangione. He went on to perform in the bands of Woody Herman, trumpeter Maynard Ferguson, and Art Blakey during the mid- to late 1960s. At this point in his career, he was successfully emulating the sound of Miles Davis and Clifford Brown, but in the following decade, Mangione began composing simple, catchy tunes laid bare of improvisation and featuring only rudimentary accompaniment. Two such, *Feels So Good* and *Land of Make Believe,* caught on big. The 1977 A&M album featuring these and other Mangione originals, titled *Feels So Good,* went platinum with more than two million copies sold.

One does not want to begrudge Mangione his success, but it seems a pity that instead of turning a lot of people onto jazz, *Feels So Good* made a lot of people think that what Mangione had written *was* jazz instead of jazz-based pop. And they demanded more of it. While *Feels So Good* is pretty music, much more interesting is Mangione's pre-crossover work, such as the 1972 *Chuck Mangione Quartet* from Mercury, which is genuine jazz.

Saxophone in a New Key: "Contemporary Jazz"

Fusion (Chapter 20) lost much of its momentum in the late 1970s as rock 'n' roll became more slickly commercial and, therefore, less fertile ground for jazz work based on it. Yet musicians (as well as record producers!) were loath to abandon fusion, which had given jazz record sales a much-needed boost. The solution they came up with was dubbed "contemporary jazz," and it was played on electric instruments but often featured the saxophone as the lead instrument. Indeed, while the trumpet was perhaps *the* jazz crossover instrument of the 1970s, the saxophone family, from tenor on up to soprano, has been the focus of much 1980s and '90s "contemporary jazz."

Talk the Talk

Contemporary jazz is a term often applied to the pop-oriented jazz of the 1980s and '90s; another word for it is *instrumental pop.*

The New Alto Men

For David Sanborn, the saxophone was a way of life—quite literally. Born in 1945, he was stricken with polio and, as a child, used the instrument to strengthen his lungs. By 14, Sanborn was playing R&B professionally in St. Louis, where he was raised, but he went on to get academic credentials at Northwestern University (1963–64) and the University of Iowa (1965–67). He also studied saxophone in the '60s with Roscoe Mitchell of the Art Ensemble of Chicago. He toured with the Paul Butterfield blues band, with soul singer Stevie Wonder, and with edgy rocker David Bowie, but he has also worked as a soloist with Gil Evans's jazz orchestra sporadically through the 1970s and into the '80s, while also touring and recording as a leader.

Sanborn's music may best be described as contemporary jazz or crossover with a large dose of R&B and soul. While he is not a bold improviser, he combines impeccable technique with genuine passion. It is his heartfelt sound that has made him one of the most influential reed men of the '80s and '90s.

Although Sanborn's recordings can hardly be called adventurous, his musical interests are wide ranging. In 1991, he recorded *Another Hand* (Elektra), which features the avant-garde compositions of alto saxophonist Julius Hemphill (compatriot of Anthony Braxton and other jazz artists on the edge), and in 1995, *Pearls* (Elektra), which goes in the opposite direction with a full orchestra backing him on melodic renditions of standards ranging from "Try a Little Tenderness" to "Smoke Gets in Your Eyes." More typical of Sanborn are *Voyeur* (Warner Bros., 1980) and *Upfront* (Elektra, 1992): soulful pop music.

Sanborn has influenced a number of recent artists, one of the most interesting of whom is Brandon Fields, a West Coast-based musician whose *The Other Side of the Story* (Nova, 1985) breathed fresh life into the crossover idiom.

In the Winelight

If David Sanborn is arguably the most influential contemporary altoist, Grover Washington, Jr., (1943–), playing alto as well as tenor and soprano saxophone (and occasionally flute and baritone saxophone as well), may be the most commercially successful.

Washington has taken contemporary jazz closer to the R&B camp, and *Winelight*, released by Elektra in 1980, is his best-known album in this vein. "Just the Two of Us" was a huge single hit from the album, which does not, however, forsake "traditional" jazz values for the sake of pop success. The solo improvisation on the album is first-rate and genuinely exhilarating.

Dig This

If you like *Winelight*, you'll love the earlier *Mister Magic*, a 1975 Motown release, which, if anything, is even more R&B-oriented.

More Tenor Men

Washington's high visibility on the tenor should not cause us to overlook other important recent players. Philadelphian Michael Brecker (1949–) spent much of his early career as a studio musician before recording *Michael Brecker* (1987, MCA/Impulse!), a high-energy pop-fusion teaming with Pat Metheny on guitar and Jack Dejohnette on drums.

Dig This

Nexus for Duo and Trio has not been reissued on CD, but Bluebird has released *Nexus One (for Trane)*, a CD featuring five cuts from the original two-LP vinyl set.

Like Brecker, Ernie Watts (1945–) played primarily in non-jazz contexts (mostly straight pop and R&B) but proved himself a fine jazz musician with *Ernie Watts Quartet* (JVC, 1987) and *Reaching Up* (JVC, 1993). This is not easy-listening pop, but a popular sound that is very high-energy, flavored with a combination of bop-like improvisation and fusion volume. Those who find a lot of crossover music blandly commercial are in for an ear-opening experience.

Chicagoan John Klemmer (1946–) is another crossover innovator, who uses an electric saxophone as well as the conventional acoustic instrument. Klemmer enjoyed popular success in the 1970s with what is best described as easy-listening music, then suddenly and surprisingly recorded *Nexus for Duo and Trio* (Novus, 1979), which smacks of hard bop.

Return of the Soprano Saxophone

The rather piercing and certainly insistent, nasally plaintive sound of the soprano saxophone is strong medicine. In the hands of Sidney Bechet (Chapter 8), the instrument glowed eloquently—save for advanced work on the instrument by Coltrane, Steve Lacy, and Wayne Shorter—receded in popularity after his death in 1959.

Then came Kenneth Gorelick, better known as Kenny G, who recorded *Duotones* in 1986 for Arista—light, jazzy pop played with ingratiating, shimmering lyricism on soprano. The record sold better than three million copies and catapulted Kenny G squarely into the pop arena, in which he has recorded with the likes of Aretha Franklin, Whitney Houston, and Natalie Cole.

Is this really jazz? Well, probably not. But it couldn't exist without jazz, and if you like the sound of the soprano saxophone, Kenny G is your man—though Grover Washington, Jr., offers on the instrument material of more enduring interest.

Dig This

Benson fans will want to get *New Boss Guitar*, originally recorded in 1964, when Benson was playing with bluesy jazz organist Brother Jack McDuff. Klugh, an acoustic guitarist, may be best enjoyed on his 1989 solo album, *Solo Guitar* (Warner Bros.), which is a lovely, melodic rendition of standards and recalls the melody-conscious guitarists of the 1930s.

Guitar Renaissance

The long association of rock and pop with the guitar has brought that instrument back into the forefront of contemporary jazz. George Benson (1943–) has played with major jazz figures including Miles Davis, Herbie Hancock, Freddie Hubbard, and others, but it is as a crossover artist that he has made his biggest impression, sometimes pairing lush, even florid guitar work with Nat King Cole-like vocals and sometimes even scatting a vocal accompaniment to his guitar. *White Rabbit*, a 1971 collaboration (on Columbia) with fellow crossover guitarist Earl Klugh, is perhaps the most all-around satisfying of Benson's albums.

Two more crossover guitarists, Lee Ritenour and Larry Carlton, deserve a hearing. *Larry & Lee* (GRP, 1995) brings them together in a lightweight but very pleasant showcase.

And on Keyboards…

Everyone remembers at least one line from *The Graduate*. Dustin Hoffman is offered a career. "I've got one word for you," a well-meaning adult tells the newly minted college grad: "Plastics."

The musical equivalent of "plastics" is *keyboards*—electronic keyboards capable of being molded into almost any kind of sound. They have played a central role in creating the texture and presence of pop beginning in the middle 1960s, and their importance has increased with each passing year as electronic synthesizer technology has continually advanced.

Bob James (1939–) began his recording career in 1962 with a bop-style trio set, *Bold Conceptions*, on Mercury, but he soon got into avant-garde music, his trio supplemented by taped electronic sounds (*Explosions*, ESP, 1965). By the end of the 1960s, however, he was back in the mainstream world, working with singer Sarah Vaughan and then, in the '70s, became a studio musician with everyone from Quincy Jones to Roberta Flack and produced and composed for a wide range of popular jazz musicians.

Beginning in the mid-1970s, James began recording lightweight jazzy pop, including the laid-back but bouncy theme music of the popular TV sitcom *Taxi* (1978–83). James has been very influential in creating much of the pop-jazz crossover sound of the 1980s and beyond.

Houston-born (1939–) Joe Sample made his name as a keyboardist with the group he formed in high school, first called the Swingsters, then the Modern Jazz Sextet, then the Jazz Crusaders, and finally simply the Crusaders, when the group moved from hard bop to rock. During his early period, Sample created what came to be called the Gulf Coast Sound—funky blues combined with instrumental R&B and a liberal helping of soulful jazz.

Keyboardists have also taken jazz in a "New Age" direction—that is, creating spacey, floating, less rhythmically driven "mood" or even "background" music conducive, perhaps, to meditation, relaxation, or (depending on the personalities involved) romance. This sounds like the antithesis of jazz, but it can be made to work, as David Benoit (1953–) demonstrates with a style one critic, Alex Henderson, described as "New Age with a beat." *Waiting for Spring* (GRP, 1989) is typical of this keyboardist's work.

At its best, crossover jazz is refreshing popular music. That jazz can hold on to its roots in pop

Riffs

Think the electronic sound is "unnatural?" The important classical conductor and composer Pierre Boulez once addressed this question with another question: "What's 'natural' about the sound of a violin?" he said.

Dig This

A typical James album is *Lucky Seven* (Warner Bros./Tappan Zee, 1979). If you're intrigued, his more recent Warner Bros. release, *Grand Piano Canyon* (1990), is a lot jazzier—though still classifiable as crossover.

Dig This

The Crusaders' highlight funky hard bop album was titled simply *I* and was released in 1970 by Chisa (it is available on CD). For Sample sans Crusaders, the 1994 *Did You Feel That?* (Warner Bros.) is a fine crossover album strongly grounded in jazz.

contexts—even in the relative formlessness of the New Age style—attests to the durability, versatility, and adaptability of the musical tradition.

The Least You Need to Know

- Jazz *aficionados* may draw hard lines between jazz and pop, but jazz *musicians* have been "crossing over" into pop since at least the days of Louis Armstrong.
- Armstrong, Cole, and Eckstine crossed over with vocals; most of the more recent jazz crossovers have been instrumental.
- While most crossover music strives for a contemporary sound, Pete Fountain and Al Hirt created successful careers by updating the traditional Dixieland sound.
- "Contemporary jazz" is an electric crossover sound that developed in the late 1970s as increasingly bland commercial rock failed to inspire new fusion.

Chapter 22

Ear and Now: Jazz Today

In This Chapter

- Jazz today: anything goes
- Wynton Marsalis and followers embrace tradition
- The new avant-garde
- Important new performers

Writing about jazz would be a whole lot easier if you could put down your pen (okay, shut down the computer) right after getting through the fusion era. Up to then, jazz more or less neatly divided itself into identifiable styles or movements. Sure, there was overlap, and many musicians played in a number of styles. But at least the labels were there, and it's hard to get along without labels.

By the early 1980s, the labels, already faded, began to disappear entirely. There were still plenty of musicians playing jazz, but no single style—or even set of styles—emerged as dominant. Jazz seemed fragmented. Worse, many of the fragments drifted off into rock or pop.

Then came Wynton Marsalis, a young trumpet prodigy who wanted to lead jazz back to basics. Contentious and controversial, Marsalis has provided much of what focus there is for present-day jazz. We'll start with him and his followers, then look to the future that is currently in the making.

Notes from Underground

For some, jazz is and always will be about freedom. Freedom means pushing the envelope: from the collective improvisation of New Orleans jazz to the individual improvisation of a Louis Armstrong; from melodic improvisation in swing to chordal improvisation in bop; from jazz versus classical music to the third stream; from jazz against rock to a fusion of the two.

Trouble is, if you push the envelope hard enough, it tears.

By the 1980s, the jazz envelope had burst, and the music was spilling out all over the place. Some found this exciting. Some—including a lot of jazz fans—found it depressing. Their music, it seemed, had disappeared into a sea of rock or pop or easy-listening soprano saxophone tunes. Disgruntled jazz fans went "underground," losing interest in "contemporary jazz" (the very term had come to mean pop crossover) and hunkering down with old bebop records, waiting for *their* music to return.

The Young Lions

In 1981, a 20-year-old trumpet virtuoso made his first recording for Columbia, titled simply *Wynton Marsalis*. While young Marsalis dazzled listeners with the maturity and technical facility of his playing, his style was not entirely his own. It had echoes of Freddie Hubbard and, even more, of Miles Davis.

But decidedly not the Davis of *Bitches Brew* fusion. Rather, it was Davis of the hard bop vintage, and hearing Marsalis resurrect hard bop—with straight bop thrown in—the underground stirred and awakened. Their time, it seemed, had come at last.

Wynton Marsalis and his year-older brother, tenor and soprano saxophonist Branford, played with tremendous conviction. Initially, they had a few detractors, who protested that bop and hard bop were fine—*in their own time*—but that that time had passed and imitations of bebop, no matter how good, could never equal the original.

Dig This

Wynton Marsalis is at home in a variety of musical traditions, jazz as well as classical. His albums of trumpet concertos by Haydn, Hummel, and Leopold Mozart (CBS Masterworks) have been critically acclaimed.

Marsalis countered these objections in two ways. The first was simply by his playing. An imitator? Maybe—but the fact was that he really was *that good*. Stunningly good.

His second response was more philosophical. Jazz, he argued, is a set of traditions in much the same way that classical music is. Nobody objects when today's performers play Brahms, who lived in the 19th century, or Haydn, who lived in the 18th. Why, then, should anyone object to revisiting the traditions of jazz?

It was a convincing argument. But Marsalis didn't use it just to defend his music. He soon took the offensive, and that's where the controversy began. For Marsalis defined the jazz "tradition" quite narrowly, excluding from it avant-garde work after about 1965 and roundly condemning fusion as a barren betrayal of jazz. In effect, for Marsalis, jazz began with Louis Armstrong and culminated in bebop and the ambitious tone poems of Duke Ellington. Anything outside of these limits may or may not have been good music, but it wasn't jazz. If you wanted to be a *jazz* musician, you would play within these limits.

Dig This

Black Codes (from the Underground), on the Columbia label, is a 1985 Marsalis album in the Miles Davis vein. It represents a vigorous return to acoustic jazz. More Ellingtonian is *In This House, on This Morning,* an ambitious 2-CD Columbia set from 1993 musically depicting an African-American church service.

Marsalis not only created controversy and very impressive music, he also created a following. Critics called them the "Young Lions."

Trumpeter Terence Blanchard (1962–) is obviously inspired by Marsalis as well as Freddie Hubbard. To date, his most ambitious album is the *Malcolm X Jazz Suite* (Columbia, 1992), developed from the score he wrote for director Spike Lee's film biography of the African-American leader.

Pianist Marcus Roberts (1963–) might be described as retrospective, exploring not only the hard bop idiom when he served with Wynton Marsalis's band, but also stride—a style born in the '20s—and even ragtime. Like Marsalis, Roberts invites controversy and is vocal about his jazz judgments. In *As Serenity Approaches* (Novus, 1991), Roberts dips into the past at least as far as Jelly Roll Morton but successfully reinvents it, never sounding as if he is merely copying a style. This reinvented originality is the controversial magic of the movement that began with Wynton Marsalis.

Of all "Wynton's children," perhaps the most promising of all is trumpeter Roy Hargrove (1969–), who burst upon the scene while he was still a teenager and has been growing as an artist by investigating different musical environments—from bands bubbling with Cuban percussionists to drummerless trios. The album to listen to first is *Parker's Mood* (Verve).

Turning from the Pride

By no means are all the young musicians Young Lions. The very success of Wynton Marsalis and those in his orbit has driven many other musicians away from the leonine pride. Some deliberately sought innovation. Some aggressively followed their own idiosyncracies. Others also turned to the past—but a past very different from the one Marsalis embraced. A number of 1990s musicians have reached back to 1960s free jazz and to 1970s fusion.

Acid Jazz

One of the very few recent jazz styles to get a label that has stuck borrows heavily from 1970s fusion. "Acid jazz" is a sort of free funk or free soul jazz. Its principal practitioner is alto saxophonist Steve Coleman (1956–). Coleman organized a group he dubbed M-Base (shorthand for "macro-basic array of structured extemporization"!). *Rhythm People (The Resurrection of Creative Black Civilization)*, a 1990 Novus release, is unpredictably improvisational funk. Fasten your seat belt.

Talk the Talk

Acid jazz developed in the late 1980s as a freer, funkier form of '70-style fusion.

Alto saxophonist Greg Osby (1960–) was a member of M-Base, who went on to create original tunes into which he injects angular solos even as the tunes themselves travel unexpected paths. Even open-minded jazz enthusiasts may have a problem with the rap lyrics he sometimes also inserts into his music; however, *Zero* (Blue Note) is an exciting album that suggests we will hear a great deal more from Osby.

Improvisational funkist and M-Base leader Steve Coleman.
Image from Novus Records (via Internet).

A Knitting Factory?

By the mid-1980s, Lower Manhattan was the focus of much avant-garde musical activity, a lot of it centered in a club called the Knitting Factory, which fashioned an amalgam of advanced jazz and rock into something chic and highly marketable.

Two Knitting Factory alumni in particular are making exciting music, the first being Don Byron, who has reintroduced the clarinet—an instrument neglected since the end of the swing era. Byron lives and breathes multiculturalism, having explored klezmer, Latin jazz, hip-hop, classical chamber music, and small-ensemble swing—excelling at all. Part of the interest in following Byron's career is guessing where his tastes will take him next. For now, *Tuskegee Experiments* (Elektra/Nonsuch, 1991) offers an exciting array of alternately twisting and soaring solo work.

Pianist-composer Myra Melford (1957–) studied with avant-gardists Henry Threadgill and free jazz violinist Leroy Jenkins. Her approach to the piano falls somewhere between the lyrical Keith Jarrett (Chapter 19) and the angular Marilyn Crispell. Her extended pieces for quintet flow through alternately mellow and downright aggressive moments, as if influenced equally by classical chamber music textures and the architecture of Frank Lloyd Wright. *The Same River, Twice* (Grammavision, 1996) reveals her as one of the leading avant-garde musicians of the 1990s.

Take Five

Though hardly newcomers, Henry Threadgill (1944–) and Marilyn Crispell (1947–) have continued through the 1990s as driving forces in avant-garde jazz. Saxophonist Threadgill was a member of the important group Air, active from the mid-1970s until its break-up in 1986. Threadgill has a knack for arranging unexpected and unconventional sounds into marvelously moody or vibrant tone poems; for example, one sextet features two tubas and two guitars, while another Threadgill group puts accordion front and center. Recommended listening: *Where's Your Cup?* (Columbia, 1997).

Marilyn Crispell is an avant-garde pianist in the Cecil Taylor mold who also has a special affinity for the music of John Coltrane. Try *Nothing Ever Was, Anyway* (ECM, 1997).

Composer and saxophonist Henry Threadgill. Image from author's collection.

Strangers on a Train

For those who think the avant-garde takes itself too seriously, another downtown Manhattan group, Jazz Passengers, may be just the ticket. Fronted by trombonist Curtis Fowlkes and reedman Roy Nathanson, the group developed from the Lounge Lizards and now runs the improvisational gamut, freely indulging in post-bop explorations that encompass everything from free jazz to Dixieland, to funk, rock, and the blues—and usually with a very good sense of humor. Their rich mix can be enjoyed on *Live at the Knitting Factory* (Knitting Factory, 1991).

...to Z

"Wynton's children" could well cite the work of John Zorn (1953–) to support their case for holding onto tradition. This alto saxophonist screams on his instrument more than he plays it, and, when that isn't enough, he may even bring in a duck call or two. He disdains jazz tradition by dipping into *any* tradition available, from rock to film music to pop, as well as bebop.

In live performance, Zorn has produced particularly strange sounds by blowing his mouthpiece underwater. But Zorn gets a whole lot stranger. For example, in a multi-part work titled *Cobra* (after a kind of war game), Zorn uses mathematical game theory to "structure" the pieces, creating various combinations of sounds from a group of 87 musicians playing a variety of instruments or simply using their voices. In effect, Zorn establishes the rule of a "game" that the musicians play out. Thus elements of structure and spontaneity are combined.

Is this jazz? Is this even music? Is this at least interesting? You can decide by listening to *John Zorn's Cobra Live at the Knitting Factory* (Knitting Factory, 1992).

If the 1980s and 1990s have seen a return to tradition in Wynton Marsalis and others, they have also witnessed a vigorous, wild, and often aggressively marketed avant-garde scene. Zorn's albums vary widely in content—with *Cobra Live* the wildest to date; a good place to sample his work is *Naked City* (Elektra/Nonesuch, 1989).

Real Square

In Chapter 19, which treated the subject of avant-garde and free jazz, you were warned that this music isn't for everybody. In fact, some of the experiments from lower Manhattan may not appeal to anybody! In any case, much of this is music for the truly adventurous. As a bungee jumper should make certain his cord is securely tied (and not too long) before taking the plunge, you might want to check out the store's return policy before making the purchase.

No Labels, Just Music

"Wynton's children," "acid jazz," "downtown music." Labels all. But really, recent jazz has been stuck with remarkably few labels. Mostly, it's just music—music played by some very exciting young musicians who not only have great ability, but, typically, the advantage of education in academic programs that regard jazz as vital and worth cultivating.

If *The Complete Idiot's Guide to Jazz* were strictly a jazz history, maybe I'd have no business speculating about where to aim your ears to hear the musicians who are building the future of jazz. But this book offers consumer advice in the here and now as well as the story of jazz past. So let's take stock:

- **James Carter** is a Detroit-born student of past saxophone styles who brings enormous enthusiasm and quick wit to his music. He's liable to leap from bebop filigree to rhythm and blues squeals in the space of a single solo. He also loves to resurrect long-neglected tunes. Recommended CD: *JC on the Set* (DIW).
- **Dave Douglas** is among the most in-demand of sidemen. Why? This trumpeter has all the chops in the world and uses them wisely. His own albums reveal a remarkable stylistic breadth, essaying post-Miles Davis eclectic fusion, third stream, folk-ethnic rhythms, free jazz spontaneity, and generally highly sophisticated post-bop tactics. A modern master. Recommended CD: *Five* (Soul Note).
- Trumpeter **Nicholas Payton** hails from New Orleans and looks like Louis Armstrong. Sometimes he *sounds* like Armstrong, too. Payton plays the trumpet with power and savvy, fitting comfortably into traditional styles, mainstream, and more modern groups. Recommended CD: *Payton's Place* (Verve).
- **Ralph Peterson** is a take-no-prisoners drummer out of the Art Blakey school of percussion, but he's also an important young bandleader, who has produced several imaginatively and colorfully programmed recordings with his Fo'tet (as he calls his quartet). Recommended CD: *The Fo'tet Plays Monk* (Evidence).

- **Matthew Shipp** combines Cecil Taylor-like impulses with carefully crafted classical designs to produce piano improvisations of dazzling variety and complexity. The marvel is that Shipp never loses the thread of his intricate explorations and, indeed, crafts cohesive, full-length suites. Recommended CD: *By the Law of Music* (Hat Art).

Has anyone been left out of this list? Plenty, you bet. Certainly far more than are included in it. But the musicians just mentioned are a few to focus on, here and now, because they are so likely to figure in the future of jazz.

Doubtless, there are many more. We are fortunate to be living in a time when jazz is recognized—and, yes, argued about—as a valuable tradition and national heritage. Many thoughtful, creative, and well-trained musicians share in it. Keep your ears open. You might also read the pages of the jazz magazines listed in Chapter 23. They'll extend the range of your hearing and alert you to new performers and new albums.

But why limit yourself to recordings, wonderful as they are? Check out the club action and college-performing scene in your city. Attend a festival. Listen to the local talent. Relish jazz wherever you hear it.

The Least You Need to Know

- Today's jazz scene cannot be defined by any dominant movement or style. Anything goes.
- Wynton Marsalis's advocacy of a narrow jazz tradition has polarized the jazz world: the "Young Lions" (as Marsalis's followers were sometimes called in the 1980s) versus everyone else.
- The new avant-garde is wilder than ever—but also more savvy about marketing itself.
- Today, exciting new performers can be found across the spectrum of jazz styles; many individuals perform work in a variety of styles.

Chapter 23

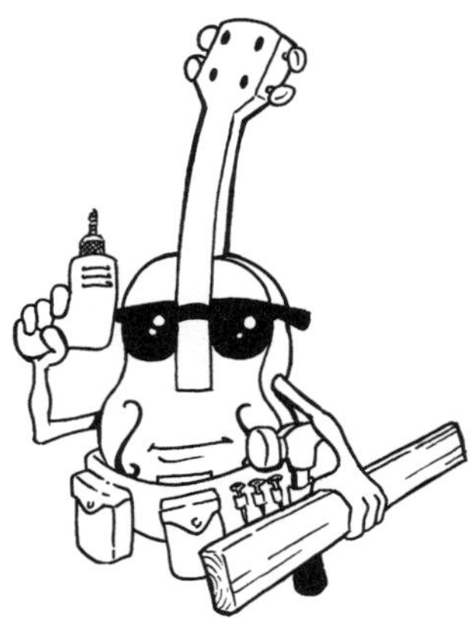

Getting Personal: How to Build Your Own Jazz Archive

In This Chapter

- Planning your music-shopping expeditions
- Learning what you like
- Strategies for building a collection
- Music sources: in person, mail order, and online
- The "desert island" list

Becoming a jazz collector requires no special qualifications—other than curiosity and an interest in the music. You'll need to decide whether you just want to get the music on CD or tape, or if it's important to you to have it in its "first edition" form, on vinyl, in the 78-, 45-, or $33^1/_3$-rpm formats. Either way, there's never been a better time to build your own jazz archive. New jazz is being recorded, CD reissues of historical and classic albums abound, and if you're interested in seeking out original vinyl LPs, most major cities (and many college towns) have secondhand record stores, and this chapter also identifies some Web sites for online collecting.

The good news is that the choices are overwhelming. The bad news is that the choices are overwhelming. This entire book is intended to make the choices a bit clearer, and this particular chapter should help, too.

The Kid in the Candy Store

Depending on your personality, a trip to the local record store—especially one of those chain superstores—can be an exhilarating hunting expedition or a dazzling exercise in frustration. If you have some idea of what you want, it's fun and gratifying to *get it.* It's also delightful to let your focus blur, as you are lured by additional possibilities: *Mmm. I came here looking for some John Coltrane, but this Monk album looks pretty good, too.* But if you just wander into a store without any idea of what you want, it's easy to become overwhelmed and frustrated by the choices. Maybe you'll end up making a careless choice. Maybe—heaven forbid!—you'll even walk out of the store with *nothing.*

Dig This

The end of this chapter includes a "desert island" short list of key jazz albums. Also: Why not actually *tear out* the tearout card at the front of this book and take it with you to the record store? It lists important jazz styles and genres, with key musicians and standout albums.

The more jazz you hear, the easier and more exciting the shopping becomes. Of course, the more buying you do, the more jazz you'll hear. This, however, need not be a catch-22 situation. You can do a lot of your jazz listening on radio first. If you have friends who are into jazz, prevail on them to play their favorites for you—even to lend you albums.

Another aid to wise shopping is reading books like this one. The more you know about the stylistic and historical context of the music, the more informed your choices can be. If you're shopping at a store with both books and CDs, refer to a jazz encyclopedia in the book section before you hit the jazz CDs, and repeat as necessary.

Can You Go Wrong?

You purchase your dream house. It takes all your money, but it's worth it. Then you find out about the freeway that's going in next door, the pig farm opening up across the street, and the fact that the house site is something called a "sanitary" landfill.

Bummer.

Dig This

Always give new music a chance. Jazz is typically complex music that you can't fully take in on the first listen. You may not like an album the first time you spin it. Resist the urge to run it back to the record store. Choose another time, and give it another hearing.

The fact is, life is loaded with opportunities to make disastrous buying decisions. Fortunately, it's actually pretty hard to buy a truly terrible jazz album—though it is certainly possible to buy an album, take it home, play it, and discover you just don't like it. What should you do?

- Check out the store's return policy before you make your purchase. Many stores will accept exchanges. Save your receipt!
- If you can't return the album, consider trading it with a friend.

- If you can't trade it, consider *giving* it to a friend.
- Sell it to a secondhand record store.
- Or just keep it. Tastes and moods change and evolve. You didn't spend *that* much on the album. Set it aside. Go back to it later. Listen again. Give it a chance. You may end up liking it.

So relax. You can't really go far wrong, even if you buy an album or two or more you just don't like. On the other hand, cash, free time, and life itself are all limited. Not only is life too short to spend listening to bad music, it would be a shame if you miss the real gems. Do a little homework—not so much to avoid making a bad purchase, but to ensure that the good ones don't get away.

Real Square

Don't be a criminal. Some people purchase a CD, tape it, then return it. This is not only illegal (hey, you are *stealing* the product, the music!), it is wrong. Everyone has to make a living. You're not just cheating the store and the record company, you're robbing the musicians of royalties (most performers are paid on the basis of sales).

Plan Your Approach

If you have oodles of cash and a lot of time on your hands, there is little reason to devote much effort to making a plan or deciding how you will focus your jazz record collection. Assuming, however, that one or both of these resources are limited, you might give some thought to ways to help you structure your collection in order to make your purchasing decisions easier, more efficient, and more cost-effective.

Few books that issue advice (regardless of subject) manage to avoid quoting Yogi Berra at least once, and this volume is no exception.

"You got to be very careful if you don't know where you're going," Yogi once said, "because you might not get there."

Before you jump in, think about your approach.

Surveying the Territory

There is nothing wrong with buying recordings randomly or as the spirit moves you, or buying something you heard—and liked—on the radio or at a friend's house. But if you take one thing from this book, I hope it is the understanding that jazz musicians don't create in a vacuum. Their music has a context, a history, a heritage, a set of traditions. The music has developed and evolved. The music has also diverged from tradition. It has gone backward, forward, sideways. The contextual dimension of *all* jazz adds to the significance of any *particular* piece of music, and because it adds to significance, it also adds to understanding and, most important, to enjoyment.

If you give some thought to acquiring recordings by a certain musician, or in a certain style, or of a certain time period, the pleasure you take in the music is enhanced by understanding where the music comes from and what it leads to. With a grasp of context, you become an insider—a jazz buff on the way to becoming a jazz maven.

How do you begin to survey the various jazz contexts? A good place to start is with this book. It lays out the historical periods and the major styles, along with the chief practitioners in each. Target something that you think will appeal to you, and purchase a recommended album.

Listen to it. What do you like about it? Do you want to hear more in this style? More from this performer? More from this time period?

If the answer to any of these questions is an *emphatic* yes, consider the album the seed from which your collection in this particular context (style, performer, time period) will begin to grow.

If you are indifferent to the album (or don't even like it), think about what it is you don't like. If it is too old-fashioned sounding, move on to a more recent period or style. If it is too dissonant, move back to something more traditional. Use the album to locate territory you'd like to stake out.

The Historical Approach

Some people are historians by nature; that is, they think in terms of eras or time periods. If this is you, you might find it most natural to build your jazz collection chronologically, perhaps even following the basic outline of Parts 3, 4, and 5 in this book.

You might decide to concentrate your initial forays on a particular time period—say the mid-1930s to mid-1940s—or you may choose two or three periods, contiguous or not (say, 1920s, 1930s, and 1940s—or 1920s and 1960s). Or you may not want to limit yourself at all, but go about purposely putting together a collection that represents a number of periods.

The point is *your* awareness of the historical period. If you hear how one piece from the '30s relates to another from the same era or from a different era, both pieces become that much more interesting and enjoyable.

As we have seen repeatedly in this book, no piece of jazz exists in a vacuum. It relates to music that came before and music that will come after. Listening to Bud Powell play bop is exciting in and of itself, but the experience is more meaningful if you know enough to play some Art Tatum first. It's hard *not* to enjoy Armstrong's Hot Five recordings. Listen to a little King Oliver or other traditional New Orleans jazz, *then* to the Armstrong, and you hear where Satchmo came from and the remarkable places he was going.

The Stylistic Approach

Style is often linked to historical period; for example, most of the jazz from the mid-1930s to the mid-1940s is swing. It's the "swing era." However, at various times, a number of styles coexisted or even competed—as in the 1950s, say, when bop duked it out with the "moldy figs" of trad jazz, and then when hard bop and the cool school diverged from bop.

You may find that a particular style so interests you that you want to acquire many recordings of the type. This is a common and efficient way to build a collection. Many serious jazz collectors, for example, focus almost exclusively on swing or on bebop.

By Performer

You probably won't want to restrict your jazz collection to the work of a single performer or band—though some (like Louis Armstrong) are so significant and so prolific that such a collection would be quite large; however, you might use individual performers or bands to focus your collection.

Perhaps you've identified Louis Armstrong, Duke Ellington, and Count Basie as your favorite jazz figures. Why not build your collection by focusing on them? You can always branch out later.

Taking this a step further, pay attention to the other players on an album—chances are they have albums of their own in a similar or at least compatible style. If you like the vibes on a particular album, see if the player has a CD section of his own. Jazz networking like this can take you a long way.

By Instrument

Some people really love the sound of a particular instrument. Others are amateur musicians, who may play a particular instrument, so have a special interest in it. You might find it rewarding to start your collection by concentrating on a single instrument or a few.

Of course, this assumes that your target instrument is one that is important to jazz. You may dig the bassoon or the bagpipes, but your jazz collection will be pretty slim. If, however, you love the sound of the tenor saxophone or you play the piano, the jazz repertoire for either of these is enormous.

Dig This

For every three CDs in your area of focus, buy one outside of that area. A magic formula? Of course not. Maybe you'd rather do a 2-to-1 ratio or a 4-to-1, 5-to-1, 10-to-1. The exact ratios don't matter. The point is to allow for diversity without becoming random and thereby losing the benefits of a collecting plan.

A Strategy for Diversity

If there's a downside to focusing your collection it's that it may arbitrarily blind you to other good stuff. How do you get the benefits of planning without the liabilities of tunnel vision? Consider a strategy of diversified buying.

It works like this. For every three CDs you buy in your focus area (let's say its swing) buy one CD outside of the area.

Dig This

Some retailers maintain sites on the World Wide Web. Indeed, jazz-oriented Web sites of all kinds now abound on the Internet. Invaluable links to many of them can be found at The JazzWeb, www.nwu.edu/jazz/internet.html. Within this site, try clicking on the "Jazz Retailers" link to find CD sources. You can also check out the "Jazz Labels" link to connect directly with jazz-oriented record companies.

You may want to continue the logic of your focus by purchasing every fourth CD in some areas related to your focus. For example, after buying three swing CDs, why not take a step ahead (in time) and buy a bebop record? Or a step *back*, into classic jazz?

Or you may decide to throw caution to the wind. After purchasing three swing CDs, you might buy some Ornette Coleman.

Where to Get It

Most large record stores carry most of the popular jazz CDs. In addition, many will be happy to order items for you. If you're truly fortunate, your city or town will have one or more jazz specialty record shops—or shops that specialize in secondhand (politely called "collectible") albums, including jazz. If you don't live near a large record store or specialty shop, or if you want to browse harder-to-get items, you can obtain catalogs from the following mail-order sources:

- Africassette, P.O. Box 24941, Detroit, MI 48224
- Audiophile Imports, Dept. JT, P.O. Box 4801, Lutherville, MD 21094-4801
- Cadence Mail Order, *Cadence*, Cadence Building, Redwood, NY 13679
- Coda Sales, Coda Publications, P.O. Box 1002, Station O, Toronto, ONT M4A 2N4, Canada
- Descarga, 328 Flatbush Avenue, Suite 180-L, Brooklyn, NY 11238
- Double-Time Jazz, P.O. Box 1244, New Albany, IN 47151-1244
- I.M.D., 160 Hanford Street, Columbus, OH 43206
- Jaybee Jazz, P.O. Box 411004, Creve Coeur, MO 63141
- Original Music, R.D. 1, P.O. Box 190, Lasher Road, Tivoli, NY 12583
- Rick Ballard Imports, P.O. Box 50063, Dept DB, Berkeley, CA 94705
- Roots and Rhythm, 10341 San Pablo Avenue, El Cerrito, CA 94530
- Stash-Daybreak Express, 140 22nd Street, 12th Floor, New York, NY 10011
- Worlds Records, P.O. Box 1922, Novato, CA 94948

You should also browse some of the following magazines for news of new recordings and the availability of old ones:

- *Cadence*, Cadence Building, Redwood, NY 13679
- *Coda,* Coda Publications, P.O. Box 1002, Station O, Toronto, ONT M4A 2N4, Canada
- *Down Beat*, P.O. Box 906. Elmhurst, IL 60126-0906
- *Jazz Now*, Jazz Now Building, 3733 California Street, Oakland, CA 94619-1413
- *The Jazz Report,* 14 London Street, Toronto, ONT M6G IM9 Canada
- *Jazz Times*, 7961 Eastern Avenue, Suite 303, Silver Spring, MD 20910-4898
- *Jazziz* 3620 N.W. 43rd Street, Gainesville, FL 32606
- *The Mississippi Rag,* P.O. Box 19068, Minneapolis, MN 55419

Dig This

"You'll find that happiness lies right under your eyes," the old song goes, "right in your own backyard." Before venturing very far afield, turn to your local Yellow Pages. You may find a jazz specialty store close to you.

Making the Scene

Where do you go to meet other jazz enthusiasts? Try going to the places jazz is kept. To concerts. To clubs. To festivals. Jazz festivals (see Chapter 2) are ideal for finding others who already share your interest in the music. The festival atmosphere is typically informal and conducive to meeting other fans and conversation. Refreshments are often available. By definition, a festival is a gathering, a kind of party, a time and place to be social.

If you're really serious about jazz and about meeting others who are really serious about the music, check out your local college or community college for jazz-appreciation courses. Typically, these are non-graded evening or weekend classes taught by a musician or music instructor. You'll do plenty of listening, and some field trips to local jazz venues may be included. Almost certainly, you'll have ample opportunity to discuss the music with others in the class.

And then there is that now-ubiquitous hangout, the Internet. Use The JazzWeb (at www.nwu.edu/jazz/internet.html) or Yahoo, Excite, or some other Web search engine to find newsgroups devoted to jazz. (A newsgroup is a focused discussion group on the Web. The contents of a newsgroup are contributed by the users of the group, who post articles and respond to posted articles.) These are ongoing discussion groups, typically open to anyone who cares to join in. You'll probably find a variety of newsgroups dedicated to specific subgenres within jazz, such as bop, fusion, avant garde, and so on, as well as to individual performers.

How to Save Money

There's good news, bad news, and more good news regarding the state of jazz recording these days. The good news is that more jazz is available than ever before, including historical reissues. The bad news is that many jazz albums go out of print at the drop of a hat (or the dip of a sales figure). The good news is that discontinued albums (called *cut outs*) are usually available at bargain prices. Many record stores have special cut-out sections, which you can browse.

Buying secondhand recordings is another great way to save. Most cities and many college towns have one or more used record stores. One benefit of the CD revolution is that the recording medium, the CD, is much more durable and less subject to wear than vinyl, which means that most used CDs (unless obviously damaged) are in better shape than most used vinyl recordings. Properly cared for, CDs don't wear out with repeated playing. In contrast, even well cared-for vinyl recordings do deteriorate a little each and every time the needle is applied.

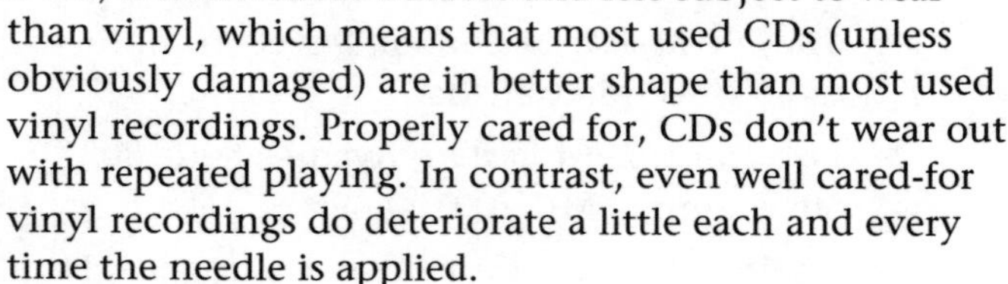

Talk the Talk

A **cut out** is a record album that has been discontinued and is made available at a greatly reduced price.

If you want free recordings, visit your local library. Many public libraries loan CDs. It's likely that some very good jazz will be among them.

Finally, recycle. Swap and sell albums among your jazz-loving friends.

Real Square

You can save money by tape recording your friends' CDs for your own use. But, in most cases, it's illegal (copyright infringement) and just plain wrong. It deprives retailers and record companies of income, and it steals from the artists—most of whom are paid royalties based on CDs sold. Do the right thing. If the album is in print and available, buy it. The artists and everyone else involved has earned your money. If the album is out of print and difficult to find, feel free to tape it.

The World of Vinyl

The six-year-old daughter of a friend of mine was watching television with her father. One of the actors dialed a call on a rotary phone.

"What's *that*, Daddy?" the little girl asked, having only seen touch-tone phones.

I expect soon to encounter a kid who looks at a 12-inch black vinyl disc with a hole in the center and asks, "What's *that*?"

It is amazing how vinyl recordings, ubiquitous and universal for some 80 years, have all but disappeared from the mainstream marketplace. While most of the history of jazz unfolded during the vinyl era, the reissue on CD of the major recordings is proceeding apace. However, you may want to hunt up vinyl originals:

- Maybe the recording you're interested in has yet to be reissued on CD.

- Maybe you like the idea of owning a treasured recording in its "original" form with full-size album cover art.
- Maybe you like the analog sound of vinyl more than the digital sound of CD. Some dedicated audiophiles insist that analog recordings sound more natural than digital recordings or remasterings (the transfer of an analog original to digital form).

Whatever your reason, if you're into vinyl, check out the availability of this format in your town and also look into these Web sites:

- John Wright's Homepage/Vintage Jazz and Dance Band Music on 78 rpm and Film specializes in 78s (http://ourworld.compuserve.com/homepages/jabw-vintage).
- Soul Records (www.chez.com/funky/) features jazz 45s.
- Millenium (*their* spelling!) Records offers the entire range, 78, 45, and 33$^{1}/_{3}$ rpm (www.record.albums.com/).

A Core Collection: The Essential Jazz Albums

It's hardly a new gimmick. You ask someone, "If you were stranded on a desert island, what 10 books would you want to have with you?" (*Books!?* Just get me off this stinking island!) Anyway, here's a short "desert island" list of 25 essential jazz albums.

1. Louis Armstrong, *Hot Fives and Sevens*, vol. 3 (Columbia)
2. Jelly Roll Morton, *Jelly Roll Morton* (Milestone)
3. Fats Waller, *Fats Waller and His Buddies* (Bluebird)
4. Coleman Hawkins, *A Retrospective 1929–1963* (Bluebird)
5. Benny Goodman, *Benny Goodman Carnegie Hall Jazz Concert* (Columbia)
6. Count Basie, *The Complete Decca Recordings (1937–1939)* (Decca Jazz)
7. Billie Holiday, *The Complete Decca Recordings* (Decca Jazz)
8. Duke Ellington, *Fargo ND, November 7, 1940* (Vintage Jazz)
9. Woody Herman, *Keeper of the Flame: Complete Capitol Recordings* (Capitol)
10. Art Tatum, *Piano Starts Here* (Columbia/Legacy)
11. Charlie Parker, *Complete Dial Sessions* (includes work with Dizzy Gillespie; Stash)
12. Bud Powell, *The Complete Blue Note and Roost Recordings* (Blue Note)
13. Thelonious Monk, *The Thelonious Monk Orchestra at Town Hall* (Original Jazz Classics)
14. Ella Fitzgerald, *75th Birthday Celebration* (GRP)
15. Miles Davis, *The Complete Birth of the Cool* (Capitol Jazz)
16. Art Blakey and the Jazz Messengers, *Moanin': Art Blakey and the Jazz Messengers* (Blue Note)
17. Charles Mingus, *Pithecanthropus Erectus* (Atlantic)

18. Miles Davis, *Kind of Blue* (Columbia/Legacy)
19. John Coltrane, *Giant Steps* (Atlantic)
20. Bill Evans, *Sunday at the Village Vanguard* (Original Jazz Classics)
21. Ornette Coleman, *At the "Golden Circle" in Stockholm*, vol. 1 (Blue Note)
22. Art Ensemble of Chicago, *Live* (Delmark)
23. Miles Davis, *Bitches Brew* (Columbia/Legacy)
24. Keith Jarrett, *Köln Concert* (ECM)
25. Wynton Marsalis, *In This House, on This Morning* (Columbia)

Are these the best recordings ever made? Well, I think some of them are. But, more important, they are representative of the range of jazz. "From the tiny acorn, the mighty oak doth grow," goes an old, old saying. Think of these twenty-five as the acorn of the oak that will be your personal jazz archive.

Dig This

Twenty-five is an arbitrary but manageable number. After all, these CDs aren't free. You'll find many additional recordings listed in Appendix C.

Feel free to reject the "help" offered in this chapter. If you prefer to follow your nose—or, rather, ears—into and around the record store, by all means do so. Jazz is to be enjoyed, not systematically or dogmatically hoarded.

A few last words before we leave you to your own ears. Be sure to check out the appendixes that come next. You'll find a handy jazz who's who, a chronology of key dates in the story of jazz, some more albums to add to your collection, and even books for your library. You'll also come across a glossary of the language of jazz.

The Least You Need to Know

- You'll enjoy your music-shopping expeditions more if you plan them.
- You can extend your shopping range by checking out jazz vendors on the World Wide Web.
- Don't overlook the many small specialty jazz labels. The small labels feature a lot of great old jazz as well as music from the cutting edge.
- Take notes on the music you hear.
- A collecting strategy based on historical period, style, performer, or instrument can make building your personal jazz collection more cost-effective and can enhance your understanding and enjoyment of the music.

Appendix A

Main Men (and Women): Who's Who in Jazz

The following men and women (and a few groups) have been central to the development of jazz.

Muhal Richard Abrams (1930–) Pianist and composer; a founder and president of the avant-garde AACM.

Cannonball Adderley (1928–75) Alto saxophonist; major figure in hard bop.

Nat Adderley (1931–) Trumpeter brother of Cannonball; major figure in hard bop.

Larry Adler (1914–) Harmonica virtuoso; helped make his humble instrument a legitimate jazz vehicle.

Air Important avant-garde group of the 1970s. Principal members included Henry Threadgill (reeds), Fred Hopkins (bass), and Steve McCall (drums).

Henry "Red" Allen (1908–67) Major Dixieland trumpeter.

Mose Allison (1927–) Singer and pianist who specializes in hard bop and "folk jazz."

Albert Ammons (1907–49) Swing/boogie-woogie pianist.

Gene Ammons (1925–74) Bop and hard bop tenor saxophonist noted for his "big" tone.

Louis Armstrong (1901–71) New Orleans-born trumpeter and vocalist who was the first great jazz soloist; one of the towering giants of jazz.

Art Ensemble of Chicago Important avant-garde jazz group, whose principal members include Roscoe Mitchell (saxophone), Lester Bowie (trumpet), Joseph Jarman (saxophone), Malachi Favors (bass), and Don Moye (percussion).

Albert Ayler (1936–70) Saxophonist important in free jazz.

Chet Baker (1929–88) Ultra laid-back trumpeter and vocalist; figure in the cool school.

Charlie Barnet (1913–91) Tenor saxophonist and swing bandleader whose "Cherokee" became a favorite bop anthem.

Count Basie (1904–84) Pianist and bandleader; towering giant of the swing era.

Sidney Bechet (1897–1959) Clarinetist and (especially) soprano saxophonist; a major figure in New Orleans jazz.

Bix Beiderbecke (1903–31) Legendary classic jazz trumpeter celebrated for his intense lyricism.

George Benson (1943–) Guitarist and vocalist specializing in hard bop, crossover, and pop.

Bunny Berigan (1908–1942) Important swing trumpeter and vocalist.

Art Blakey (1919–1990) Drummer, hard bop guru, and founder/leader of the Jazz Messengers.

Anthony Braxton (1945–) Multi-reed player and avant-garde innovator.

Michael Brecker (1949–) Post-bop tenor saxophonist and crossover artist.

Clifford Brown (1930–1956) Extraordinary hard bop trumpeter whose career was cut short by a car accident at age 25.

Dave Brubeck (1920–) Innovative and popular cool school pianist, leader, and composer.

George Cables (1944–) Hard bop and pianist and leader.

Benny Carter (1907–) Important and long-lived swing alto saxophonist, trumpeter, arranger, composer, and leader.

Betty Carter (1930–1998) Leading avant-garde and bop vocalist.

Doc Cheatham (1905–1997) Veteran Dixieland and swing trumpeter and vocalist.

Charlie Christian (1916–1942) First important electric guitarist; featured musician in Benny Goodman band.

June Christy (1925–1990) Cool school vocalist.

Buck Clayton (1911–1991) Swing trumpeter and arranger who "invented" mainstream jazz.

Nat King Cole (1919–1965) Great swing pianist and sensational pop vocalist.

Ornette Coleman (1930–) Avant-garde and free jazz alto saxophonist, composer, leader, who is also a trumpeter and violinist.

John Coltrane (1926–1967) Multi-reed player called the most influential jazz musician of the past 35 years; worked in hard bop, avant-garde, and free jazz.

Eddie Condon (1905–1973) Popular Dixieland leader and guitarist; owned a famous nightclub in New York.

Chick Corea (1941–) Keyboardist, leader, and composer in fusion, post-bop, and free jazz styles.

Marilyn Crispell (1947–) Exciting avant-garde pianist.

Bob Crosby (1913–1993) Dixieland and swing vocalist and leader; brother of Bing.

Tadd Dameron (1917–1965) A central bop arranger and composer.

Eddie Lockjaw Davis (1922–1986) Tough tenor saxophone hard bop and swing stylist.

Miles Davis (1926–1991) Trumpeter, leader, and composer in bop, cool school, hard bop, avant-garde, and fusion styles; one of the most influential jazz innovators ever.

Wild Bill Davison (1906–1989) Fine Dixieland cornet player.

Jack DeJohnette (1942–) Avant-garde and fusion drummer, keyboardist, and leader.

Baby Dodds (1898–1959) Considered the first important jazz drummer; played in the New Orleans style.

Johnny Dodds (1892–1940) New Orleans-style clarinetist; brother of Baby Dodds.

Eric Dolphy (1928–1964) Multi-reed avant-garde musician.

Lou Donaldson (1926–) Fine bebop alto saxophonist.

Kenny Dorham (1924–1972) Hard bop trumpeter.

Jimmy Dorsey (1904–1957) Major swing bandleader and alto saxophonist; brother of Tommy.

Tommy Dorsey (1905–1956) Major swing leader and trombonist; brother of Jimmy.

Roy Eldridge (1911–1989) High-energy swing trumpeter.

Duke Ellington (1899–1974) Great pianist, composer, arranger, and leader; one of the most important figures in American music.

Herb Ellis (1921–) Bop and swing guitarist.

Bill Evans (1929–1980) Sublime bop and cool school pianist and leader.

Gil Evans (1912–1988) Great jazz arranger in cool, fusion, and the late bop styles.

Art Farmer (1928–) Cool school and hard bop trumpeter and flugelhorn player.

Maynard Ferguson (1928–) Bop, hard bop, and pop crossover trumpeter.

Ella Fitzgerald (1917–1996) The definitive female jazz vocalist.

Pete Fountain (1930–) Popular Dixieland clarinetist.

Dave Frishberg (1933–) Original swing and bop lyricist, pianist, and vocalist.

Kenny G (1959–) Crossover soprano saxophonist.

Erroll Garner (1921–1977) Popular swing and bop piano stylist.

Stan Getz (1927–1991) Leading cool school tenor saxophonist who introduced the bossa nova into American jazz.

Dizzy Gillespie (1917–1993) Pioneering bebop trumpeter, leader, and composer.

Jerry Gonzalez (1949–) Afro-Cuban jazz trumpeter, percussionist, and leader.

Benny Goodman (a 1909–1986) King of swing, greatest jazz clarinetist of all time, and major big band leader.

Dexter Gordon (1923–1990) Bop and hard bop tenor saxophonist.

Stephane Grappelli (1908–) The great swing violinist.

Grant Green (1931–1979) Hard bop guitarist.

Johnny Griffin (1928–) Bop and hard bop tenor saxophonist who is often called the "world's fastest saxophonist."

Lionel Hampton (1909–) First and foremost jazz vibraphonist.

Herbie Hancock (1940–) Fusion and pop pianist, leader, and composer.

Coleman Hawkins (1904–1969) First important tenor saxophonist; a great classic jazz, swing, and bop musician.

Fletcher Henderson (1897–1952) Classic jazz and swing pianist, leader, and arranger; especially important work for Benny Goodman.

Joe Henderson (1937–) Hard bop tenor saxophonist.

Woody Herman (1913–1987) Major swing, bop, and hard bop clarinetist, alto saxophonist, and band leader.

Andrew Hill (1937–) Avant-garde pianist.

Earl Hines (1903–1983) Dubbed the first modern jazz pianist; great swing and classic jazz stylist.

Billie Holiday (1915–1959) Most famous of all jazz singers; the soulful "Lady Day."

Freddie Hubbard (1938–) Hard bop trumpeter and flugelhorn player.

Helen Humes (1913–1981) Swing and blues vocalist.

Dick Hyman (1927–) Stride, classic jazz, and swing pianist and historic re-creator.

Illinois Jacquet (1922–) Bop and swing tenor saxophonist; also plays alto.

Keith Jarrett (1945–) Exciting avant-garde pianist, especially noted for his solo concerts.

Antonio Carlos Jobim (1925–) Brazilian songwriter, guitarist, and pianist who introduced the bossa nova to jazz.

Bunk Johnson (1889–1949) New Orleans trumpeter.

J.J. Johnson (1924–) Perhaps the greatest jazz trombonist ever; specializes in bop and hard bop.

James P. Johnson (1894–1955) Dean of stride pianists and important classic jazz composer.

Philly Joe Jones (1923–1985) High-energy hard bop drummer.

Quincy Jones (1933–) Best known as a popular jazz composer specializing in bop and crossover styles.

Louis Jordan (1908–1975) Swing-era alto saxophonist and vocalist.

Stan Kenton (1911–1979) Inventor of "Progressive Jazz;" controversial but a popular pianist, leader, and composer.

Freddie Keppard (1890–1933) New Orleans jazz cornetist.

John Kirby (1908–1952) Underrated but important swing leader and bass player.

Andy Kirk (1898–1992) Successful swing leader.

Rahsaan Roland Kirk (1936–1977) Wild bop, hard bop, swing, avant-garde, and New Orleans jazz multi-reed player.

Lee Konitz (1927–) Major cool school alto and soprano saxophonist.

Gene Krupa (1909–1973) Most famous swing era and Dixieland drummer; a featured player in Benny Goodman's band.

Steve Lacy (1934–) Free jazz soprano saxophonist.

Lambert, Hendricks & Ross Leading bop vocal group.

George Lewis (1952–) Avant-garde trombonist and electronic music specialist.

John Lewis (1920–) Cool school and third stream pianist, leader, and composer; musical director of the Modern Jazz Quartet.

Meade "Lux" Lewis (1905–1964) Boogie-woogie pianist.

Abbey Lincoln (1930–) Post-bop vocalist.

Jimmie Lunceford 1902–1947) Swing era band leader.

Machito (1912–1984) Afro-Cuban jazz musician and innovator.

Herbie Mann (1930–) Popular jazz flutist.

Shelly Manne (1920–1984) Hard bop and cool school drummer and leader.

Branford Marsalis (1960–) Hard bop tenor saxophonist.

Wynton Marsalis (1961–) Versatile superstar trumpeter, leader, and composer; specializes in New Orleans jazz, swing, bop, and classical music.

Bobby McFerrin (1950–) Unique bop and pop vocalist who uses his voice as an extraordinarily flexible instrument.

John McLaughlin (1942–) British-born fusion guitar virtuoso.

Jackie McLean (1932–) Hard bop alto saxophonist.

Carmen McRae (1920–1994) Mainstream and bop vocalist.

Jay McShann (1916–) Swing and blues pianist and vocalist.

Pat Metheny (1954–) Avant-garde and crossover guitarist, leader, and composer.

Glenn Miller (1904–1944) Most famous big band leader of World War II.

Charles Mingus (1922–1979) Phenomenal bass virtuoso, pianist, leader, and important jazz composer; a master of the avant-garde and bop.

Hank Mobley (1930–1986) Hard bop tenor saxophonist.

Modern Jazz Quartet Long-lived and highly influential cool school and third stream "jazz chamber music" group.

Thelonious Monk (1917–1982) Highly original pianist, composer, and leader; essentially unique but usually classified as a bop or avant-garde musician.

Wes Montgomery (1925–1968) Great jazz guitarist, specializing in hard bop and crossover.

Jelly Roll Morton (1890–1941) Called himself the inventor of jazz; a very important early pianist, composer, and leader.

Bennie Moten (1894–1935) Kansas City band leader best remembered as the leader of the band Count Basie took over after his death.

Gerry Mulligan (1927–1996) Baritone saxophonist, composer, arranger, and leader; a cool school luminary.

Fats Navarro (1923–1958) Great bop trumpeter.

Anita O'Day (1919–) Bop and swing vocalist.

Chico O'Farrill (1921–) Cuban composer, arranger, and trumpeter, best known for the music he wrote for Goodman, Kenton, Machito, Parker, and Gillespie.

King Oliver (1885–1938) Cornetist and leader of an early New Orleans jazz band; hired Louis Armstrong.

Kid Ory (1886–1973) Pioneering Dixieland trombonist.

Charlie Parker (1920–1955) Legendary bebop alto saxophonist, whose improvisations have been widely studied and imitated.

Joe Pass (1929–1994) Bop guitarist.

Jaco Pastorius (1951–1987) Fusion bassist.

Art Pepper (1925–1982) Cool school and post-hard bop alto saxophonist.

Oscar Peterson (1925–) Very popular and widely recorded pianist specializing in bop and swing.

Jean-Luc Ponty (1942–) Fusion and crossover violinist.

Bud Powell (1924–1966) Bop composer and piano virtuoso; a keyboard giant.

Tito Puente (1923–) Latin jazz leader and percussionist.

Flora Purim (1942–) Brazilian and fusion jazz vocalist.

Don Redman (1900–1964) Instrumentalist and major swing and classic jazz composer-arranger.

Django Reinhardt (1910–1953) Swing guitarist who often partnered with violinist Stephane Grappelli.

Buddy Rich (1917–1987) Billed as the "world's greatest drummer" and many would agree. Played with major swing orchestras and successfully fronted his own big band from 1966 until his death.

Max Roach (1924–) Highly versatile drummer and leader who has played avant-garde, bop, and hard bop.

Luckey Roberts (1887–1968) Stride pianist.

Sonny Rollins (1930–) Hard bop tenor saxophonist.

Annie Ross (1930–) Bop vocalist and member of Lambert, Hendricks & Ross.

Pharoah Sanders (1940–) Free jazz tenor saxophonist.

Artie Shaw (1910–) Major swing clarinetist and leader.

George Shearing (1919–) Popular pianist, specializing in bop, cool, and Latin jazz; known for the block-chord "Shearing sound."

Archie Shepp (1937–) Tenor and soprano hard bop and avant-garde saxophonist.

Wayne Shorter (1933–) Fusion and hard bop soprano and tenor saxophonist.

Horace Silver (1928–) Most important hard bop pianist-composer.

Zoot Sims (1925–1985) Bop and cool school tenor saxophonist.

Frank Sinatra (1915–1998) Swing and pop vocalist.

Bessie Smith (1894–1937) Classic jazz and blues vocalist.

Jimmy Smith (1925–) Hard bop organist.

Muggsy Spanier (1906–1967) Dixieland cornetist.

Billy Strayhorn (1915–1967) Arranger and composer closely associated with Duke Ellington.

Maxine Sullivan (1911–1987) Swing vocalist.

Sun Ra (1914–1993) Avant-garde and free jazz pianist, keyboardist, and leader of the "Arkestra;" highly colorful, highly controversial.

Art Tatum (1909–1956) Virtuoso swing pianist, who influenced Bud Powell and many other pianists.

Cecil Taylor (1929–) Free jazz pianist and leader.

Jack Teagarden (1905–1964) Dixieland and swing trombonist, vocalist, and leader.

Clark Terry (1920–) Swing and bop flugelhorn player.

Toots Thielemans (1922–) Foremost jazz harmonica player.

Claude Thornhill (1909–1965) Unique pianist, leader, and arranger in the cool school style.

Cal Tjader (1925–1982) A non-Latin band leader who specialized in Latin jazz.

Mel Tormé (1925–1997) Bop and swing vocalist.

Lennie Tristano (1990–1978) Cool school pianist and leader.

Stanley Turrentine (1934–) Hard bop tenor saxophonist.

McCoy Tyner (1938–) Avant-garde pianist and leader.

Sarah Vaughan (1924–1990) Bop vocal stylist.

Joe Venuti (1903–1978) Dixieland, swing, and classic jazz violinist.

Fats Waller (1904–1943) Major stride, classic jazz, and swing pianist, vocalist, composer, and leader; Waller also played the organ.

Dinah Washington (1924–1963) Blues vocalist.

Grover Washington, Jr. (1943–) Foremost crossover multi-reed musician.

Weather Report Key fusion group.

Chick Webb (1909–1939) Drummer and swing band leader who gave Ella Fitzgerald her start.

Ben Webster (1909–1973) Big-toned swing tenor saxophonist.

Randy Weston (1926–) Hard bop pianist and composer.

Paul Whiteman (1890–1967) Pop and classic jazz band leader who commissioned George Gershwin's *Rhapsody in Blue.*

Clarence Williams (1896–1965) Classic jazz and blues pianist and vocalist.

Teddy Wilson (1912–1986) Swing pianist.

Phil Woods (1931–) Hard bop alto saxophonist who sometimes doubled on clarinet.

Lester Young (1909-1959) Sophisticated swing tenor saxophonist; nicknamed "Prez" by an adoring Billie Holiday.

John Zorn (1953–) Avant-garde composer and performer who has brought game theory to compositions for large forces.

Appendix B

Counting Time: A Brief Chronology of Jazz

1619: The first African slaves are sold to Virginia planters.

1817: New Orleans city council establishes "Congo Square" as an official site for slave music and dance.

1892: Tom Turpin writes "Harlem Rag," the first known ragtime composition.

1895: Scott Joplin begins publishing his rags.

Buddy Bolden's first band is formed.

1899: Joplin's "Maple Leaf Rag" launches a national ragtime craze.

1917: Joplin dies; the classic era of ragtime ends.

Original Dixieland Jass Band makes the first-ever jazz recording.

The U.S. Navy closes New Orleans's Storyville red-light district; jazz musicians begin to leave the city for the North.

1918: King Oliver leaves New Orleans for Chicago.

1919: Sidney Bechet leaves New Orleans to tour Europe.

1920: Mamie Smith cuts "Crazy Blues," the first blues record.

1923: King Oliver, Jelly Roll Morton, Sidney Bechet, and Louis Armstrong make their first recordings.

King Oliver's Creole Jazz Band (with Louis Armstrong on board) makes it big in Chicago.

Don Redman becomes the first major jazz arranger (for Fletcher Henderson).

Bennie Moten puts Kansas City jazz on the map with his band's first recordings.

1924: Bix Beiderbecke records with the Wolverines.

Paul Whiteman commissions *Rhapsody in Blue* from George Gershwin.

1925: Louis Armstrong begins the Hot Five series of recordings.

1926: Jelly Roll Morton makes his Red Hot Peppers recordings in Chicago.

1927: Duke Ellington appears at Harlem's Cotton Club.

1928: Louis Armstrong records the landmark *West End Blues*—and the first great recorded jazz solo.

1929: Armstrong records with big bands.

The important Casa Loma Orchestra makes its debut recordings.

Count Basie joins the Bennie Moten Orchestra.

1930: Cab Calloway becomes a Cotton Club regular.

1932: Sidney Bechet kicks off a New Orleans jazz revival with his New Orleans Feetwarmers.

Ellington records his first big swing hit: "It Don't Mean a Thing If It Ain't Got That Swing."

1933: Art Tatum cuts his first records.

Billie Holiday makes her first recordings.

1934: Jimmie Lunceford's band begins recording.

The Benny Goodman Orchestra is broadcast nationally on radio.

Ella Fitzgerald debuts with the Chick Webb Orchestra.

Fats Waller and His Rhythm record.

1935: Bob Crosby Orchestra combines Dixieland and swing.

After much struggle, the Benny Goodman Orchestra becomes an "overnight" sensation at the Palomar Ballroom, Los Angeles; the swing era is officially underway.

Bennie Moten dies; protege Count Basie forms his own orchestra with many Moten players.

Tommy and Jimmy Dorsey break up the successful Dorsey Brothers Band; each forms his own band.

1936: Woody Herman forms his first band.

Record producer John Hammond "discovers" the Count Basie band while listening to his car radio.

Lester Young cuts his first record.

Artie Shaw forms his first orchestra.

1937: Trumpeter Bunny Berigan forms a big band.

Basie begins recording.

Glenn Miller forms his first band.

Dizzy Gillespie makes his first recordings.

Duke Ellington's Puerto Rican valve trombonist Juan Tizol composes "Caravan," introducing Latin jazz.

1938: Benny Goodman triumphs at Carnegie Hall.

The John Kirby Sextet introduces small-ensemble swing.

Jelly Roll Morton is rediscovered; records for the Library of Congress.

Eddie Condon records Dixieland revival material.

1939: Charlie Barnet makes it big.

Harry James starts his own big band.

Glenn Miller's orchestra reaches the height of its popularity.

Ella Fitzgerald assumes leadership of the Chick Webb Orchestra when its leader dies.

Coleman Hawkins records "Body and Soul."

Charlie Christian introduces electric guitar in the Benny Goodman Orchestra.

1940: Dizzy Gillespie and Charlie Parker meet.

Bandleader Machito forms the Afro-Cubans.

1941: Gene Krupa scores several hits.

Stan Kenton forms his first orchestra.

Lu Watters makes his first Dixieland revival recordings.

Charlie Parker makes his first records.

Jam sessions at Minton's Playhouse and Monroe's Uptown House mark the beginning of bebop.

1942: Glenn Miller joins the U.S. Army Air Corps.

Lionel Hampton has a vibraphone hit with "Flying Home."

The recording strike begins.

Claude Thornhill hires arranger Gil Evans.

1943: Duke Ellington triumphs at Carnegie Hall.

Earl Hines's big band features Parker and Gillespie—fathers of bop.

1944: Woody Herman's orchestra becomes the First Herd.

Glenn Miller dies in an air crash over the English Channel.

Billy Eckstine forms a bop big band.

Coleman Hawkins leads a bop session.

Thelonious Monk composes "'Round Midnight."

1945: Recording heyday of Parker and Gillespie.

Miles Davis makes his first records.

1946: Major big bands begin to break up.

Gillespie forms a successful bop big band.

Lennie Tristano makes his first records.

1947: Gillespie introduces Cubana Bop (Afro-Cuban jazz) to bebop.

Charlie Parker forms a quintet including Miles Davis and Max Roach.

Thelonious Monk cuts his first records.

Bud Powell makes his first trio recordings.

1948: Miles Davis forms his highly influential nonet.

1949: High-watermark of the bop era; big bop concert at Carnegie Hall.

Tristano records with his sextet, which includes Lee Konitz, Warne Marsh, and other major "cool school" players.

Hard bopper Sonny Rollins makes his recording debut.

Stan Kenton and Benny Goodman both commission Afro-Cuban arrangements from Chico O'Farrill.

Lennie Tristano's "Intuition" and "Digression" are the first free jazz improvisations.

1949: Miles Davis's "Birth of the Cool" recordings are issued; "cool jazz" is born.

1950: Bop's popularity wanes.

The Dave Brubeck Trio enjoys popularity.

Horace Silver is "discovered" by Stan Getz.

1951: Brubeck forms a quartet featuring altoist Paul Desmond.

Miles Davis makes his first hard bop recordings (with Sonny Rollins and Jackie McLean).

1952: Modern Jazz Quartet makes its debut recordings.

Chet Baker and Gerry Mulligan are the core of a pianoless quartet.

Miles Davis leaves the "cool school" and starts playing hard bop.

1954: Clifford Brown and Max Roach form a hard bop quintet.

Cal Tjader records Latin jazz.

1955: Cannonball Adderley emerges as a major hard bop musician.

Art Blakey and Horace Silver start the Jazz Messengers, a major hard bop force.

Cecil Taylor records free jazz.

John Coltrane joins the Miles Davis Quintet.

Sun Ra records with his Arkestra.

1956: Tito Puente records *Puente Goes Jazz*.

Charles Mingus records *Pithecanthropus Erectus*, an early avant-garde work.

1957: Altoist Art Pepper records *Art Pepper Meets the Rhythm Section* with members of the Miles Davis Quintet.

1958: Hard bop guitarist Wes Montogmery records.

Ornette Coleman cuts his first records.

1959: Brubeck records "Take Five."

The film *Black Orpheus* features a Brazilian jazz score by Antonio Carlos Jobim and Luiz Bonfa.

Ornette Coleman's Quartet creates great controversy over free jazz.

1960: Freddie Hubbard debuts on disk.

John Coltrane forms his "classic quartet."

Mingus forms a quartet that includes Eric Dolphy.

1961: Oliver Nelson records the definitive hard-bop album, *Blues and the Abstract Truth.*

1962: Stan Getz and Charlie Byrd record *Jazz Samba*—beginning of the bossa nova craze in the United States.

1963: Bossa nova becomes ubiquitous with the release of Astrud Gilberto's recording of "Girl from Ipanema" (featuring Jobim and Getz).

1964: Louis Armstrong has a big pop hit with "Hello, Dolly!"

Pharoah Sanders makes his first recordings.

Coltrane records his spiritual *A Love Supreme.*

1965: AACM (Association for the Advancement of Creative Musicians), an avant-garde collective, formed in Chicago.

1966: Cannonball Adderley becomes one of the first hard boppers to cross over to pop.

Art Ensemble of Chicago is formed.

1967: Herbie Hancock, playing with Miles Davis, introduces an electric piano—the first step toward fusion.

1969: Fusion is born with Miles Davis's *Bitches Brew.*

1970: Classical pianist Joshua Rifkin records his first Joplin album.

1971: The seminal fusion groups Weather Report and Mahavishnu Orchestra are formed.

1972: Chick Corea's fusion group, Return to Forever, records its first two albums.

1973: *The Sting,* a hit film, features a Joplin soundtrack and launches a ragtime revival.

1974: Grover Washington, Jr., scores a crossover hit with "Mr. Magic."

1976: Jaco Pastorius plays with Weather Report.

George Benson scores a pop hit with "This Masquerade."

1977: Spyro Gyra, a pop-influenced fusion group, debuts on record.

Trumpeter Chuck Mangione scores a pop hit with "Feels So Good."

1978: The Pat Metheny Group is formed.

1980: Grover Washington, Jr. records *Winelight,* the definitive "contemporary jazz" album.

1985: Wynton Marsalis leads a revival of acoustic jazz with *Black Codes (from the Underground).*

1986: Kenny G's star rises with "Songbird."

1993: Wynton Marsalis records *In This House, on This Morning,* an ambitious jazz work depicting a Sunday church service.

1995: Jean-Luc Ponty, Al Di Meola, and Stanley Clarke form the Rite of Strings.

Beyond the Core: Ideas for Building a Bigger Collection

The following list of CDs *extends* (does not include) the list of 25 "core" CDs found at the end of Chapter 23.

Cannonball Adderley/John Coltrane, *Cannonball And Coltrane,* EmArcy

Mose Allison, *I Don't Worry About a Thing*, Rhino/Atlantic

Louis Armstrong/King Oliver, *Louis Armstrong and King Oliver*, Milestone

Charlie Barnet, *Drop Me Off in Harlem*, Decca

Count Basie, *April in Paris*, Verve

Sidney Bechet, *Master Takes: Victor Sessions* (1932–1943), Bluebird

Bix Beiderbecke, *Bix Lives*, RCA

George Benson, *Body Talk*, Columbia

Art Blakey, *A Night in Tunisia*, Blue Note

Clifford Brown, *Brown and Roach, Inc.* EmArcy

Dave Brubeck, *Time Out*, Columbia

Benny Carter, *All of Me*, Bluebird

Nat King Cole, *Jazz Encounters*, Blue Note

Ornette Coleman, *Free Jazz (A Collective Improvisation)*, Atlantic

John Coltrane, *Blue Train*, Blue Note

Eddie Condon, *Dixieland All Stars*, GRP/Decca

Chick Corea, *My Spanish Heart*, Polydor

Eddie Lockjaw Davis, *All of Me*, SteepleChase

Miles Davis, *Miles Ahead*, Columbia

Miles Davis, *Miles Smiles*, Columbia

Miles Davis, *Sketches of Spain*, Columbia

Johnny Dodds, *Blue Clarinet Stomp*, Bluebird

Eric Dolphy, *Outward Bound*, Original Jazz Classics

Roy Eldridge, *Montreux 1977*, Original Jazz Classics

Duke Ellington, *Blanton-Webster Band*, Bluebird

Duke Ellinglon, *Seventieth Birthday Concert*, Blue Note

Bill Evans, *Portrait in Jazz*, Original Jazz Classics

Gil Evans, *New Bottle, Old Wine*, Blue Note

Maynard Ferguson, *The Birdland Dream Band*, Bluebird

Ella Fitzgerald, *The Complete Ella in Berlin*, Verve

Dave Frishberg, *Can't Take You Nowhere*, Fantasy

Stan Getz, *Stan Getz and J.J. Johnson at the Opera House*, Verve

Dizzy Gillespie/Roy Eldridge, *Dizzy Gillespie with Roy Eldridge*, Verve

Dizzy Gillespie, *Dizzy Gillespie At Newport*, Verve

Benny Goodman, *Sing Sing Sing*, Bluebird

Benny Goodman, *The Birth of Swing*, Bluebird

Stephane Grappelli, *Young Django*, Verve

Lionel Hampton, *Midnight Sun*, GRP

Herbie Hancock, *Maiden Voyage*, Blue Note

Coleman Hawkins, *Body and Soul*, RCA/Bluebird

Woody Herman, *Blues on Parade*, GRP

Earl Hines, *Spontaneous Explorations*, Contact

Billie Holiday, *Billie Holiday: The Legacy Box*, Columbus

Freddie Hubbard, *Breaking Point*, Blue Note

Keith Jarrett, *My Song*, ECM

James P. Johnson, *Snowy Morning Blues*, GRP

Stan Kenton, *Retrospective*, Capitol

John Kirby, *John Kirby 1938–1939*, Classics

Rahsaan Roland Kirk, *Bright Moments*, Rhino

Gene Krupa, *Uptown*, Columbia

Lambert, Hendricks & Ross, *Sing a Song of Basie*, GRP/Impulse!

George Lewis/Jimmie Lunceford, *Stomp It Off*, Decca

Machito, *Mucho Macho Machito*, Pablo

Branford Marsalis, *Trio Jeepy*, Columbia

Wynton Marsalis, *Black Codes (from the Underground)*, Columbia

Bobby McFerrin, *Spontaneous Inventions*, Blue Note

Pat Metheny, *Letter from Home*, Geffen

Charles Mingus, *Mingus at Antibes*, Atlantic

Modern Jazz Quartet, *Django*, Original Jazz Classics

Thelonious Monk, *Big Band and Quartet in Concert*, Columbia

Wes Montgomery, *So Much Guitar*, Original Jazz Classics

Jelly Roll Morton, *Jelly Roll Morton Centennial: His Complete Victor Recordings*, Bluebird

Bennie Moten, *Basie Beginnings*, Bluebird

Gerry Mulligan, *Best Of Mulligan Quartet with Chet Baker*, Pacific Jazz

Fats Navarro, *Fats Navarro and Tadd Dameron*, Blue Note

King Oliver, *Sugar Foot Stomp*, GRP

Original Dixieland Jazz Band, *75th Anniversary*, Bluebird

Kid Ory, *Kid Ory's Creole Jazz Band (1954)*, Good Time Jazz

Charlie Parker, *Charlie Parker and Stars of Modern Jazz at Carnegie Hall (Christmas 1949)*, Jass

Art Pepper, *Meets the Rhythm Section*, OJC

Art Pepper, *Straight Life*, OJC

Oscar Peterson, *At the Stratford Shakespearean Festival*, Verve

Bud Powell, *The Amazing Bud Powell*, Vol. 1, Blue Note

Tito Puente, *Goza Me Timbal*, Concord Picante

Django Reinhardt, *Django's Music*, Hep

Buddy Rich, *Mercy, Mercy*, World Pacific

Max Roach, *Freedom Now Suite*, Columbia

Sonny Rollins, *Saxophone Colossus and More*, Original Jazz Classics

Pharoah Sanders, *Karma*, Impulse

Artie Shaw, *Personal Best*, Bluebird

George Shearing, *I Hear a Rhapsody: Live at the Blue Note*, Telarc

Horace Silver, *Song for My Father*, Blue Note

Muggsy Spanier, *The Ragtime Band Sessions*, Bluebird

Art Tatum, *Classic Piano Solos (1934–39)*, GRP

Cecil Taylor, *Jazz Advance*, Blue Note

Claude Thornhill, *Best of Big Bands*, Columbia

Cal Tjader, *Latin Concert*, Original Jazz Classics

Mel Tormé, *In Concert in Tokyo*, Concord Jazz

Lennie Tristano, *The Complete Lennie Tristano on Keynote*, Mercury

McCoy Tyner, *Supertrio*, Milestone

Sarah Vaughan, *Complete: Live in Japan*, Mobile Fidelity

Joe Venuti, *Fiddlesticks*, Conifer

Fats Waller, *Turn on the Heat: The Fats Waller Piano Solos*, Bluebird

Dinah Washington, *Dinah Jams*, EmArcy

Grover Washington, Jr., *Mister Magic*, Motown

Weather Report, *Heavy Weather*, Columbia

Chick Webb, *Chick Webb (1929–1934)*, Classics

Ben Webster, *Meet You at the Fair*, Impulse!

Teddy Wilson, *With Billie in Mind*, Chiaroscuro

Lester Young, *The Jazz Giants '56*, Verve

Words on Music: An Essential Jazz Bibliography

Balliett, Whitney. *American Musicians: 56 Portraits in Jazz*. New York: Oxford University Press, 1986.

Basie, Count, and Albert Murray. *Good Morning Blues: The Autobiography of Count Basie*. New York: Random House, 1986.

Bechet, Sidney. *Treat It Gentle: In Autobiography*. London: Cassell & Co., 1960.

Berlin, Edward A. *King of Ragtime: Scott Joplin and His Era*. New York: Oxford University Press, 1994.

Blesh, Rudi, and Harriet Janis. *They All Played Ragtime*. New York: Knopf, 1950.

Chernoff, John Miller. *African Rhythm and African Sensibility*. Chicago: University of Chicago Press, 1979.

Chilton, John. *The Song of the Hawk: The Life and Recordings of Coleman Hawkins*. Ann Arbor: University of Michigan Press, 1990.

Cohn, Lawrence, ed. *Nothing But the Blues: The Music and the Musicians*. New York: Abbeville Press, 1992.

Collier, James Lincoln. *Benny Goodman and the Swing Era*. New York: Oxford University Press, 1989.

Jazz: The American Theme Song. New York: Oxford University Press, 1993.

Louis Armstrong: An American Genius. New York: Oxford University Press, 1983.

The Making of Jazz: A Comprehensive History. New York: Houghton-Mifflin, 1978.

Crow, Bill. *Jazz Anecdotes*. New York: Oxford University Press, 1990.

Davis, Francis. *The History of the Blues*. New York: Hyperion, 1995.

Davis, Miles, and Quincy Troupe. *Miles: The Autobiography*. New York: Simon & Schuster, 1989.

Ellington, Duke. *Music Is My Mistress*. Garden City, N.Y.: Doubleday, 1973.

Erlewine, Michael, et al, eds., *All Music Guide to Jazz,* 2d ed. San Francisco: Miller Freeman Books, 1996.

Feather, Leonard. *The Encyclopedia of Jazz.* 1960; reprint ed., New York: Da Capo. N.d.

Firestone, Ross. *Swing, Swing, Swing: The Life and Times of Benny Goodman.* New York: W.W. Norton, 1993.

Giddins, Gary. *Celebrating Bird: The Triumph of Charlie Parker.* New York: William Morrow, 1987.

Satchmo. New York: Doubleday, 1988.

Gillespie, Dizzy, and Al Frazer. *To Be or Not...to Bop.* Garden City, N.Y.: Doubleday, 1979.

Gioia, Ted. *The History of Jazz.* New York: Oxford University Press, 1997.

Gitler, Ira. *Jazz Masters of the Forties.* New York: Macmillan, 1966.

Gourse, Leslie. *Louis' Children: American Jazz Singers.* New York: William Morrow, 1984.

Gridley, Mark. *Jazz Styles,* sixth ed. Englewood Cliffs, N.J.: Prentice-Hall, 1997.

Hasse, John Edward. *Beyond Category: The Life and Genius of Duke Ellington.* New York: Simon & Schuster, 1993.

Hentoff, Nat, and Nat Shapiro. *Hear Me Talkin' to Ya: An Oral History of Jazz.* New York: Dover, 1966.

Kernfield, Barry, ed. *The New Grove Dictionary of Jazz.* New York: St. Martin's Press, 1994.

Lees, Gene. *Leader of the Band: The Life of Woody Herman.* New York: Oxford University Press, 1995.

Litweiler, John. *The Freedom Principle: Jazz After 1958.* New York: William Morrow, 1984.

Ornette Coleman: A Harmolodic Life. New York: William Morrow, 1992.

Lomax, Alan. *The Land Where the Blues Began.* New York: Pantheon, 1993.

Marquis, Donald. *In Search of Buddy Bolden, First Man of Jazz.* Baton Rouge: Louisiana State University Press, 1978.

Mingus, Charles. *Beneath the Underdog.* New York: Knopf, 1971.

Owens, Thomas. *Bebop: The Music and Its Players.* New York: Oxford University Press, 1995.

Pearson, Nathan W., Jr. *Goin' to Kansas City.* Urbana: University of Illinois Press, 1987.

Pepper, Art, and Laurie Pepper. *Straight Life: The Story of Art Pepper.* New York: Schirmer, 1979.

Porter, Lewis, ed. *A Lester Young Reader.* Washington, D.C.: Smithsonian Institution Press, 1991.

Roberts, John Storm. *The Latin Tinge: The Impact of Latin American Music on the United States.* New York: Oxford University Press, 1979.

Rosenthal, David H. *Hard Bop: Jazz and Black Music 1955–1965*. New York: Oxford University Press, 1992.

Russell, Bill. *New Orleans Style*. Compiled and edited by Barry Martyn and Mike Hazeldine. New Orleans: Jazzology Press, 1994.

Russell, Ross. *Bird Lives!: The High Life and Hard Times of Charlie (Yardbird) Parker*. New York: Charterhouse, 1973.

Jazz in Kansas City and the Southwest. Berkeley: University of California Press, 1971.

Sales, Grover. *Jazz: America's Classical Music*. Englewood Cliffs, N.J.: Prentice-Hall, 1984.

Santoro, Gene. *Dancing in Your Head: Jazz, Blues, Rock and Beyond*. New York: Oxford University Press, 1994.

Schuller, Gunther. *Early Jazz*. New York: Oxford University Press, 1968.

The Swing Era: The Development of Jazz 1930–1945. New York: Oxford University Press, 1989.

Sudhalter, Richard, and Philip R. Evans. *Bix: Man and Legend*. New York: Arlington House, 1974.

Tesser, Neil. *The Playboy Guide to Jazz*. New York: Plume, 1998.

Tucker, Mark, ed. *A Duke Ellington Reader*. New York: Oxford University Press, 1993.

Wilder, Alec. *American Popular Song: The Great Innovators*. New York: Oxford University Press, 1972.

William, Martin. *Jazz Masters of New Orleans*. New York: Macmillan, 1967.

The Jazz Tradition, revised ed. New York: Oxford University Press, 1983.

Appendix E

Talk the Talk: The Words of Jazz

arranger Not a composer, but one who orchestrates an existing composition to make the most expressive use of a particular ensemble.

articulate To separate musical notes precisely rather than to blur them or run them together.

atonal music Music that is not written in a particular key. To ears accustomed to music centered on a particular key or scale (conventional Western music is always centered on a key or keys), atonal work sounds dissonant.

audiophile A person who is both fanatical and knowledgeable about hi-fidelity sound.

avant-garde jazz See *free jazz.*

axe Also spelled *ax*. To a jazz musician, any instrument but especially a saxophone.

battle of the bands See *cutting contest.*

bent note A musical effect produced by attacking a note on pitch but then sliding up or down a bit before returning to the "correct" pitch again.

big band A jazz orchestra of 10 to 15 instruments or more. Typically, big bands are associated with music of the swing era.

blue note See *blues*.

blues A style of popular music derived from southern African-American folk song tradition and usually characterized by slow tempo and the use of flatted third and sevenths ("blue notes"). Emotionally, the blues is typically intense and plaintive.

bomb A loud, unexpected accent on the bass drum. "Dropping bombs" became a trademark of bebop drummers.

bongo drums A pair of small Afro-Cuban drums played with bare hands and capable of producing a range of tones, timbres, and musical effects.

bossa nova Brazilian Portuguese for "new wrinkle" or "new wave"; a musical style of Brazilian origin that blends elements of the *samba* with elements of cool jazz.

cakewalk Originally a strutting, high-stepping dance popular among African-American slaves and performed in the presence of their masters, the cakewalk (which did not get its name until much later) was actually a sly parody of white ballroom dances. By the end of the 19th century, the cakewalk had become a stage dance for couples and was subsequently adapted as a ballroom dance. It played an evolutionary role in dance steps accompanying ragtime and jazz.

changes Term jazz musicians use for the *chord progressions* on which a jazz piece is based.

chart What jazz musicians call sheet music or a musical score.

chops Synonymous with technique and musical skill—the ability to play fast, loud, and nimbly.

chord progression A succession of chords that have a certain harmonic coherence, a recognizable harmonic pattern.

collective improvisation A musical style in which each member of an ensemble contributes a musical line of equal importance. Characteristic of traditional New Orleans jazz, it was supplanted by *individual improvisation* (improvisation focusing on soloists) during the late 1920s.

color In music, color refers to tonal quality and is a product of the instrument as well as the player.

combo Any small jazz ensemble up to about nine players; it plays the jazz equivalent of what classical musicians call chamber music.

contemporary jazz A term often applied to the pop-oriented jazz of the 1980s and '90s; another word for it is "instrumental pop."

counterpoint Music in which two or more melodic lines are combined in a harmonic relationship that also retains the linear individuality of each line.

cover To "cover a song" is to appropriate a song or a style composed or originated by another performer.

cubop Short for Cubana Bop and pronounced "QUE-bop." The name applied to a Latin-inspired form of bop introduced by the Afro-Cuban musicians Machito and Mario Bauzá and additionally developed by Dizzy Gillespie.

cut out A record album that has been discontinued and is made available at a greatly reduced price.

cutting contest A type of *jam session* in which musicians compete to determine who has superior skill, inventiveness, and stamina. When entire bands compete in this way, the cutting session is often called a "battle of the bands."

Dixieland Traditional New Orleans jazz as played by white musicians. Also see *New Orleans jazz.*

dynamic range Applied to an instrument, voice, or piece of music, the span separating the softest from the loudest passages.

field holler A song fragment, half sung, half yelled, that was popular among African-American slaves and Southern African-American agricultural workers. It is one of the roots of the blues tradition.

free jazz The terms free jazz and avant-garde jazz are often used interchangeably to describe the free-form jazz of Ornette Coleman and a number of later musicians. Some critics differentiate between the terms, however, reserving "free jazz" for music that is wholly improvisational and follows no rules or prescribed pattern whatsoever, and "avant-garde" simply to describe experimental music in general, which may or may not adhere to rules or pattern. A synonym for free jazz is action jazz, while some commentators in the early 1960s referred to avant-garde jazz simply as the New Thing.

funk May be taken as a synonym for *soul jazz,* but it is also a style of African-American soul music, characterized by complex syncopation in duple meter.

habanera A Spanish word meaning dance of Havana; describes a slow Cuban folk dance that has provided composers with one of the most familiar of Spanish rhythms.

harmony The combination of two or more notes played simultaneously to produce chords, which are, in turn, combined successively to produce chord progressions.

heterophony The playing of roughly harmonized and only approximately parallel musical lines.

individual improvisation Jazz improvisation that focuses on soloists rather than the ensemble. Also see *collective improvisation.*

jam session An assembly of jazz musicians for the purpose of improvisation together.

jam To jam is to improvise, usually with other musicians.

jazz A highly improvisational form of music primarily developed by African-Americans who combined European harmonic structures with African complex rhythms. These are, in turn, overlaid with European and white American dance and march rhythms and with elements borrowed from the *blues* tradition.

jazz festival A series of performances by a large number of jazz performers over a limited period of time.

juke joint Historically, a roadhouse or tavern that played dance music, the blues, or even early jazz; the term connotes a rough place or dive.

klezmer Pronounced "klets-mare." Developed late in the Middle Ages as a form of instrumental music among the Jews of eastern Europe. (The name is derived from the Hebrew kele zemir, "instuments of song.") Jewish folk musicians (klezmorim in the plural) played in ensembles consisting of a violin, flute, bass viol, and cymbals. Later, the clarinet was very prominently featured. They played at family festivals, such as weddings, and on certain special festival occasions. A number of *swing* clarinetists used elements of the *klezmer* style in their playing.

legato In musical performance, connecting each note played, moving seamlessly from one to another. The opposite of *staccato*, attacking and articulating each note sharply, separating one from the next.

liner notes Packaged with a CD (or found on the back of a vinyl LP), liner notes are a brief essay by an expert or the performers explaining some aspect of what's on the recording.

melody A series of notes arranged rhythmically to form a recognizable unit.

modal jazz Jazz based on modal scales (such as those that characterize non-Western music), which dictate melodic and harmonic content. Modal jazz, popular in the 1950s, provided an alternative to jazz built on conventional scales.

multiphonics The sounding of simultaneous notes, like a chord, on an instrument (for example, a saxophone) conventionally capable of playing only one note at a time.

New Orleans jazz Traditional jazz of New Orleans as played by African Americans. Also see *Dixieland.*

nonet A nine-person musical ensemble.

polyphonic Describes music with more than one melodic line sounded together; a polyphonic instrument can play such music without accompaniment.

polyphony A form of music in which instruments play simultaneous melodies and countermelodies.

polyrhythm A complex musical structure in which one rhythmic pattern is superimposed on another. In other words, the simultaneous playing of two or more distinct rhythms.

polytonality The simultaneous use of more than one key in a single piece of music. While frequently encountered in various non-Western ethnic musical traditions, polytonality is rare in Western music.

portamento A musical technique or style in which the singer or instrumentalist glides from one note to another rather than articulates each note separately. Portamento is a characteristic of the *blues* and much jazz.

progressive jazz A term coined by Kenton to describe his idiosyncratic, elaborately arranged, and classically inflected music. While progressive jazz (perhaps surprisingly) appealed to mainstream audiences, some critics classify it with "cool jazz."

ragtime A jazz precursor characterized by elaborate *syncopation* in the melody played against a steadily accented accompaniment. Ragtime was most popular at the end of the 19th century and in the early 20th, before the 1920s.

reggae Popular music of Jamaican origin, combining strains of calypso, soul, and rock 'n' roll. Rhythmically, the offbeats are strongly accented, and politically, the lyrics often pack a protest punch.

rhythm A beat pattern or patterns formed by a series of notes of varying duration and accent or stress.

riff A short melodic ostinato (constantly repeated) phrase, usually two to four bars long. Born in Kansas City jazz, the riff became a mainstay of large-ensemble jazz.

rubato A relaxation of strict musical time; a rhythmic flexibility within a musical phrase or measure. It is very widely used in jazz.

samba A popular ballroom dance in the United States by the late 1930s, it originated as a lively, complexly syncopated, duple-meter folk dance of Afro-Brazilian descent.

scat singing Putting nonsense syllables to melody. At its best, scat singing is a way of using the human voice as an instrument, eliminating the need for words entirely.

shouting A style of *blues* singing in which a rough-voiced male performer shouts (or shout-sings) the lyrics.

sideman A supporting player in a small jazz ensemble.

soul jazz Another word for hard bop, a style combining elements of bebop with elements of the blues, rhythm and blues, and African-American gospel music, all at intense, hard-driving tempos.

speakeasy A place where illegal alcoholic drinks could be obtained during Prohibition. Many speakeasies featured jazz entertainment and were important in the early history of the music.

staccato In musical performance, attacking and articulating each note sharply, separating one from the next. The opposite of *legato*, connecting the notes, moving seamlessly from one to another.

stride A style of jazz piano playing in which the left hand athletically "strides" the keys in aggressive accompaniment to the right hand's melodic line. The style was a bridge between ragtime and mature jazz.

studio group An ensemble that does not tour or perform live, but records exclusively. It is often an ad hoc group.

swing A style of music, chiefly associated with big bands, popular in the 1930s and 1940s. *Swing* is also a difficult-to-define rhythmic quality that characterizes most jazz, an interplay or conflict between the accents and duration applied to musical notes versus the overall fixed pulse of the music.

symphonic jazz Music that combines elements of classical orchestral music with jazz but is fully written out, leaving no room for improvisation.

syncopation A rhythmic device whereby weak beats rather than the main beats are accented. The rhythm becomes at once freer and yet more compelling to listeners.

tailgate trombone A style of trombone playing that uses the slide frequently and with gusto to draw attention to an instrument typically "trapped" between the trumpet and clarinet. The name is derived from the way early bands played crowded onto advertising wagons with the slide trombonist standing out on the tailgate so that he'd have room to play his instrument.

timbre Sometimes spelled timber and pronounced either "tamber" or "timber," it's the distinctive tone of an instrument or instruments or singing voice.

Tin Pan Alley Collective reference to the popular music industry during the early 20th century. Tin Pan Alley was the nickname of an actual New York City neighborhood on Seventh Avenue between 48th and 52nd streets, which housed most of the major music publishers. The phrase is derived from 19th-century musician's slang for a cheap, tinny piano.

tone clusters Dissonant chords consisting of adjacent notes. clusters are often heard in *atonal* music.

vibrato A tremulous or pulsating musical tone. Trombonists create vibrato by rapidly moving the instrument's slide back and forth.

vocalise Pronounced "vocal-ease," a general term for singing meaningless syllables or a single syllable (usually fa). *Scat singing* is a form of vocalise.

zoot suit The "uniform" of the late 1930s and early 1940s swing hipster. Typically of gaudy color, it featured full-legged, tight-cuffed (pegged) trousers and a very long coat with exaggerated lapels and padded shoulders. Knobby-toed shoes, a broad-brimmed fedora, and a long watch chain completed the zoot suit look. Cab Calloway wore a trademark yellow zoot suit.

Index

A

B

C

E

F

H

I

N

O

P

Q

R

S

T

U-V

W

Y

Z